5/85

791.43 R816c   M
ROSENZWEIG
CASABLANCA AND OTHER MAJOR
FILMS OF MICHAEL CURTIZ
                                39.95

WITHDRAWN

Casablanca
and Other Major Films of
Michael Curtiz

Studies in Cinema, No. 14

Diane M. Kirkpatrick, Series Editor

Associate Professor, History of Art
The University of Michigan

Other Titles in This Series

No. 11   *Balkan Cinema: Evolution after the Revolution*   Michael J. Stoil

No. 12   *The Rhetoric of Filmic Narration*   Nick Browne

No. 13   *Bertolt Brecht,* Cahiers du Cinema, *and
Contemporary Film Theory*   George Lellis

No. 15   *Old Hollywood/New Hollywood*   Thomas Schatz

No. 16   *Donald Duck Joins Up: The Walt Disney Studio
During World War II*   Richard Shale

No. 17   *The High Noon of American Films in
Latin America*   Gaizka S. de Usabel

No. 18   *The Spanish Civil War in American and
European Films*   Marjorie A. Valleau

No. 19   *Antonioni's Visual Language*   Ned Rifkin

No. 20   *Cinema Strikes Back: Radical Filmmaking
in the United States, 1930-1942*   Russell Campbell

Casablanca and Other Major Films of Michael Curtiz

by
Sidney Rosenzweig

UMI RESEARCH PRESS
Ann Arbor, Michigan

Produced and distributed by
UMI Research Press
an imprint of
University Microfilms International
Ann Arbor, Michigan 48106

Library of Congress Cataloging in Publication Data

Rosenzweig, Sidney.
Casablanca and other major films of Michael
Curtiz.

    (Studies in cinema ; no. 14)
    Revision of thesis (Ph.D.)—University of Rochester,
1978.
    Bibliography: p.
    Filmography:
    Includes index.
    1. Curtiz, Michael, 1888-1962.   I. Title. II. Series.
PN1998.A3C9 1982   791.43'02333'0924   82-1848
ISBN 0-8357-1304-0   AACR2

For My Parents

Frontispiece: Humphrey Bogart *(l.)* and Michael Curtiz on the set of *Passage to Marseille.*

Contents

Acknowledgments   *ix*

Introduction   *1*

1 "All Right M'Hearties, Follow Me":
    Captain Blood   *13*

2 The Castle and the Forest: *The Adventures
    of Robin Hood*   *29*

3 Pirates and Politics: *The Sea Hawk*   *43*

4 Out West and Other Places: Variations on
    the Swashbuckler   *61*

5 "A Hill of Beans": *Casablanca*   *77*

6 In the Shadows of *Casablanca:* Hawks's
    To Have and Have Not and Curtiz's *Passage
    to Marseille*   *97*

7 Convicts and Kids: The Art of Heroic
    Sacrifice   *109*

8 Aprons and Minks: *Mildred Pierce*   *121*

9 Artists, Athletes, and Tycoons: Ambition
    as Self-Destruction   *145*

Conclusion   *157*

viii   *Contents*

Plates   *161*

Notes   *173*

Filmography   *197*

Bibliography   *207*

Index   *215*

Acknowledgments

Filmmaking is a collaborative art. No individual has ever made a feature film without help from a lot of people. It also seems as though no one can write about these films without receiving such help. In preparing this study of Michael Curtiz's films, I was given assistance by many people, and I'm happy to have the chance to thank them now.

Perhaps the most difficult aspect of writing film criticism is getting to see the films. I was fortunate enough to meet Bob Kline and through him contact Erwin Ezzes and Jack McLaughlin of United Artists Television, as well as Herbert Schottenfeld and Ira Michaels of United Artists. Without the extraordinarily generous cooperation of these men, and their staffs at United Artists, it would have been impossible for me to complete the early stages of my work. I also want to thank Patrick Sheehan and the Motion Picture Section of the Library of Congress, including David Parker, for making my work there as comfortable and productive as possible. The staff of the British Film Institute not only gave me the rare opportunity to see two of Curtiz's surviving European films, but also helped me find my way around London. William K. Everson and Eric Spilker also generously helped me locate prints. Finally, I must thank at least a dozen anonymous film programmers for various television stations, who had the wisdom to schedule Curtiz films when I could see them.

I also had help in locating written reference material, and want to thank the University of Rochester Library, especially Gerri Martone, Sally Roche, and Ann Schertz of Interlibrary Loans, Phyllis Andrews and Brad Smith of the Reference Department, and the anonymous librarian at the Lincoln Center Branch of the New York Public Library who alerted me to Jeffrey Richards's work on the swashbuckler.

Professor Richard Gollin has been not only an advisor, but a good and valued friend; he knows best how much he endured in seeing this work to its completion. Sylvia Moukous let me have, not only the use of her typewriter, but also her time and her warm-hearted, sympathetic support. Ruth Kimmerer typed the final draft, which meant translating from my nearly indecipherable original draft, and cheered me along and boosted my spirits in the final stage of my work.

I regret the poor quality of some of the photographs, which are frame and video blow-ups. However, there would have been no photographs at all if I had not received much needed help from John Mueller, Alexandra Egbert, Dan Rorabaugh, Charles Ilardi, Nic Hambas, Richard Reisem, and Linda McAusland.

Finally, I want to mention a group of people whom I am lucky to call my close friends and who have kept me going for several years. They know who they are and how much they mean to me, so I will mention only one name, Harold M. Frank.

Introduction

The motion picture can be called the first art form invented since the Greeks. Earlier civilizations had painting, sculpture, music, and drama, but the motion picture was not invented until the late nineteenth century. Unlike other art forms it cannot exist without technology; it needs electricity, heavy equipment, laboratories; it is literally an art of and for the machine age.

Film is not only a combination of industry and art, it is also a combination of many arts.[1] Containing elements of music, painting, and drama, it approaches Wagner's ideal *Gesamtkunstwerk*. Of course, narrative films are primarily a form of drama and use traditional conventions of plot, character, and dramatic structure. But they also express themselves through visual means unique to the medium, such as camera movement and editing. The artist reponsible for organizing all these elements into a coherent whole is the director. Michael Curtiz (1888-1962) was one of the world's most talented and prolific directors. The creator of *Casablanca*, over a hundred other feature films in America, and at least fifty others in Europe, he worked in almost every film genre: swashbuckler (*Captain Blood*, 1935), romantic melodrama (*Casablanca*, 1942), *film noir* (*Mildred Pierce*, 1945), musical (*Yankee Doodle Dandy*, 1942), gangster (*Angels with Dirty Faces*, 1938), western (*Dodge City*, 1939), costume spectacle (*The Egyptian*, 1954), and horror (*Dr. X*, 1932). This study will examine certain of his major American films in depth, focusing on both their dramatic elements and their visual style, and will argue that within the large variety of Curtiz's films lies a consistent core of themes and attitudes, and a consistent cinematic style that expresses them.

My original title for this book, *Talking Shadows*, plays on words. All movies are literally shadows on a screen, produced by light passing through a transparent celluloid strip. But Curtiz's films contain shadows within shadows. One of the characteristics of his visual style is high-contrast lighting, which produces areas of bright light and dark shadows. These shadows "talk" in that they are part of his expressive cinematic style. My intent in this study is to interpret what those shadows have to say.

Despite the massive number of books and articles now being published about American film directors, almost nothing has been written about Michael Curtiz. John Davis has written a number of important articles for *The Velvet Light Trap,*[2] and other writers have contributed scattered essays in numerous magazines.[3] Kingsley Canham wrote a short, superficial survey of Curtiz's films for the *Hollywood Professionals* series.[4] Perhaps the most admiring words on Curtiz come from John Baxter, who surveyed Curtiz's thirties films for his book, *Hollywood in the Thirties*: "Inescapably one of the best directors ever to emerge in the cinema, Michael Curtiz lays a substantial claim to being the greatest director of the thirties."[5] Charles Higham and Joel Greenberg surveyed Curtiz's films of the following decade for their work in the same series, *Hollywood in the Forties,* and had similarly high praise:

> ... greatest of all, Michael Curtiz, the forties' magnifico whose films embraced all genres ... and whose wholly American drive, energy and flair expressed themselves in the forties' most characteristic single film, the unforgettable *Casablanca.*[6]

Sections on Curtiz are also included in the recent critical anthology, *Passport to Hollywood,*[7] the equally recent *The Warner Brothers Directors,*[8] and the American Film Institute's anthology, *The American Film Heritage.*[9]

However, because of the large number and variety of his films, Curtiz has generally been viewed as a studio work-horse, competent in many genres, willing to do whatever was asked of him, but with no distinctive style or theme.[10] As recently as the winter 1976 issue the *Journal of Popular Film,* Ina Rae Hark echoed this view by dismissing Curtiz as simply an "able craftsman."[11]

Curtiz did spend twenty-seven of his thirty-six years in America working exclusively for one studio, Warner Brothers. He was part of the studio system and therefore, to understand his films, we must first understand that system.

The term "studio system" defines the means of production of the vast majority of American feature films released from the late twenties to the mid-sixties. Six to eight major companies (M-G-M, Warner Brothers, Paramount, Twentieth Century-Fox, RKO, Universal, and Columbia) and a fluctuating number of minor ones (including Monogram, PRC and Republic) produced and distributed most of the American films made during those years.

Moreover, until the Supreme Court decision of May 1948 forcing the studios to divest themselves of the theater chains they owned or controlled,[12] the major companies also controlled the exhibition of films. Because their income came directly from the dollars deposited at the box office, the studios were keenly aware of their audience and tried to cater to their sense of the public's likes and dislikes. This led, in John Baxter's words, to Hollywood's being "ruthless in its pursuit of excellence in the film-making process," at least technical excellence, which created a "policy of purchasing the best talent, no matter where it came from."[13] Often it came from Europe; during the late twenties and early thirties, scores of European performers, directors, and technicians were invited to join the Hollywood studios. Among them was Michael Curtiz.

As a result of this stockpiling of European and American talent, the major studios became, in effect, repertory theaters. Each had under contract a stock company of leading and supporting players, together with writers who could tailor scripts to fit the performers' special abilities, directors who understood those abilities as well as the demands of the genres to which the scripts belonged, and a host of craftsmen (such as cameramen, editors, sound engineers, and costume and set designers) who helped create the films' visual and aural texture. The repeated combination of these talents in film after film gave each studio an identifiable thematic and visual style.

Warner Brothers, during the early 1930s, gained the reputation of being the "proletarian" studio; it made films for, and about, the working man.[14] Characters were often defined by their occupation, and the plots concerned how they made their living. Usually they were lower- or middle-class workers, such as taxi drivers, truckers, newspapermen, linemen, prizefighters, detectives, gangsters, or chorus girls; far less often were they professionals such as doctors or lawyers. The villains were usually people who held or wanted power, usually financial, often political. Even in lighter Warner Brothers films, such as comedies and musicals, sympathies were directed towards the "little guy," the average man. For example, the gold diggers of the well-known musical series (*Gold Diggers of 1933,* etc.) were for the most part shown to be good-hearted working girls, trying to advance their careers while avoiding the advances of the lecherous businessmen who backed the shows they danced in.

These characters and their stories were often cynical and hard-boiled. The films were filled with violence and death. Stylistically they were marked by simple sets, high contrast lighting, and ruthlessly fast-paced editing that filled them with a sense of furious energy. They were most often set in a contemporary American city and, taken as a whole, they created a highly stylized but recognizable urban landscape—the Warner Brothers city.

In the later thirties and forties some of these conventions changed. During the war years, for example, Warners joined the other studios in making morale-building propaganda, stories of courage at home and on the battlefield. Melodramas retained their urban setting, but often involved wealthier, more leisured characters. Despite such changes, audiences remained able to identify the films of each studio. Usually the star was the major clue; Bogart or Cagney meant a Warners film, for example, and Gable or Garland meant an M-G-M film. To the audience, however, directors were invisible and unknown forces, mere names at the end of long, ignored lists of production credits.

Directors were invisible even to most critics. American film historians and critics had long agreed that film is the "director's medium"; whether he has written the script or not, the director determines a film's style, structure, and content. But, until recently, they applied this assumption primarily to European directors, discussing their work as carefully and respectfully as any playwright's.[15] They had difficulty discerning the thematic and stylistic signatures of American directors because they thought the director's individual identities were lost within the studios they worked for. Because of the highly efficient studio system, they considered most Hollywood films to be factory-made products, and tended to ignore the differences between the work of individual directors.

Ironically, it was a group of postwar European critics, especially those who, in the early 1950s, wrote for the French film magazine *Cahiers du cinéma* (including André Bazin and future directors like François Truffaut, Jean-Luc Godard, and Claude Chabrol), who first focused attention on these differences by formulating the "politique des auteurs," which was mistranslated as the "auteur theory."[16] Reduced to its simplest essentials, the auteur theory reiterated that the director is the controlling creative force behind a film (i.e., the "auteur"), and suggested that within the conventions of style and subject that identified each studio and each genre within the studio, one could further identify the particular style and attitudes of an individual director. As Andrew Tudor says, no one ever denied the importance of the director; what "the *Cahiers* critics did was to find *auteurs* where none had been dreamt of before,"[17] within the studio system. They argued that the only way to understand a director's films was to consider them "in relation to one another."[18] The French auteurists drew up lists ranking directors and gave the films of their favorites exhaustive analyses.

Eventually, the auteur theory reached the United States, and Andrew Sarris became one of the leading American auteurists. His article "Notes on the Auteur Theory in 1962", which first appeared in *Film Culture*,[19] expounded his version of the theory for American readers. Though attacked by some, most notably Pauline Kael,[20] it was revised into the introduction to Sarris's *The American Cinema*, an influential work which ranked and commented on 199 American directors. In recent years, numerous studies of formerly "invisible" American directors have appeared,[21] but, as I have remarked, little work has been done on Curtiz.

The auteur approach seems to raise an important question: how much control did Curtiz have over his studio-made films? Actually, for my purposes, the question is neither as important nor as real as it may seem. I am not a pure auteurist; I do not argue that a film director working within the studio system is an "author" in the same sense that a novelist or playwright is an author. Filmmaking is a group project; writing is a solitary, lonely craft. Even Sarris claims he never intended to "forget about writers and actors and photographers and scenic designers."[22] Curtiz himself spoke of filmmaking as a team effort.[23]

I believe that looking at the films of one director is nonetheless a valid approach to film criticism, one important method of isolating a group of films for discussion. Tudor states this position most succinctly: "The *auteur* principle directs our attention to groups of films having in common one thing—the director."[24] We could just as easily examine a group of films whose common factor is their writer, or cameraman, or editor, or actor or genre, and in fact such studies do exist.[25] What matters is not so much who created the films but what is in them. The important thing is to give them "close textual analysis rather than brief critical comment."[26]

Nevertheless, the question of Curtiz's control can be answered in a general fashion. Like all studio directors, Curtiz was responsible to the studio's head of production. He could be assigned to unpalatable projects or see his films altered or recut. But within the limitations of the studio system, Curtiz actually had considerable control over his films. Much of this came from Curtiz's own personality, and the prestige he brought from his past history as a major filmmaker in Europe. To understand this, we need to look briefly at Curtiz's biography.

Mihaly Kertesz (his name was anglicized upon his arrival in the United States) was born in Budapest on December 24, 1888.[27] His parents were Jewish, [28] probably moved to Vienna when he was a child, and most likely were comfortable, middle-class citizens. But Curtiz changed the stories he told to American interviewers. To some he said his father was an architect, his mother an opera singer, and himself an extra in one of her performances when he was eleven. To others, he said his father was a poor carpenter.[29] He also claimed to have joined a touring circus at age seventeen as a strongman, acrobat, juggler, and pantomimist, and was once reported to have been on the Hungarian fencing team in the 1912 Stockholm Olympics.

We do know that he attended Markoszy University and the Royal Academy of Theater and Art in Budapest, and then joined the National Hungarian Theater as an actor and director. In 1912 he acted in and may have helped direct and write one of the first films made in Hungary, *Ma Es Holnap (Today and Tommorow)*. After directing at least one other Hungarian film, he went to Denmark's Noridsk studio in 1913 to learn as much as he could about every phase of filmmaking from directors like Mauritz Stiller and Victor Seastrom. While there he acted in and perhaps assisted August Blom in directing *Atlantis* (1913), and directed a film of his own whose title is now unknown. Six months later he returned to Hungary and began directing popular commercial successes. When World War I broke out he served in the Austro-Hungarian artillery, but a year later he was filmmaking again, first as a newsreel cameraman and then at the commercial studios. In 1915 or 1916 he married Lucy Doraine, a seventeen-year-old aspiring actress who began appearing in his films. By 1917

Curtiz was director of production at Phoenix Films, an important and influential European company noted for its high technical and dramatic quality.

Curtiz left Hungary in 1919, while in the middle of a film version of Molnar's *Liliom*, because Béla Kun's Communist government had nationalized the film industry. Once again the biographical facts grow hazy. He may have directed in Sweden a film known in France as *Odette et l'histoire des femmes illustrée* (1919), in which a fourteen-year-old Greta Garbo played Marie Antoinette; he may have directed in Berlin a version of the first part of Fritz Lang's serial, *Die Spinnen: der goldene See* (1919). Eventually he settled in Vienna and joined Count Alexander Kolowrat's Sascha Films company, where he directed at least twenty-one films in the seven years between 1919 and 1926. He also showed his talent for "star-making." Until they were divorced in 1923, Curtiz continued to use Lucy Doraine in his films, and she became quite popular. Curtiz's last three Austrian films turned their leading lady, Lily Damita, into an equally famous actress.[30]

Thus, while some of the details of Curtiz's European career may be unclear, its meaning is unquestionable. Curtiz learned his craft from some of the great European pioneers, at some of the best-equipped European studios, and from his own long, intense experience. He started in film almost as early as D.W. Griffith; by the time he arrived in America on July 4, 1926, he was the popular, highly successful director of sixty to seventy feature films.[31] He understood every phase of the industry. He was used to molding new talent and working with sympathetic technical assistants. He knew that filmmaking was a team effort, but he also firmly believed that the director was the captain of the team,[32] and he carried that belief with him to America.

What brought Curtiz to Hollywood was a film called *Die Slavenkönigin* (Austrian—1924, literally translated as *The Slave Queen*, but known in the U.S. as *Moon of Israel*) and a man named Jack Warner. Many of Curtiz's works for Sascha Films were elaborate, expensive biblical and historical spectacles,[33] similar to those produced by Cecil B. DeMille. Warner wanted to compete with DeMille in his own territory and had planned a lavish biblical epic to be called *Noah's Ark*. When he saw *Moon of Israel* in 1926 he was "laid in the aisles by Curtiz's camera work...[by] shots and angles that were pure genius."[34] He knew Curtiz was the man to direct *Noah's Ark* and offered him a contract. Curtiz accepted, but he didn't make *Noah's Ark* until 1928, after he had proven he could accommodate to American methods by making five films in two years.

Moon of Israel indicates that Curtiz also brought to America his own highly developed visual style and thematic interests. That style, heavily influenced by postwar German Expressionism, is marked by certain pictorial effects: high crane shots to establish a story's environment; unusual camera angles and complex compositions in which characters are often framed by physical objects; much camera movement; subjective shots, in which the camera becomes the character's eye; and high contrast lighting, with pools of shadows. *Moon of Israel*'s plot and structure show Curtiz's fondness for romantic melodrama, for setting a small, personal love story against events of vast, historical importance, for driving his characters to crises and forcing them to make moral decisions. In short, *Moon of Israel* bears a stylistic and thematic resemblance to the films Curtiz would make in Hollywood.

Almost as little is known about Curtiz's private life in America as about his life in Europe. Soon after his arrival he met and later married the screenwriter Bess Meredyth; they were divorced about a year before his death, from cancer, on April ll, 1962. He was an active athlete, supposedly fond of polo, and may have been a bit of a lecher; Jack Warner states that "he was the only director in history who, after his death...was adjudged the father of an illegitimate child."[35]

During his lifetime, the publicity that Curtiz received in popular magazine and newspaper articles centered on two features of his personality. One was his heavy Hungarian accent and his comic problems with spoken English, which he may have exaggerated to give himself a public image. His garbled phrases were laughingly compared with Samuel Goldwyn's "Goldwynisms," but they were less malaprops than, as one journalist put it, "a redeployment of the language."[36] There were stories of Curtiz asking extras to "separate together in a bunch," claiming that a scene would "make your blood curl," and angrily dismissing an assistant by saying, "Next time I send a damn fool for something, I go myself."[37] What is probably his most famous request, for a technician to "bring on the empty horses," was used by David Niven as the title for a book of memoirs.[38]

The other reputation Curtiz gained is more relevant to the immediate question. He was known as an arrogant, tyrannical perfectionist, a hard driving, excessively demanding director who overworked himself and everyone else on his set. He had little respect for those who wouldn't work as hard as he did, and his own dedication to work was almost fanatical. He was known for arriving on the set early, for leaving late, for completing complicated projects in record time, and for starting a new film as soon as the last one was finished.

Again, there are many stories of his feuds with actors and actresses. Errol Flynn claimed Curtiz removed the rubber tips from the swords used in *Captain Blood*'s dueling scenes.[39] Bette Davis never forgot Curtiz muttering under his breath that she was a "goddamned nothing no good sexless son of a bitch."[40] Nevertheless, he had an instinct for uncovering new talent, and he made stars of many unknowns by giving them strong first roles. These include: Errol Flynn (in *Captain Blood*, 1935), John Garfield (in *Four Daughters*, 1938), and Doris Day (in *Romance on the High Seas*, 1948). Under his direction James Cagney and Joan Crawford each won acting Oscars (for *Yankee Doodle Dandy*, 1942, and *Mildred Pierce*, 1945, respectively).

Because of his speed and efficiency, during the twenty-seven years that

Curtiz remained under contract to Warner Brothers (1926-54), he made eighty-six feature films and one short. In April of 1953 he announced he would leave the studio rather than submit to a pay cut required by an economy move. The next year he began freelancing, and between 1954 and 1962 he made another fifteen feature films, including one more for Warners. He completed his last film, *The Comancheros*, only months before his death.

Curtiz's large output, however, does not mean he worked carelessly. If we look closely at popular magazine and newspaper articles about him, we can find in them a third recurring theme, Curtiz's awareness of his own artistic ambitions. He often spoke of his attempts to balance these ambitions with the commercial demands of Hollywood filmmaking. He knew his films had to be entertaining and he tried to insure their mass appeal, while making them as artistically as possible.[41]

However, it was less the art than the continued commercial success of Curtiz's films that appealed to Warner Brothers. Because of this, Curtiz gradually became one of the studio's more important and influential directors. By 1934 he was considered an "A" director; that is, he was assigned the bigger budgeted, higher prestige films.[42] With this prestige went greater authority, the opportunity to be more selective about scripts, casts, and crew. William Dieterle, another "A" director at Warners in the thirties, reports that all Warners directors were given three "refusals," that is, three chances to reject scripts they didn't like before starting their next project.[43] Whittemore and Cecchetini argue that by 1938 Curtiz's position was so strong he could actually demand that certain films be given to him rather than other directors at the studio.[44] John Davis notes that Curtiz

> controlled the contributions of his various collaborators and especially those of his cameramen. . . . Tom Flinn and I interviewed several cinematographers (Charles Rosher, Ray Rennahan, James Wong Howe, Ted McCord, . . . Hal Mohr and Ernest Haller) who worked with Curtiz. While some of them did not exactly love Curtiz, all admitted that he took particular care over the angle, composition, lighting, and often movement, of each shot. Hal Mohr called Curtiz a "finder director" (meaning he used a viewfinder to compose his shots). . . . Curtiz also influenced the editing of his pictures, shooting only what he knew would be necessary. If an editor put the shots together wrong, Curtiz would make him do it again.[45]

Howard Koch, one of the scriptwriters on *Casablanca* (1942), admits that Curtiz's "directorial prerogatives" enabled him to insist that certain scenes be added to that film's script.[46] After Curtiz won the best director Oscar for *Casablanca*[47] his prestige grew even further. In fact, in the late forties Curtiz formed his own production unit within Warner Brothers. Michael Curtiz Productions gave him greater control of script, cast, and crew, as well as a direct financial interest in the films. *The Unsuspected* (1947) was one of the films that resulted. Curtiz dissolved the unit after a few years because it was less profitable than he had hoped, but the venture shows his taste for independence and control.

This study is not based on pure "auteurist" assumptions; it involves a combination of auteur and genre approaches. Recently the idea of film genre has received as much critical attention as auteur theory.[48] The major problem seems to be to define exactly what a genre is. Andrew Tudor, for example, elaborately explains how difficult the problem is, but he realizes that the idea of genres is too deeply imbedded in our ordinary experience of film to be dismissed.[49] He is forced to return to common sense by using this experience to conclude that we must "lean on a common cultural consensus as to what constitutes a genre."[50] He adds, "We feel we know a 'Western' when we see one. . . . Genre is what we collectively believe it to be."[51] A critic may create his own arbitrary definition of a genre, which may prove to be a useful critical tool. But, generally speaking, the most practical definition of genre for Tudor is "the rather loose way in which an audience classifies its films."[52] I would agree, adding only that genre is also the way the Hollywood studios classified its films. But of course these two sets of classifications are synonymous. Audiences drew their conceptions of genre from what the studios produced; they then went to the movies with certain genre expectations, and the studios set out to satisfy them.

Stanley Solomon provides a slightly more specific definition of genre. He says that a "genre film is one in which the narrative pattern, or crucial aspects of that pattern, is visually recognizable as having been used similarly in other films."[53] The "defining aspect of genre" is a "core of narrative meaning" that can have varied sources.[54] For example, though a western can be defined by its locale, or a private-eye film by its hero's occupation, in both cases a familiar narrative pattern evolves from the central "core."[55] Finally, Solomon, like Tudor, refers to the popular sense of a genre, and says it is usually based on its "iconography," that is, its recurring visual and aural elements, such as the cowboy's six-gun or the detective's tough, clipped dialogue.[56]

Although this study examines the work of one director, it concentrates on the films of certain genres within that work. What makes Curtiz's films worth examining is precisely what makes them difficult to examine: their number and their generic variety.

Robin Wood has recently suggested that the problem with most genre theorists is their "tendency to treat the genres as discrete."[57] Genres, for Wood, "represent different strategies for dealing with the same . . . tensions. . . . In the classical Hollywood cinema, motifs cross repeatedly from genre to genre."[58] He cites as an example the "home/wandering opposition," that is, a character's internal conflict between the urge to remain free from emotional involvements, and the desire to settle into a domestic routine, which structures not only westerns, but many musicals and melodramas as well. Because this form of structural or archetypal criticism goes beyond traditional considerations of genre to probe personal or cultural predilections, it allows us to discuss the interplay of directorial and generic concerns.

One of my main intentions here is to use Curtiz's films to pursue Wood's suggestions. What kinds of stylistic and thematic motifs do Curtiz's films share? Do their differences in genre outweigh the similarities imposed by their common director? Answering these questions will require the close analysis of a number of films. Obviously, the detailed examination of all of Curtiz's films would be an impossibly massive project. On the other hand, a few brief remarks on a large number of films can reveal only the most superficial connections between them. I have tried to balance depth and breadth. I have chosen six of his films for consideration in depth: *Captain Blood* (1935), *The Adventures of Robin Hood* (1938), *The Sea Hawk* (1940), *Casablanca* (1942), *Passage to Marseille* (1944), and *Mildred Pierce* (1945).

Each one merits such close analysis for several reasons. First, with the exception of *Passage to Marseille*, each one was a critical and commercial success at the time of its release, and continues to be popular in revivals today. *Captain Blood* launched Errol Flynn's career; Joan Crawford won an Oscar for *Mildred Pierce*; *Casablanca*, Curtiz's best-known film, has become an extraordinarily popular cult film. *Passage to Marseille*, one of Warner Brothers' attempts to imitate *Casablanca*, has never been as popular, but does provide an important point of comparison.

More important, each film is an outstanding example of a particular genre or mix of genres. The chapters are grouped into three sections corresponding to these genres. Thus, *Captain Blood, The Adventures of Robin Hood,* and *The Sea Hawk* are swashbucklers; *Mildred Pierce* is a *film noir*; *Casablanca* and *Passage to Marseille* are transitional films containing elements of both the comic swashbucklers and the tragic *film noir*. These specific genre labels will be defined later. The point here is that focusing on these films enables us to pose the cross-genre questions mentioned earlier. After each section I deal far more briefly with four or five other Curtiz films which may belong to different genres, but which still bear notable stylistic and structural similarities to the films of that section. For example, at the end of the first section I discuss a number of films which can be considered variations on the swashbuckler, including three westerns.

It may seem that I have given disproportionate emphasis to the swashbuckler, since three of the six films I discuss in detail belong to the genre. However, the three films form a kind of trilogy and are conveniently discussed together. Still, the emphasis is deliberate. It is my effort to help fill a gaping hole in film criticism. While other genres have been written about at length, there is virtually no study of the swashbuckler; there is less serious criticism of the genre than there is of Curtiz.[59]

I hope my work will have the additional function, which should arise naturally from the critical analysis of any film, of furthering the understanding and appreciation of the specific films I discuss. Earlier I mentioned Curtiz's desire to balance the commercial and artistic aspects of his films. He once summed up his attempts by saying, "I put all the art into my pictures I think the audience can stand."[60] What that art consists of is a central theme of the following pages.

1

"All Right M'Hearties, Follow Me": *Captain Blood*

Synopsis of the Film

Captain Blood begins in England in 1685, during the revolt-filled reign of King James II. Dr. Peter Blood (Errol Flynn) is arrested while operating on a wounded rebel, tried for treason, and sentenced to be sold into slavery in Port Royal, a Caribbean colony. Arabella Bishop (Olivia de Havilland), niece of the cruel and powerful Colonel Bishop (Lionel Atwill), buys him and helps him win favor by telling the island's gouty governor (George Hassel) of his medical skill. When Spanish pirates attack the colony, Blood and several other slaves escape, take over the Spanish ship, and sail off to new careers as pirates. Blood becomes partners with Levasseur (Basil Rathbone) until the Frenchman breaks their agreement by taking a woman prisoner, Arabella. She had been en route to Port Royal with an English emissary, Lord Willoughby (Henry Stephensson). After Blood kills Levasseur, Willoughby announces that James has been deposed; "good King William" rules in his stead, and needs sailors to defeat the French fleets now attacking England and her colonies. Blood and the other reformed pirates shout their allegiance to the new king, return to Port Royal, and defeat the French. Blood completes his victory by being appointed the island's governor and marrying Arabella.

Two pirates face each other on a windswept, rock beach. Handsome, long-haired, with swords at their sides, they argue angrily over who owns the beautiful woman prisoner. "You'll never take her while I live," cries one. "Then I'll take her when you die," answers the other. They draw their swords and duel across the beach until one lies dead.

Night, aboard ship, in the pirate captain's cabin: through the porthole we see the stars over the sea and hear the rigging creak. The beautiful woman prisoner stares at the pirate. They kiss, then they quarrel; he storms onto the deck shouting, "Set sail for Port Royal."

A pirate ship fires a broadside against an enemy French vessel, turning it into a wall of flame. Ragged French sailors scurry across the smoke-filled deck. The pirate captain grabs a torn rigging line and swings aboard the enemy ship, crying to his crew: "All right, m'hearties, follow me!"

These images of menace, romance, and violence, all from Curtiz's *Captain Blood*, summon up a fantasy world of gallant pirates and cruel slave masters, of beautiful women, bountiful treasure, and bloody death—the world of the swashbuckler. I want to begin this chapter by putting the film swashbuckler into a larger literary context. Then I will examine *Captain Blood* in detail, looking closely at the structure and characters. Finally, I will define some of the major features of Curtiz's cinematic style and show how they stamp the film with his directorial signature.

Of all the popular film genres, the swashbuckler has received the least amount of serious critical attention. Recent studies of a broad range of genres by Kaminsky[1] and Solomon[2] completely ignore the swashbuckler; and John Cawelti's informative analysis of formula films and literature, although provocatively titled *Adventure, Mystery and Romance*,[3] concentrates on detective stories and westerns and has almost nothing to say about the swashbuckler. The genre seems to inspire nothing better than oversize, coffee-table books, crammed with gossip and pictures but with little intelligent critical analysis. For example, in Parish and Stanke's *The Swashbucklers*[4] the title refers to the performers, not the films; the book consists of brief biographies of actors who specialized in swashbuckling roles. Another series of star biographies is *Cads and Cavaliers: The Film Adventurers.*[5] *The Great Adventure Films*[6] does concentrate on films but offers only superficial comment on fifty films, most of them not swashbucklers. Ian Cameron's *Adventure in the Movies*,[7] a general survey organized by topics rather than by film or star, is the best study thus far, but still much too sketchy.[8] The best essay I have found on the genre is Jeffrey Richards' "The Swashbuckling Revival,"[9] which consists of the most interesting and useful parts of his book, *Swordsmen of the Screen.*[10]

To explain this critical neglect I can offer only a few speculations. One is that modern critics look down on tales of adventure and high romance, considering them juvenile escapism rather than serious literature.[11] Two other popular film genres, the western and the gangster film, were similarly thought escapist, though recently they have received considerable serious study. Even so, these genres differ from the swashbuckler in several significant ways. First, the western is closely associated with several critically popular directors, most notably John Ford and Howard Hawks, and initial interest in Ford and Hawks spilled over into interest in the western in general. There is no comparable figure associated with swashbucklers.[12]

More important, both the western and the gangster film are completely American in origin and are among our most influential contributions to world culture. The iconography of the western, for example, is recognized and imitated everywhere. Moreover, critics find in both genres expressions of America's changing values and ideals. Changes in the western, which is always set in the past, may reflect changes in our attitude towards our own history.[13] Similarly, changes in the gangster film, which is always set in its own present, may reflect changes in our view of twentieth-century urban America.[14] The swashbuckler, on the other hand, is not an American invention, nor does it deal with America's past or present. As Richards points out, the genre's characteristics have remained relatively unchanged over the years, so critics cannot approach it with the same methods they apply to the western and gangster film.[15]

The swashbuckler's general features seem to be its setting in a remote time (usually pre-twentieth century) and place (usually not the U.S.), its clearly defined heroes and villains, and its emphasis on action, especially swordplay, and romance. The story may involve medieval English knights, seventeenth-century French musketeers or eighteenth-century Spanish pirates, but it always climaxes in the violent confrontation of good and evil, and concludes with the hero and heroine embracing. Jeffrey Richards adds that

> it is basically in form and ethos that the swashbuckler is to be distinguished from other genres. Stylization rather than realism, fictional adventure and not historical fact are the keynotes. Settings, costumes, stories, action, are all stylized.[16]

The genre's identifying iconography is its lavish, colorful costumes and sets, its graceful, balletic action and, most important of all, its swords. American film genres do seem to be identified by weapons. Where the cowboy uses the six-gun, the gangster the automatic, the swashbuckler uses the sword; without at least one major duel, a film cannot really be called a swashbuckler.

This iconography, the screen swashbuckler's form and style, was first established by Douglas Fairbanks, Sr., in the series of films he made that started with *The Mark of Zorro* (1920) and ended with *The Iron Mask* (1929). Historical films appeared fairly early in film history; for example, *Robin Hood and His Merry Men* and *The Count of Monte Cristo* were both produced in 1909,[17] and numerous similar films were made before *The Mark of Zorro*. But these were not swashbucklers as we know them. Slow and heavy, too closely based on stage plays, they were, as Richards says, "literal and literary in concept."[18] With Fairbanks, "the swashbuckler took off as a cinematic genre, in which physical movement and visual style predominated."[19] Although Fairbanks did not direct his films, he can be called their auteur because he

> masterminded their creation, writing the screen stories, collaborating on stunt design, selecting the cast, supervising the production details.... The ingredients [of the swashbuckler]—character archetypes, elaborate sets, acrobatic setpieces and stylised [sic] content—were definitively established by Doug's [sic] films.[20]

The immediate literary ancestors of the swashbuckling films are the romantic historical novels and plays on which so many of them are based. Sir Walter Scott can be called the father of historical fiction. He had been influenced by the late eighteenth-century's gothic revival, with its interest in chivalry and medieval romances, and its tales of mystery, adventure, and the supernatural that became the Gothic novel. From these, he fashioned a new form, the serious historical novel, based on careful research into the past but using history to illuminate unchanging aspects of human personality.[21] Under Scott's influence, nineteenth-century novelists like Edward Bulwer-Lytton, R.D. Blackmore, and W. Harrison Ainsworth produced a flood of historical novels. But Scott's most important disciple was Alexander Dumas, who transformed the serious historical novel into the popular swashbuckler.[22] Dumas

> laid down the characters and the archetypes, the settings and the ingredients...[of] the swashbuckling novel as opposed to the historical novel *per se*. The bulky historical detail, the concern with the recreation of actual historical events and periods is pared down. The costumes, settings, milieu and ambiance of the period remain, but as the accoutrements of romance.[23]

Historical events are replaced by duels, chases, and escapes, a "ritual of action-pieces,"[24] built around two basic hero types, the gentleman outlaw and the gentleman adventurer. Dumas' many works, such as *The Three Musketeers* and *The Count of Monte Cristo*, and those of his many nineteenth- and twentieth-century followers, such as Baroness Orczy *(The Scarlet Pimpernel)*, Anthony Hope *(The Prisoner of Zenda)*, and Robert Louis Stevenson *(Kidnapped, The Black Arrow, Treasure Island)*, were often turned into popular stage plays which later became the basis for those early swashbuckling films.

These nineteenth-century cape-and-sword plays[25] are but one variety of melodrama, and the swashbuckler has much in common with melodrama as a whole. Both tend to exteriorize their characters' emotional lives, stressing encounters between rather than conflicts within them, transforming internal problems into external events.[26] At their core is the clash between good and evil. Peter Brooks has written of melodrama's "manicheanism," its habit of polarizing the world into good and evil.[27] These moral forces are also personified as heroes and villains. As Robert B. Heilman has said, the clash is not between the good and evil within man, but between good men and evil men. Melodrama "attributes whatever is wrong to evil men and its faith is that good men can decontaminate or eliminate evil men and thus restore . . . a normal state of serene well being."[28] In melodrama, therefore, moral issues are usually resolved by violence;[29] similarly, the climax of most swashbucklers is the inevitable duel betwen hero and villain.

The duel is not the only inevitable aspect of the swashbuckler, for the genre is one of the most strongly conventionalized, and those conventions have not changed since Fairbanks' era. In fact, Jeffrey Richards insists that what separates the swashbuckler from other film genres is its resistance to change, its inherent inability to take on "the psychological complexity of the latter-day western, the social significance of the problem drama, the violence and cynicism"[30] of recent gangster films. He defines the swashbuckler by its morally black-and-white world where action "is ritualized, emotions stereotyped, the characters are archetypes rather than individuals."[31]

In its dependence on convention and its expectation of audience familiarity with those conventions, the swashbuckler enrolls itself in a tradition that dates back to the earliest forms of drama we know. From ancient Greek amphitheaters to modern living rooms, audiences familiar with the pattern of their plays have always enjoyed anticipating movements of plot and discovering unexpected variations, finding satisfaction in their sense of the inevitability of dramatic fate. They are like a man watching a building under construction after having read the blueprints, gazing in fascination as each brick is put in place, each story added, until the building becomes a single, unified structure and the form it has been growing into stands before him completed.[32]

Moreover, with its world of moral absolutes, its archetypal characters, and its almost ritual-like form, the swashbuckler begins to resemble the earliest forms of modern drama that we know, the medieval mystery and morality play.[33] Certainly its popular emotional function is similar, to provide a ritual celebration of the exorcism of evil and the triumph of good. A darkened theater replaces the medieval church, the characters are somewhat more complex than the abstractly named allegorical figures of morality plays, and the action is more intricate. But the dramatic representation of the struggle against evil and the coming together of an audience to witness and vicariously participate in this representation remain comparable.

Northrop Frye finds that all forms of narrative, including drama, belong to one of four basic kinds: comedy, romance, tragedy, irony or satire. The swashbuckler is commonly thought to be a type of romance; several critics have adopted this view, including Richards[34] and Thomas Agabiti,[35] both of whom specifically cite Frye.[36] The swashbuckler does have its roots in romance. Frye, for example, tells us that in romance the essential plot element is adventure and the essential formal element is a tendency to polarize the world into an innocent idyllic realm and a demonic nightmare realm, and the characters into heroes and villains.[37] The structure of romance, for Frye, is that of the

successful quest, and such a completed form has three main stages: the stage of the perilous journey and the preliminary minor adventures; the crucial struggle, usually some kind of battle in which either the hero or his foe, or both, must die; and the exaltation of the hero.[38]

But I would argue that the film swashbuckler is as much a form of comedy as romance, primarily because of the importance it gives to the relationship between hero and heroine. On several occasions Frye has asserted that the structure of comedy is based on the effort of a young man to overcome various barriers and win the young woman he loves.[39] The villains in the swashbuckler, as in comedy, are those figures who separate hero and heroine.

Furthermore, while romance exalts the individual hero, comedy has a strong social implication, celebrating the "festive society."[40] Frye notes that comedies move

> from one kind of society to another. At the beginning of the play the obstructing characters are in charge of the play's society, and the audience recognizes that they are usurpers. At the end of the play the device in the plot that brings hero and heroine together causes a new society to crystallize around the hero. . . . [41]

In the swashbuckler the villain is also usually a political figure, a tyrant of some sort, and by the end of the film the hero not only removes him from government but often replaces him himself. In fact, the three part structure of the typical swashbuckler combines that of romance and comedy. In the first section, hero and heroine meet and fall in love (although they may not express it and may even act as if they dislike each other), while the villain plots to destroy the hero and expand his tyranny. In the second section, the villain seems triumphant; the society suffers under his rule while hero and heroine are separated and surrounded by danger, including the threat of death. In the final section, the hero escapes the dangers, conquers the villain, thus freeing the society from his cruelty, and marries the heroine.

I now want to look at *Captain Blood* from this dual perspective of romance and comedy. The film was produced by Warner Brothers in 1935, with a script by Casey Robinson, based on the 1922 novel by Rafael Sabatini (1875-1950). Sabatini was one of the most prolific writers of swashbucklers;[42] many of his novels, including *Scaramouche, The Sea Hawk,* and *The Black Swan,* have been filmed, a few several times. *Captain Blood* itself was originally filmed in 1924.[43] The 1935 version was Warner's first big-budget, talking, costume film, and helped inaugurate among all the studios a cycle of similar films that lasted until the start of World War II.[44] The film was originally to star Robert Donat, chosen because of his performance in *The Count of Monte Cristo* (1934), but when Donat refused the part because of a salary dispute,[45] Errol Flynn was given his first leading role. *Captain Blood* was also the first time Flynn played opposite Olivia de Havilland; they were to work together frequently. Finally, the film was the first for which Erich Wolfgang Korngold wrote the music; along with Max Steiner, he was to become one of Warner Brother's leading composers.[46]

Captain Blood's plot possesses an important quality of romance; its hero suffers a loss of identity. Northrop Frye tells us that most romances end "with a return to a state of identity, and begin with a departure from it."[47] This "loss or confusion or break in the continuity of identity" often takes the form of a "sharp descent in social status, from riches to poverty, from privilege to a struggle to survive, or even slavery."[48] In *Captain Blood,* Peter Blood undergoes a series of identity changes. He starts as a doctor, suffers a "sharp descent" into slavery, becomes a pirate and finally a colonial governor. The film ends with Blood returning to a social position higher than when he began, but along the way he plunges into the demonic, nightmare realm of romance. As we will see, that realm seems to be one of Curtiz's favorite subjects; it is often one of the two contrasting worlds that seem to appear in almost all of Curtiz's films. I will discuss these worlds more fully in the next chapter. In *Captain Blood* the nightmare world appears in the images of imprisonment that form one of the film's major visual motifs.

Curtiz introduces this motif with his first shot of Blood. The film begins with Jeremy Pitt's frantic ride to Blood's home, to ask him to treat a wounded rebel. Pitt pounds on Blood's door; the peephole slowly opens, revealing a small, barred window. Behind those bars, partly masked by them and framed by the window, is Peter Blood (Plate 1). The implication of imprisonment is appropriate here, for this innocent act of opening the door and admitting Jeremy Pitt begins Blood's odyssey from freedom to slavery and back.

This image, Blood's face behind bars, is repeated several times in different contexts; the contrast of contexts comments on Blood's changing fortunes. When it next appears, Blood really is a prisoner; we see him peering through the bars of a porthole aboard the slave ship bound for Port Royal and the auction block (Plate 2). The last time we see it Blood's fortunes have reached a turning point. He and the other escaped slaves have climbed aboard the Spanish ship lying at anchor off Port Royal. As they are about to descend upon the Spanish sailors below deck, there is a low angle shot of Blood gazing down through the grating of a hatch cover (Plate 3). Again he is framed and masked by bars, but here the image is an ironic reversal; it is the Spaniards, not Blood, who soon will be prisoners.

But it is not altogether ironic. Blood escapes to the sea, yet the sea is only a subtler form of imprisonment. Frye notes that in romance the sea often functions as part of that demonic lower world.[49] Blood is free only within the confines of his ship and a few pirate islands; he cannot return to England, nor to Port Royal and the woman he loves. As John Davis says, of all his crew, "only Blood fully feels the desperation of being a man without a country."[50]

Curtiz uses the physical details of sailing ships to express this form of imprisonment. In all the shipboard sequences, from the boarding of the Spanish ship to the final sea battle against the French, he entwines his characters in a chaotic tangle of ropes and rigging (Plate 4). When Blood and his crew first reach the Spanish ship, for instance, we see a long shot of the backs of the men climbing aboard. Small and centered in the frame, the men seem squeezed between the webs of rigging and rope ladders that fill the right and left foreground. Later sequences include long, high shots that look down onto tiny figures trapped by networks of crisscrossing lines, disorienting low angle shots dominated by heavy masts slanting across the screen, and shots with flapping sails covering half the frame (Plates 5 and 6).

Throughout the film, in shipboard scenes and elsewhere, high-contrast, fretted lighting adds to the impression of imprisonment. Light, streaming through bars, grates and other shadow-making objects, falls across the characters in heavy stripes of jet black and bright white, pressing against them like a physical force.

Blood's imprisonment and adventures relate him to the heroes of romance; his personality relates him to the heroes of comedy. In his important book, *The Adventurer,* Paul Zweig distinguishes between what he calls the adventurer and the hero. The adventurer dives into the demonic world of romance because he belongs to it as much as to the world of men. He travels "between the worlds,...condemned to a life of endless mobility. Because he is at home everywhere, he will be at home nowhere." The hero is

> a heightened man who, more than other men, possesses qualities of courage, loyalty, resourcefulness, charisma, above all, selflessness. He is an example of right behavior; the sort of man who risks his life to protect a society's values, sacrificing his personal needs for those of the community.

The adventurer has all the hero's qualities but one; he "is the opposite of selfless...a self-determined man who defends, not us, but himself. His inner destiny is his law." The adventurer discovers within himself "a mirror of the demonic world...the dark furies against which his bravery..." battles. The hero, on the other hand, "chooses loyalty, and the clear light of the human world."[51]

Zweig believes swashbuckling heroes are adventurers; he says the adventurer "flits across the screen in forgettable pirate movies."[52] But by his own definition, Peter Blood, like most film swashbucklers, is really the tamer, more civilized, highly moral hero. In one of his very first speeches, he states explicitly his decision to give up the adventurer's homeless life. Mrs. Barlow, his housekeeper, suggests that some have called him coward for not involving himself in the rebellion against King James. Blood answers

> Mrs. Barlow me darlin...I've fought for the French against the Spanish and the Spanish against the French and learned my seamanship in the Dutch navy. Having had adventure enough in six years to last me six lives I came here and changed my sword for a lancet....[53]

He has chosen to rejoin society as a doctor, to be a "healer" and not a "slayer" of men.

He is clearly a creature of courage, confidence, and intelligence, but his Irish brogue and cocky manner give him distinctly human dimensions. Almost every one of his speeches is punctuated by a broguish "bedad," "me darlin'," "methinks," or their equivalent. He shows his conceit in his first speech to Mrs. Barlow; while talking, he adjusts his collar and smiles into the mirror with great satisfaction. At times his conceit seems more foolhardy than courageous, but we enjoy it because it is one of his defenses against the villains. For example, when the officer who arrests him for treating a rebel misunderstands his Latin, he says, "If your wit were as big as your voice, me dearest, it's a great man you'd be." Later, during the slave auction, he refuses to bare his teeth for Colonel Bishop's inspection. Angered, the colonel slaps his face; he answers the slap with a mocking smile.

Blood's intelligence, shown during his slavery by his manipulation of Port Royal's doctors and governor, becomes his most dangerous weapon when he begins his piratic career. As he and his crew sail away, a superimposed title declares: "And thus Captain Blood began his career of piracy... with a ship, a handful of men, and a brain...." It is Blood's intelligence that most appeals to Levasseur, who suggests their partnership by saying, "Your brain is the greatest in all the Caribbean... with your brains and my strength there is nothing we cannot do."

Despite his brain, Blood can make human errors, such as agreeing to this partnership. He does, at least, give voice to his suspicions: "Well, bedad, methinks the greatest captain on the coast has just made the greatest mistake the most common ordinary fool could make." Of course this is a bit of melodramatic foreshadowing, preparing us for the climactic duel between Blood and Levasseur. But it also indicates that our hero retains his accurate instincts, though he does not always follow them.

Blood's most important quality, however, is his sense of justice and humanity, his moral code. We see it first in his unhesitating willingness to care for the wounded rebel, despite the personal dangers. We see it again, at his trial when he verbally collides with the chief judge, Baron Jeffries (Leonard Mudie). Blood condemns the "injustice of keeping a man locked up for three months" without a hearing. Jeffries declares that anyone aiding a traitor is himself a traitor; Blood answers that he was only doing his duty as a doctor.

Jeffries: Your duty is to your king.
Blood: I thought it was to my fellow man.

Throughout the film, Blood aims his anger at those who, like Colonel Bishop, treat their fellow man with savagery and cruelty.

With all this talk of Blood's morality, we should not forget that he is, after all, a pirate. But rather than threatening his moral position, his piracy simply enrolls him in the venerable literary society of the outlaw-hero. Dating back to the medieval Robin Hood legends, becoming highly popular in nineteenth-century melodrama,[54] the noble bandit is usually seen as not only more courageous and clever than the official law keepers but also morally superior to them. Authority is the oppressor, protecting privileged aristocracy, representing arrogance and selfishness. The outlaw protects the common man, and represents compassion and human decency. The bandit, in fact, becomes a kind of political rebel and, as John Davis remarks[55] and as we will see in later chapters, the rebel-hero appears in many of the Curtiz-Flynn adventure films.

Blood himself is as gallant a pirate as a lady could hope to meet. He joins with Levasseur on the condition that they do not take any women prisoners. Jeffrey Richards notes his strong "adherence to the gentlemanly code" which prevents him "from doing anything violent to Bishop, the chief perpetrator of the evils of slavery."[56] Most significantly, Blood becomes a pirate and attacks English ships only because of the English government's corruption. When Arabella asks him how many lives it cost to procure his plunder, he answers, "As few as possible . . . it wasn't lives I was after." What he is after is revenge against the "unclean tyrant," King James, and his representatives, and once James is removed from the throne Blood becomes a loyal Englishman again.

King James's representatives are the film's villains. Like its hero, they seem related less to the mythic world of romance than to the social world of comedy;[57] they are the masters of the old society which the hero overthrows. Baron Jeffries (Leonard Mudie), for example, has clearly prejudged Blood and hears his defense unwillingly. He refuses to believe that Blood is a doctor and will not allow him to call witnesses to prove it because, "We haven't the time." When Blood declares his allegiance to his "fellow man" instead of his king, Jeffries convicts him because of these words that have come "out of his own rascally mouth." Aristocratic, emotionless, deathly somnolent in speech, he cloaks his sadism in patriotism.

Colonel Bishop (Lionel Atwill) is far more active a villain, his cruelty more energetic, his sadism more passionate. As aristocratic as Baron Jeffries, he prides himself on his personal friendship with King James. He considers the prisoners at the slave auction to be less than human, traitors worthy of being "hanged, drawn, and quartered." He treats them like cheap cattle, smacking their stomachs, inspecting their teeth and muscles. Later, he takes obvious pleasure in whipping Jeremy Pitt and branding a recaptured runaway.

But the blindness of his brutality can turn him into a fool. After the Spanish attack on Port Royal, he rows out, alone and unarmed, to the captured Spanish ship to see who has saved the city. His arrogance becomes idiocy when he offers the escaped slaves the possibility of a "slight reduction" in their sentences as a reward. Quite naturally, they want to hang him on the spot, but Blood cries out that "hanging is too good for him . . . throw him overboard." Although the film denies us the satisfaction of his death, it does end with his complete humiliation.

When he returns to Port Royal after unsuccessfully searching for the infamous Captain Blood, he learns that, as a friend of the now deposed James, he must beg mercy from the new governor. As Governor Blood slowly raises his head and reveals his face, Bishop's expression changes from shock to submission; his only response is wordlessly to remove his hat.

Port Royal's governor, Mr. Steed (George Hassel), is more fatuous than ferocious, his villainy stemming from ignorance rather than action. But it is an ignorance bred of aristocratic privilege and selfishness that blinds him to other people's suffering. Bishop's branding of the runaway dissolves to a closeup of Steed's fat, foolish face, his lips pursed in a silly grimace as he says, "What a cruel shame that any man should suffer so...." Then the camera pans down to a closeup of his leg resting on a pillow, as he completes his sentence, "with beastly gout." Curtiz's little joke reveals Steed's utter self-absorption, the complete reversal of Blood's selflessness. He is not malicious, simply ineffectual; he does not actively create evil, but he does nothing to stop it.

The only villain who is not part of the Establishment, nor even an aristocrat, is Levasseur. Although he is one of the film's most memorable characters, he appears in only two major sequences, the first, to establish his partnership with Blood, the second, to end it with his death. He seems, at first, to have three functions: he is an evil pirate, whose taking of women prisoners contrasts with Blood's chivalry; his capture of Arabella allows Blood to become reunited with her; and he creates the excuse for one of the film's major set pieces, the duel between him and Blood.

A title introduces him as the "hard fighting, hard gaming French rascal, Captain Levasseur." The word "rascal" (despite Baron Jeffries' use of it) implies a kind of amiability, a youthful exuberance and animal vitality which he certainly possesses. As the duel begins, there is a shot of him with sword drawn, eyes blazing, curly hair blowing wildly about his head, his teeth bared in an ecstatic grin as if his face could not contain all the energy pouring out of him.

What all this lusty animal energy means, of course, is that Levasseur's real function is to be the only villain who is a sexual threat. We first see him at a boisterous pirate feast, surrounded by greasy men tearing at a fat, roasting pig. He signs the articles of partnership with Blood, drinks heartily, then lets his eyes wander to the whores at the party, while Blood prophetically remarks that women will be the death of him. He captures Lord Willoughby and Arabella and informs them that the Englishman will be sent to collect a ransom while Arabella will remain with him. "I get very lonely on this island," he says. Blood offers to buy her, but he chooses to fight. Because he is the only direct threat to Blood's sexual supremacy, he is the only villain to die. Bishop's virulent sadism may represent a repressed and perverse sexuality, but it remains repressed and he remains alive. Levasseur is just too plainly potent; when he draws his sword, he signs his death warrant.

Levasseur's role as a sexual rather than a social threat confirms what I said earlier about the importance of the hero/heroine relationship to the swash-buckler. What most distinguishes Peter Blood from the heroes of romance and relates him to the heroes of comedy is his pursuit of the heroine. Paul Zweig tells us that the adventurer's most dangerous adversary is woman. Woman represents home and family, both the immediate one and the larger one of community, society, all the civilizing forces from which he flees. Like Huck Finn, the adventurer feels free only when he lights out for the territory.[58] Peter Blood is simply too amorous to be an adventurer in this sense. As soon as he sees Arabella Bishop, he is determined to have her; that determination gives the film a comic shape; their final union gives it a comic conclusion.

The lovers are separated not only by the villains, social and sexual, but also by their own personalities. Arabella, a worthy and equal companion for Blood, shares his human sympathies, witty vitality, and, most of all, his stubborn pride. But this pride imprisons their affection; indeed, emotional imprisonment is as important to the film as physical imprisonment. Arabella and Blood act like Shakespeare's quarrelling lovers Beatrice and Benedick; their romance is a continuing power struggle with the upper hand alternating until at last they learn to exchange embraces instead of arguments.

This struggle begins at the slave auction. Arabella, attracted to Blood by his insolent refusal to humble himself before Bishop, buys him above her uncle's objections, then is angered when he directs his insolence at her. She soon asserts her power over him by helping him without his knowledge. Knowing that Governor Steed has gout, she slyly suggests that he try the services of her slave, a former physician, then laughs at the thought of how "annoyed Peter Blood would be if he knew" she had helped him.

Shortly after, Arabella coyly pretends not to see Blood emerge from his new patient's house, then flirts with him until he admits he hates the "unclean tyrant" King James. She warns him that such traitorous talk could earn him a flogging, but he answers that he'll not be flogged while the governor has gout, and the scene ends with his self-satisfied grin.

They clash again at their next meeting, their dialogue a series of halting steps towards each other, until again Blood steps too far. He admits that Arabella is his master, but he would prefer to call her friend. She answers that she would be glad to be his friend. Then he kisses her. She slaps him. He must not forget his slavery, she says; he answers, grimly, that remembering is a "characteristic the Irish have in common with the elephant."

The pattern continues when Blood, now Levasseur's pirate partner, tries to buy the captured Arabella. She claims she has "no wish to be bought" by Blood; but he, now in the dominant position, reminds her that, as "a lady once said to her slave," her wishes are unimportant. After he has killed Levasseur, they talk in his cabin aboard ship and again come together briefly. He offers her jewels but she rejects them, calling him, not slave, but words more stinging, thief and pirate. Only after they have returned to Port Royal are the internal, as well as external, obstacles to their feelings swept away. Arabella, recognizing the risk he took to return her there, admits her love for him; Blood, now not only a free man but the governor of Port Royal, admits his love for her.

All of this is presented in a distinctive visual style, the directorial signature of Michael Curtiz. I have already suggested one aspect of this style in talking about the visual motif of imprisonment: Curtiz's fondness for shadows and for elaborate, complex compositions in which objects surround and entrap the characters, often obscuring them from the camera. This technique allows Curtiz to comment on relationships between characters, and to give scenes an emotional depth they might otherwise lack.

As an example, let us consider in detail the relatively brief scene in which the Spanish leader demands from Bishop, Steed, and another English officer a huge ransom to spare the city. It begins with a medium shot of the Governor's office (Plate 9). At lower frame-left the three Englishmen sit around a desk; they are small, background figures. Looming above them are three enormous black shadows cast by three unseen Spaniards. In the center of the frame, in midground (i.e., closer to the camera and therefore larger than the Englishmen) stands the Spanish pirate leader, casting an even larger shadow behind him. A bright chandelier hangs in the upper right part of the frame. Cut to a full shot of the three seated Englishmen, the bare wall above them black with shadow (Plate 10).

The effect of these two shots seems to depend on a contrast between large, dark masses, associated with the Spanish, and small, bright ones, associated with the English. In the first one, the dark power of the Spanish shadows dwarfs the tiny Englishmen; the shadows have more substance than the figures. In the second shot, the English are again in an isolated pool of light trapped by the enveloping darkness.

The third shot seems to reverse this dialectic of light and dark: we look down onto the Spanish leader, still in midground and the center of the frame; the English are glimpsed in the far left background (Plate 11). But the visual emphasis is not on shadows; the entire right half of the frame is filled with a huge closeup of the brightly blazing, multi-tiered chandelier. Here, the Spaniard seems associated with light, his power over the English linked to the chandelier's splendor.

Actually, this image's effect depends partly on its total visual contrast with the preceding one, the contrast between a simple image and a complex one. The flamboyant, gaudy closeup of the chandelier, dominated by the candles' dancing flames, follows the stark, simple full shot of the Englishmen, dominated by the bare, shadowed wall. These images create two different visual worlds; seeing them so juxtaposed, we experience the conquest of one world by the other.

Another of Curtiz's favorite techniques is the high shot that establishes both an environment and a character's relationship to the environment. In later films, by placing his camera on a crane, Curtiz adds a downward movement to the shot so that the audience not only surveys the scene from an objective, godlike perspective, but is literally pulled into it. In *Captain Blood,* a high shot of a prison courtyard begins the scene of Blood's trial (Plate 8). We look down, past three large gallows in the foreground, to a street in the background, running diagonally across the upper half of the frame. The gallows loom over a tiny line of prisoners who march along the street to their trial. The shot's meaning is unmistakable: the men are quite literally under the threat of death.

A similar shot introduces us to Colonel Bishop's plantation, a garden of delights dominated by an enormous water wheel. Stretching across the screen like some colossal tinker toy, the water wheel is the machine on which the slaves sweat away their lives (Plate 7). At frame-right is a large, horizontal gear from which long spokes radiate. Slaves, tied to these spokes, turn this gear, which meshes with a vertical one in center-frame. An axle connects it to a second, larger vertical wheel at frame-left. Water buckets hang from it like the seats of a ferris wheel; as the wheel turns the buckets are lowered into an immense watering trough. One slave walks the wheel, like a rat on a treadmill, and hands the filled buckets to other slaves waiting on the ground. Curtiz follows the initial high shot with images that associate the water wheel with prison bars; he keeps parts of it in the foreground and shoots through them to slaves in the background, framing the figures within the all-powerful structure.

Curtiz uses Korngold's music, low, mournful, and ominous,[59] as well as sound effects, to add to the overall effect. A drum's slow, deep beat blends into the sound of a whip; a huge, bare-chested black slave beats time for the others; in another shot, in the background, a man is flogged, the whip striking his back with precisely the same rhythm.

We can see how a number of Curtiz's cinematic devices work together in the scene of Bishop branding the runaway. It opens with a shot of Colonel Bishop on horseback; in the left foreground a slave is tied to a tree. Bishop explains that the slave was caught trying to escape and will be branded with the letters "FT," for "Fugitive Traitor." As he speaks the medium shot cuts to a closeup of the victim, his scarred arms stretched out on a crossbeam above his head. Cut to a close high shot, looking straight down at a pit of burning coals. A branding iron is pulled out of the coals, turned directly to the camera and thrust at the audience, the letters "FT" glowing in closeup. Cut to a medium tracking shot along a row of prisoners; they watch silently, fear and anger mingled on their faces. Cut to a low angle three-quarter shot of Colonel Bishop on horseback, warning the prisoners to brand the letters in their brains lest they be branded on their hides. Cut to a closeup of the victim, the smoking iron pulling away from his face, his cheek bearing the FT brand. Dissolve to the shot of Governor Steed complaining of gout.

Although this scene's editing adds to its force, each shot is composed for maximum emotional effect. The low angle view of Colonel Bishop bellowing emphasizes his brute power; the reaction shot of the prisoners acts as a momentary choral comment on the events, while the camera movement maintains the forward thrust of the action to its climactic moment of pain; the dissolve to Governor Steed is a black joke that first relieves the tension, then reinforces it with new villainies. Most impressive of all, the subjective shot of the branding iron forces the audience to participate emotionally in the action.

Both the moving camera and the subjective shot are also part of Curtiz's stylistic signature. As John Davis remarks, Curtiz "loved to move the camera if there was a narrative justification. . . . Often he would use a short dolly-in on a character to emphasize an emotion or a line of dialogue. . . ."[60] The subjective shot extends our identification with a character. By showing us only what the character sees, the camera transforms our eyes into his; we momentarily become that character.

I would, in fact, agree with Davis' assertion that all of Curtiz's technical proficiency

> served the single functional purpose of involving the audience in the action on the screen . . . Curtiz always knew exactly how far from the action, and at what angle, to place the camera to achieve maximum emotional identification from his audience.[61]

But Curtiz's ornate, baroque style, with its emphasis on the physical environment surrounding a character, has other effects as well. Ultimately, that style suggests that Curtiz's characters are identified by their environment. Each of the visual devices we have considered, the patterns of light and shadow that entrap a character, the complex compositions in which objects block the camera's view of him, the high crane shots that look down on him lost within the world on screen, the subjective shot that draws the audience into that world—each expresses the force of environment on the character's life.

In *Captain Blood* this force becomes associated with fate, an equally powerful element in Blood's life. Blood himself repeatedly refers to it. As a prisoner on his way to Port Royal, he muses about the destiny that has rescued him from execution only to send him to the "living death" of slavery, and concludes, "Faith, it's an uncertain world." Later, when an unexpected explosion prevents Bishop from beating him, he comments, "This is what I call a timely interruption, though what will come of it the Devil only knows." The timely interruption is the Spanish attack on Port Royal, and what comes of it is Blood's escape into piracy.[62] Fate, in fact, impels him on all his adventures; we first see him behind the bars of his door-window, because he is already fate's prisoner.

Earlier I spoke of another kind of fate, the dramatic fate imposed by the conventions of structure and situation that shape the swashbuckler genre. I mentioned that our familiarity with those conventions is an essential element of our experience of any single film. The strongest convention in comedy is, of course, that of the happy ending. However, for a film to be fully effective, we must feel some threat against that convention. At some level we must believe that the triumph of evil is a real possibility, and we must experience a tension between that possibility and our expectation of a happy ending.[63] Curtiz's style expresses an understanding of this need. His talking shadows, the eloquent images that form his visual worlds, allow us to play a double role. We are both the godlike observer looking down from the safe distance of the crane shot, and the participant, forced by the subjective camera to become the hero and share his adventures.

2

The Castle and the Forest: The Adventures of Robin Hood

Synopsis of the Film

When King Richard of England (Ian Hunter) is captured during a crusade, his brother, Prince John (Claude Rains) takes over the Regency and begins a reign of oppression against the Saxons. Sir Robin of Locksley (Errol Flynn) stops John's ally, Sir Guy of Gisbourne (Basil Rathbone), from arresting Much the Miller's son (Herbert Mundin), then arrives uninvited at a feast in Nottingham Castle, where he tells John he will organize a revolt against his tyranny.

Outlawed for his actions, Robin and his friend Will Scarlet (Patric Knowles) convince Little John (Alan Hale) and Friar Tuck (Eugene Pallette) to join their growing band. The merry men capture a procession carrying gold for King Richard's ransom, led by Gisbourne and the Sheriff of Nottingham (Melville Cooper). With them is Maid Marian (Olivia de Havilland), who falls in love with Robin. In revenge, the prince plots to trap Robin at an archery tournament; the trap works, but Robin is saved from execution with help from Marian, who is herself arrested and condemned to death. Richard returns to England in disguise, hiding from would-be assassins in Sherwood. When Much tells of Marian's impending execution and John's plans to crown himself king, Richard reveals himself and, with Robin, leads an attack on Nottingham Castle. Robin kills Gisbourne and rescues Marian; Richard banishes John and announces Marian's marriage to Robin.

Perhaps the best known, best loved figure from Anglo-Saxon legend is Robin Hood. First mentioned in the 1377 version of *Piers Plowman,* he appeared in ballads throughout the fourteenth and fifteenth centuries, early plays of the fifteenth and sixteenth centuries, and remained so popular that he found his way into nineteenth century novels such as Scott's *Ivanhoe,* and onto the American stage via the de Koven-Smith light opera of 1890, *Robin Hood.*[1] He was the subject of some of the earliest film swashbucklers[2] and of one of Douglas

Fairbanks' greatest successes, the 1922 *Robin Hood* (directed by Alan Dwan). But the definitive Robin Hood film[3] is Curtiz's *The Adventures of Robin Hood,* produced by Warner Brothers in 1938.

In the previous chapter I spoke about *Captain Blood* as romance and comedy. In this chapter I want to pursue this notion of the swashbuckler by looking at *The Adventures of Robin Hood* as a comedy/romance of the green world. I will argue that the central opposition between an innocent green world and a corrupt court world molds every aspect of the film by considering first its structure and characters and then its visual style.

The Adventures of Robin Hood, with a script by Norman Reilly Raine and Seton I. Miller, and a score by Erich Wolfgang Korngold (who also scored *Captain Blood*), was the first Curtiz-Flynn film shot in technicolor. It won academy awards for Carl Jules Weyl's art direction, Ralph Dawson's editing, and Korngold's music. Although Curtiz directed most of the film, he shares screen credit with William Keighley, who began the film but was removed after about eight weeks work. I have already cited Whittemore and Cecchetini's claim that Curtiz's power and influence enabled him to persuade Jack Warner to reassign the film to him. The usual explanation is that Keighley's direction was felt to be too weak; Rudy Behlmer says this, and provides the most complete account I have found of who directed what:

> Late in '37 the cast and crew, under the guidance of director William Keighley, traveled 600 miles to Bidwell Park in the town of Chico, California, to film the Sherwood Forest sequence. There, while Keighley handled the principals, B. Reeves ("Breezy") Eason, specialist in action sequences involving horses, directed the scenes of the treasure-train party en route through the forest, all of the horse action, and some of the scenes of the merry men dropping on Sir Guy's party from the tree tops. Eason had originally been engaged to handle a spectacular jousting sequence which was to open the picture but was eliminated in the final script.
>
> After the company returned from Chico shooting started on the Archery Tournament at Busch Gardens in Pasadena, but after a few days it was decided, by Jack Warner, Hal Wallis and Henry Blanke, to replace Keighley with Warner's top director, Michael Curtiz. The reasons seem to have been Keighley's too lighthearted approach and the lack of impact in the action sequences.
>
> Curtiz completed the picture and shot additional material, possibly with Eason, at Hidden Valley, just outside Los Angeles in the San Fernando Valley, to embellish and punch up the action scenes previously shot at Chico.[4]

In summary, then, Keighley (and Eason) directed most of the Sherwood Forest scenes; Curtiz directed all the Nottingham Castle and town scenes, all the other interiors, and apparently some of the archery tournament and additional forest scenes.[5]

Although the film does seem to have a strong stylistic consistency,[6] it is possible to detect some differences between the Keighley and Curtiz sections. In general the Sherwood scenes do seem to have less visual "impact"; they are flatter, more two-dimensional; characters are arranged horizontally across the screen, rather than diagonally to create perspective effects; there are fewer subjective shots, fewer camera movements,[7] and foilage simply frames faces, rather than coming between camera and character as often in Curtiz's images.

In his *Anatomy of Criticism* and elsewhere, Northrop Frye discusses a form of romantic comedy he calls the "drama of the green world" whose theme is the "triumph of life and love over the waste land."[8] In such a comedy, the action "begins in a world represented as a normal world, moves into the green world, goes into a metamorphosis there in which the comic resolution is achieved, and returns to the normal world."[9] The normal world of court and city suffers some form of corruption, be it moral, political, or romantic; the green world forest is a place of healing and renewal. Characters flee the court and enter the green world where all problems are solved, injustices corrected, and romantic complications untangled. Villains repent, hero and heroine are united, and all return to the court bringing with them the green world's comic spirit. In "The Argument of Comedy," Frye explicitly refers to Robin Hood as a "traditional denizen of the green world . . . the outlaw who manages to suggest a better kind of society than those who make him an outlaw can produce."[10]

The action of *The Adventures of Robin Hood* does move from a corrupt court world, Nottingham Castle, to a healing green world, Sherwood Forest, and then returns to a redeemed court. As we will see, within the forest Marian "goes into a metamorphosis," switching her allegiance from Prince John to Robin Hood.

This opposition of idyllic and demonic, innocent and corrupt worlds appears in various forms in almost all of Curtiz's films. Throughout this discussion I will call them "castle" and "forest," court world and green world, but I am not limiting these terms to Frye's definitions nor to the way they appear in *The Adventures of Robin Hood.* I use them to stand for a whole series of related oppositions within Curtiz's films, some of them far more complex than the simple opposition of good and evil, innocence and corruption. Among them are: cynicism and idealism, imprisonment and freedom, war and love, public duty and private desire. However, with this variety and complexity of meaning in mind, I do think the terms are adequate metaphors.

In *The Adventures of Robin Hood,* the opposition of court and forest structures the plot, characters, and visual style. At first glance, *The Adventures of Robin Hood* may appear rather loosely structured. Unlike the plot of *Captain Blood,* in which each event causes the next, *The Adventures of Robin Hood*'s plot seems to divide into disconnected halves; Robin's escape from execution marks a new beginning; the film then seems free to follow any direction it wants to. But we experience the film, not as a loose, meandering work, but as a tight, suspenseful one.[11] What gives the film its coherence is not the causal connection between events but the pattern these events create. During the first two thirds of the film, for almost every important action in the court world, there is an analogous action in Sherwood; further, every major action in the film's last third echoes a similar action in the first two thirds. Moreover, for every character in Nottingham, there is a comparable character in Sherwood; visually, the court world becomes associated with one group of colors, the forest world with another.

The film opens by introducing Nottingham Castle's arrogant villains, Prince John (Claude Rains), self-appointed regent of England, and Sir Guy of Gisbourne (Basil Rathbone), the Norman lord of Nottingham; they plot to prevent King Richard's ransom. Almost immediately thereafter, we meet Sir Robin of Locksley (Errol Flynn) and his friend, Will Scarlett (Patric Knowles), who protect one of Richard's loyal subjects, Much the Miller's Son (Herbert Mundin). This pattern of action and reaction continues as Robin is outlawed, expelled from the protection of the court's false law, only to become spokesman for the green world's true law, administering its solemn oath to his followers:

> ... free men of the forest, swear to despoil the rich only to give to the poor, to shelter the old and the helpless, to protect all women, rich or poor, Norman or Saxon; swear to fight for a free England, to protect her loyally until the return of our king and sovereign, Richard the Lion Heart....

Similarly, two brief montage sequences become Nottingham's statement and Sherwood's reply. The first shows the Saxons' sufferings under John's injustice: Norman soldiers steal meat from a peasant; other soldiers force another peasant into slavery. The second depicts the merry men's growing resistance: a soldier tortures a peasant until an arrow strikes his chest; other soldiers storm into a tavern, split open a wine cask and terrorize the tavernkeeper, until another arrow ends their fun.

The most obvious instance of this pattern is the contrasting feasts in Nottingham Castle and Sherwood Forest. The Nottingham scene begins with a title suggesting the castle's physical and emotional temperature:

> The great cold hall of Nottingham Castle ... knew an unaccustomed warmth this night, for John and his friends were met to celebrate a promising future.

A high shot follows, looking down at the huge hall, emphasizing its icy gray walls and inhospitable spaciousness. Then we cut to a slightly lower shot, which descends and pans left, following a procession carrying great platters of food: "haunches of venison and legs of lamb, roast chicken and roast quail, piles of fresh fruit, great chocolate cakes, flagons of wine ..."[12] The camera seems to be heading towards the dais, where the prince, Gisbourne, Maid Marian (Olivia de Havilland), the Sheriff of Nottingham (Melville Cooper), and the Bishop of the

Black Canons (Montague Love) are seated. But Curtiz ends the shot unexpectedly, commenting ironically on Prince John as he had commented on Governor Steed in *Captain Blood:* as an offscreen voice cries, "Hail to Prince John," the camera tilts to a dog tearing at a plate of food, then cuts to John licking his fingers.

The feast in Sherwood replaces the torch-lit interior of Nottingham with the sunny exterior of Sherwood. Robin, uninvited guest at the castle, now plays host to the Sheriff, Gisbourne, and Marian, whom he has captured along with John's tax money. The peasants, object of their laughter at court, now fill the air with their own laughter, tossing slabs of meat to one another, mocking the humiliated nobles.

As Ina Rae Hark notes, the Nottingham feast is a rather formal affair, with everyone seated stiffly in his place waiting to be fed by humble servants. In Sherwood, the frame

> fills with moving people and bustles with activity. Even while the feast is in progress, men and women dance in the background.... Everyone seems involved in the preparation of the meal, but unlike the situation at Nottingham, everyone shares it as well. No arbitrary division exists between servant and master in the forest.[13]

Even the comic styles of the two scenes differ. The dialogue at Nottingham allows us to feel morally superior to the villains while enjoying their deliciously wicked repartee:

John: Any more objections to the new tax from our Saxon friends?
Knight: Objections, your highness, with a Saxon dangling from every gallows tree between here and Charnwood?
(laughter)
John: Well said, Sir Knight, but not too many mind, else we'll have nobody left to till our land or pay the tax.
(more laughter)

In the Sherwood scene the laughter comes from the villains' discomfiture; we laugh at them instead of with them.

But the most important difference between the meals is the change in Marian and her relationship to Robin. At Nottingham she is a haughty little snob, whose reaction to Robin parallels Arabella Bishop's to Peter Blood:

John: Sir Robin, this is Lady Marian Fitzwalter.
Robin: I hope my lady had a pleasant journey from London.
Marian: What you hope can hardly be important.
Robin: What a pity her manners don't match her looks, your highness.

Within the forest, her manners begin to change. At first her hostility continues.

She calls Robin a "Saxon hedge robber,"echoing Arabella calling Blood a "thief and pirate." Watching the peasants grabbing hunks of meat, she calls their behavior "revolting." But Robin chastises her, saying this is the only happiness they have had since John's reign began. To prove they are not mere bandits, he asks the crowd if they want to keep the captured money for themselves, rather than for Richard's ransom. They reply with a thunderous "No!" Then Robin explains why he became an outlaw, showing her maimed and hungry peasants who have sought his protection. Marian is surprised to find Normans among them, and Robin answers:

> Robin: It's injustice I hate, not the Normans.
> Marian: But it's lost you your rank, your land, it's made you a hunted outlaw when you might have lived in comfort and security. What's your reward for all this?
> Robin: Reward? You just don't understand, do you?
> Marian: I'm sorry. I do begin to see a little now.

As Ina Hark says, Marian "begins symbolically to convert to Robin's way of looking at things when she momentarily forgets her decorum and picks up a piece of meat with her hands."[14]

Thus, a pattern of statement and counterstatement, underlining the contrast between court and forest, structures the film's first two thirds. Its final third consists of episodes which echo those in the first two. Marian's arrest and trial, for example, parallels Robin's. Both are charged with numerous crimes, capped by high treason, and are sentenced to death. The sequences are stylistically similar as well: both begin with high shots looking down on the accused, emphasizing their helplessness; both sound tracks feature almost identical musical motifs. The scenes following each trial are equally parallel. After Robin's trial, Marian goes to the tavern where his men meet to help plan his escape. After Marian's trial, Bess (Una Merkel) goes to the same tavern to warn the merry men of the danger awaiting her and Richard. The villains first plot Robin's capture, then the king's. Robin arrives at the archery tournament disguised as a tinker; Richard returns to England in a monk's garb. Finally, as Robin's rescue climaxes the first two thirds, so Marian's climaxes the last.

This structure of repetition and variation not only organizes the events in the film, it also influences the audience's response to those events. The archery tournament, for instance, orchestrates several sources of tension, each a question the audience asks itself. First, will Marian warn Robin of the trap set for him? Closeups of her worried face as she overhears the bishop, Gisbourne, and John anticipating his capture indicate her growing concern for him. Second, will Robin win? We naturally want him to, but we fear his capture if he does. Finally, will Robin evade the trap? Here, the film's structure increases the tension because that tension stems partly from our knowledge of the Nottingham feast scene. We saw Robin escape that danger through sheer energy and bravado. We therefore expect him to escape from the tournament also.

Robin's obvious awareness of the trap heightens that expectation. At the feast, shots of soldiers closing the castle doors intercut with closeups of Robin indicate he understands his danger. Similarly, at the tourney, shots of Robin are intercut with shots of John's men surrounding him, while some fairly explicit dialogue is heard:

> Friar Tuck: They've cooked up this whole thing just to take you.
> Robin: Well, what of it?
> Will: You know what'll happen if they do.
> Robin: Where's your sporting blood?

Clearly, Robin has not been fooled. His failure to escape becomes, therefore, one of the film's most effective emotional shocks, because it so directly violates our expectations.

It also becomes a new source of tension for a scene in the final third that echoes the archery tournament. When the disguised King Richard (Ian Hunter) and his followers sup at a tavern on their return to England, one of the men accidentally refers to him as "sire." The bishop, overhearing, realizes the king has come back. But Richard also realizes his identity is known; he and his men pretend to sleep while the bishop watches them, then slip away when he leaves to warn John. Again we have a disguised hero who knows his disguise has been penetrated. Now, however, we cannot be sure his knowledge will protect him.

Thus the film's structure and the tensions it creates give it the "dramatic drive"[15] Richards finds missing from the Dwan-Fairbanks *Robin Hood* of 1922. A brief comparison of the two will make this clearer. *Robin Hood* begins with a tournament at Nottingham, won by the Earl of Huntingdon (Fairbanks) who, after falling in love with Maid Marian (Enid Bennet), leaves for the Crusades with King Richard (Wallace Beery). With Richard gone, his brother John (Sam de Grasse) begins to exercise his evil. Marian sends a message asking Huntingdon to return; when John learns of this, she flees, leaving evidence of her death. Huntingdon, back in England, seeks shelter in Sherwood where he becomes Robin Hood and organizes an outlaw band. Meanwhile, John's ally Gisbourne (Paul Dickey), thinking he has killed the sleeping king, returns to England, unaware that Richard has also returned. Marian is captured by John's men, but Robin, joined by Richard and the merry men, attack Nottingham, rescue her and rout the villains.

The film does demonstrate the tripartite structure common to most swashbucklers: hero and heroine meet and fall in love while the villains begin scheming; threats to society and the lovers grow and seem to overpower them; hero and heroine are reunited and the threats are dissolved. Moreover, a close analysis might reveal, within this general structure, specific patterns of parallels and contrasts. For example, like the Curtiz film, *Robin Hood* has a montage showing John's injustice and a second montage showing the merry men rescuing his victims. Further, Richard's presumed murder parallels Marian's pretended death. John and Gisbourne celebrate the one with a planned coronation; Robin mourns the other by turning outlaw. But the Dwan-Fairbanks film does not share the specific structure of Curtiz's, the consistent pattern of contrasts between castle and forest, court world and green world.

This structure determines not only the plot but the character relationships as well. All the traditional representatives of order in the court world are corrupt: the state, in Prince John; the church, in the bishop; the law, in the sheriff. Each of these figures has his counterpart in the green world: Richard, the true king, just and compassionate; Friar Tuck, despite his fondness for food and fighting, a more humane church; Robin, an outlaw in Nottingham, defender of the true law of the forest. Even Dickon (Harry Cording), the discredited knight bribed to murder Richard, has his counterpart in Much, the king's honest peasant protector, who foils Dickon's scheme.

Only Gisbourne plays no specific social role, and only he dies. He is simply the aristocracy at its worst, arrogant, insensitive, cruel. His only counterpart is all the oppressed peasants who have fled to the green world. As Hark says, he represents the rapacity of John's reign, as Robin represents the justice of Richard's.[16] Only after his death can Richard mercifully banish the other villains, banishing "all injustice and oppression" with them.

Levasseur (also played by Basil Rathbone) is the only villain to die in *Captain Blood,* but his similarity to Gisbourne ends there. Sir Guy, a smooth talking, cunning courtier like John, lacks the exuberant energy and sexuality that makes Levasseur so attractive. During the Nottingham feast we hear that he is "desperately in love with Lady Marian." But he is clearly more concerned with throne rooms than bedrooms and when Marian interferes with his plans, he quickly arrests her. Unlike Levasseur, he dies because he is a political and moral rather than a sexual threat.

The bad men of *The Adventures of Robin Hood* do illustrate an important but rarely noted quality of adventure film villains; like those of the morality plays and Shakespearean drama, they always know they are villains. Outside the theater, an audience is never sure who the villains of real life are. Most of us, believing in our own morality, finding only the highest ideals behind our actions, see ourselves as the hero. But in swashbucklers and other melodramas, as Peter Brooks observes, the villains willingly admit their evil intentions and clearly "announce their moral identity."[17]

In the opening scene of *The Adventures of Robin Hood,* for example, John, musing with Gisbourne about his impending power, remarks, "Who would have thought my dear brother would be so considerate as to get himself captured and leave England to my tender care." He succinctly demonstrates this tenderness by gashing a piece of fruit with a knife, then accidentally spilling a goblet of blood red wine. I have already mentioned the satisfyingly wicked dialogue at the Nottingham feast, and when Robin is captured John happily assures him that his punishment will be "something special."[18] John and Gisbourne enjoy their villainies; we also enjoy them, perhaps because we purge our own hidden nasty impulses by identifying with their open ones. But their gleeful acknowledgement of them separates them from us, and we enjoy their downfall even more.

The villain's characteristic activity is plotting. We first see John and Gisbourne plotting to keep Richard unransomed; later they plan to capture Robin at the archery tournament; still later they plot the king's assassination, which for John means both regicide, the destruction of the state, and fratricide, the destruction of the family. All their conspiracies involve deceit and betrayal; they attack all forms of human relationships. "Their power to command," as Hark says, "stems entirely from fear or from promise of personal aggrandizement.... But their henchmen feel no selfless loyalty whatsoever."[19] However, within the green world relationships are based on a sense of mutual trust and respect. Ernest Callenbach describes the strong sense of camaraderie that binds the outlaws[20] which Hark calls "an enormous sense of fun concerning life and themselves."[21]

The merry men share this camaraderie because each has proven his worthiness; before admitting them to the fellowship of the forest, Robin tests each of his important companions. Much, the first to join him onscreen (Will met him before the film begins) reveals his heroism in his encounter with Gisbourne. The Norman knight has caught the poaching peasant and warns him of the severe penalties for such crimes. But Much, unafraid of "Sir Guy of the Devil," as he calls him, unleashes a bitter tirade against Norman oppression. After Robin rescues him, he promises to serve Robin as best he can. At the end of the film, he repays Robin by risking his own life against Dickon.

Several scenes later, Robin and Will first meet Little John crossing a stream on a log. Robin decides to see what the "little man" is "made of." Striding onto the log, Robin demands the stranger "give way." The stranger refuses, they fight, and Robin ends up splashing around in the water. Back on land, amid much laughter, the three exchange introductions and Little John becomes one of Robin's closest compatriots.

Still later, Robin, Much, Little John, and some others stumble onto a snoring Friar Tuck, propped against a tree, his fishing pole dangling in a pond. Robin wakes him and orders that he carry Robin across the pond. Not wishing to spoil a good joke on Robin, Much prevents Little John from telling him that the fat friar is actually "one of the most dangerous swordsmen in England." Halfway across the water Friar Tuck tosses Robin off his back, pulls out his sword, and begins whacking away at the outlaw. Eventually Robin subdues him by laughingly promising him all the food he can steal if he joins the band. Friar

Tuck becomes the group's "spiritual leader" and Robin receives a symbolic baptism. This last is not so farfetched an idea, for Robin himself has also been tested in the green world. His laughter, when he has been bested by both Little John and Friar Tuck, his willingness, as Hark says, "to lose ... [his] dignity and superiority if confronted by a moral equal,"[22] proves him worthy of leading the merry men.

Even King Richard is, in some manner, tested by the rules of the forest. Lying on a tree branch as the disguised king and his companions ride through Sherwood below him, Robin welcomes him with a jaunty "Greetings, Sir Abbot." He swings down from the tree and asks the black-robed figure for his excess money. Smiling approvingly at the outlaw, the king claims he has none, though he admits, honestly enough, that he loves no man better than the king. With these words he passes the test, and Robin leads him to his camp.

Robin's most important relationship is with Marian, and she too must earn her way into his heart. She appears at the tavern where the merry men meet with a plan to rescue him from the gallows, but Robin's followers do not trust her until Friar Tuck makes her swear her loyalty. We never actually hear what her plan is and from what follows it is obvious that the merry men could have devised it themselves. The point is that, unlike Arabella Bishop, Marian must actively commit herself to her hero. Having been so closely associated with John and the court party, she can prove her love only by risking her own life to save Robin's.

With Marian we meet a figure who will assume greater importance in other Curtiz films, the morally divided person, the character torn by contradictory moral and emotional demands. These conflicting demands become associated with the two worlds found in Curtiz's films, of which I spoke earlier. Marian, the Norman in love with a Saxon, faces a relatively easy conflict; once she has recognized the Normans' treachery, she easily converts to the Saxon side. But her love for Robin and her belief in his cause creates a second, more serious conflict. Callenbach claims that the film emphasizes "personal and emotional factors, not external and political ones."[23] On the other hand, Hark argues that "politics ... is intrinsic to the film's structure, pervading even the love theme."[24] In fact, the film focuses on the conflict between love and politics, the invasion of private lives by public events.

After escaping the hangman, Robin returns to Nottingham to find Marian. He climbs a vine outside her window and, hoisting himself onto her balcony, begins a love scene obviously patterned after the balcony scene in *Romeo and Juliet*,[25] one that temporarily transforms the castle into a lyrical green world. Robin wants Marian to join him in Sherwood, but she refuses, urging him to remain free to protect the people while she stays in the palace to spy on John. This clash between love and politics, between private feeling and public duty, is one of the most serious faced by the morally divided heroes of films we will consider in later chapters, particularly *The Private Lives of Elizabeth and Essex* and *Casablanca*.

Thus far we have concentrated on *The Adventures of Robin Hood*'s structure and characters. However, the central opposition of court world and green world, castle and forest, is also reflected in its visual style. Compared to modern films, the color of some thirties and forties films often seems too lush. Callenbach, for example, refers to "that characteristic technicolor visual fulsomeness which now seems so overripe."[26] In *The Adventures of Robin Hood,* however, the brilliance of the colors helps create the atmosphere of fable. More important, contrasting color schemes visually define the film's two worlds. Nottingham Castle's dominant colors are the stone gray of its walls and the fire orange of its torches; green, brown, and blue, the colors of earth, sea, and sky, dominate in Sherwood.

We are always outside in Sherwood on a sunny, summer afternoon; we are always inside Nottingham, surrounded by vast, forbiddingly empty spaces, enclosed by massive walls. The only light comes from flames, torches, and candles. Numerous images, in fact, associate artificial light with the deceit of John and his companions, linking fire with their burning ambition. For example, the Nottingham feast opens with a high shot of the hall. On the right edge of the frame, in close-up, a torch burns brightly. Later, when the bishop learns of Richard's return to England, Curtiz puts his camera behind a fireplace; we see a medium shot of the bishop, surrounded by flames, with the king and his men in the background. In the next scene, as John and Gisbourne convince Dickon to murder Richard, the camera again cuts to behind a fireplace; we look through flames to the treacherous group of would-be assassins.

Early in the film the camera creates another color-based visual association, between red wine and blood. When in the opening scene, John and Gisbourne celebrate the king's capture and John spills some wine, the camera follows the wine as it flows to the floor, then dissolves to the montage showing the oppression of the Saxons. Although we see no actual blood during the montage, our mind's eye adds it because the spilled wine suggests spilled blood in that context. The impression is reinforced in the second montage, Robin's men rescuing the Saxons, with a shot of soldiers watching wine from a split cask gush to the floor.

I have observed that Curtiz often defines his characters through their environment. The citizens of Sherwood and Nottingham do seem to spring naturally from their surroundings, defined by their costumes' colors. At the Nottingham feast each member of the court party wears a cloak of a single bright color. The prince wears blue green, the bishop a dark, deep purple, Gisbourne bright red. These colors, strong visual magnets attracting our eyes to them, lend power and authority to those who wear them. Set out apart from the barren gray walls, the prince, the bishop, and Gisbourne dominate the space of the hall.

On the other hand, for all the gaudy greenness of his costume, Robin blends into his surroundings. Dressed entirely in green except for his brown hat, boots, and arrow quiver, he seems to materialize from the forest itself. The emotional effect of his initial encounter with Gisbourne depends partly on their visual contrast. The iron gray of Gisbourne's chain mail suit links him to the castle's forbidding walls; his bright red cloak and the yellow crest on his breastplate mark him as a man of the court, out of place in the green world.

Ina Rae Hark has noticed another important visual contrast between the worlds of castle and forest. The Norman villains, she contends, are "controlled by an inflexible protocol, visually expressed through geometrical symmetry, which is all the more deadly because it masks sadism and greed."[27] She remarks that whether

> feasting, presiding over an archery contest, or supervising an execution, they sit in horizontal rows. Heralds with symmetrically aligned trumpets announce the commencement of these official functions. Rows of banners on straight poles surround the nobles' seats. Their soldiers march in strictly drilled ranks and . . . carry long spears which they place perpendicular to the floor.[28]

On the other hand:

> Robin and his men provide a kinetic presence which galvanizes the screen . . . [as they] use their vitality to disrupt this static Norman geometry.[29]

In general, I would agree with this thesis, which is demonstrated most clearly at the Nottingham feast. Robin's unexpected arrival and the commotion it creates fills the screen with color and movement. As John's men try to surround Robin, Curtiz cuts to a high shot, looking down on a kaleidoscope of swirling cloaks. Robin climbs to a balcony and fires arrows at his enemies; low angle frontal shots of Robin are intercut with high shots from behind him, aiming down to the crowd, including one startling, quasi-subjective shot that looks along Robin's arm, in closeup, to the tiny targets scurrying below. These shots, using Curtiz's technique of composition in depth, "galvanize" the image by creating powerful relationships between foreground and background.

The film ends with Robin (and Richard) returning to Nottingham Castle where they defeat the villains in a final battle. Curtiz signals John's surrender with a closeup of a shield with swords dropping onto it.[30] The camera then cranes up from the shield and moves left past the profiles of the defeated fighters. As it continues to rise it turns ninety degrees until, now high above the rows of beaten men, it looks down at their miniature faces.

With this one virtuoso shot, Curtiz presents the downfall of the forces of corruption. Richard, now restored to power, promises to "banish from my realm all injustice and oppression" and commands Robin to marry Marian. The swirling cloaks that sought Robin at the Nottingham feast swirl again as he and Marian escape the well-wishers through the castle's huge doors. Where once he fled from danger, now he runs towards the promised marriage, and the doors close the fable on an appropriately comic note. All the splits that severed England have been healed. Richard will rule rich and poor alike. Saxon knight will wed Norman lady. Robin will be Earl of Nottingham and Sherwood. The court world and the green world, the castle and the forest, have become one.

3

Pirates and Politics:
The Sea Hawk

Synopsis of the Film

Set in 1585, *The Sea Hawk* begins with Spain's King Philip (Montague Love) revealing his plans for world domination, complaining that only England and her pirates, the sea hawks, stand in his way. He dispatches Don Alvarez (Claude Rains) and his niece Maria (Brenda Marshall) to England as his ambassador. During the voyage they are attacked by the Albatross, captained by Geoffrey Thorpe (Errol Flynn). After its galley slaves, many of them English, are freed and its treasure taken, the Spanish ship is sunk, but Don Alvarez and Maria are deposited safely in England. Queen Elizabeth (Flora Robson) publicly scolds Thorpe, but privately assents to his plan to sail to Panama and capture Spain's gold from the New World. The traitorous Lord Wolfingham (Henry Daniell) and Don Alvarez discover his scheme and arrange for his arrest in Panama. Thorpe and his crew are caught and sentenced to life in the galleys. Eventually they escape, capture a Spanish galleon and documents proving Philip's intent to attack England, and return home where Thorpe slays Wolfingham and wins both Maria's love and a knighthood.

There is a moment in *The Sea Hawk* (1940) that epitomizes the film's grandiloquent operatic style, and our reaction to it may represent our reaction to all swashbucklers. Geoffrey Thorpe, one of the English pirates known as the sea hawks, had been captured by the Spanish and sentenced to life imprisonment as a galley slave. But he and his crew have escaped, seized a Spanish ship, and are now happily headed back to England. Thorpe orders his men to their posts: "Man the helm, Abbot . . . Pitt, the mizzen . . . " In each of the next four shots a crew man shouts some sailorly jargon, followed by a musical chord:

First sailor:	Aloft there, clear your leach lines.
Second sailor:	Clear away your mizzen vanes.
Third sailor:	Heave taut your halyards.
Fourth sailor:	Take away your trueliness.

The mounting rhythm of music, dialogue, and editing builds the scene's emotional intensity until it explodes into an ode to joy: over a long shot of the ship, an orchestra plays and an off-screen chorus sings:

> Look to your oars, strike for the shores of Dover,
> Over the seas... we'll soon be over
> Here we go, for we know, that we row,
> For home sweet home...
> Sailing for home...

This is the cinema of feeling rather than thought, a naked and unashamed appeal to our emotions which will embarrass some and arouse others. We can say the film has reached too far and tumbled into bathos, or we can allow it to move us as we are moved by ballet, opera, and other highly stylized and artificed forms.

This examination of Curtiz's swashbucklers can conclude by observing in *The Sea Hawk* and again briefly in *Captain Blood* and *The Adventures of Robin Hood* two apparently different directions the genre can follow. One is the stylization just referred to, the dramatic and cinematic techniques Curtiz uses to manipulate our emotions. The other is the direction of social and political comment. An interest in artificial style and form might seem incompatible with a desire for political relevance, but in *The Sea Hawk* both may be found in abundance.

Warner Brothers acquired the rights to Rafael Sabatini's *The Sea Hawk* in 1929, when the studio took over First National, which had made the silent version of 1924. After *Captain Blood*'s success, Warners decided to remake the film and asked Delmer Daves[1] to write a screenplay. However, the final film bears no relation to Sabatini's book other than its title. By the time production had begun, Warners had replaced Daves' script with a new one by Howard Koch[2] and Seton I. Miller[3] based on Miller's original story *Beggars of the Sea,* about a character modeled on Sir Francis Drake.[4]

The production involved a number of people who had worked with Curtiz on earlier swashbucklers, including composer Erich Wolfgang Korngold, cameraman Sol Polito (who worked on *Captain Blood*), art director Anton Grot (who designed *The Adventures of Robin Hood*) and, of course, Errol Flynn. Some of the sets, costumes, and props from Curtiz's *The Private Lives of Elizabeth and Essex,*[5] made the previous year, were used, but the studio built two full-scale ships, much larger and more elaborately detailed than the models used in *Captain Blood,* and set them afloat in the new "Warner ocean," a huge tank that occupied an entire sound stage.[6] Costing 1.7 million dollars, the film was one of Warner's most lavish and expensive to that time; the studio even thought of releasing it as a special attraction, with an intermission.[7] Ironically, when Warners re-released it in 1947, it cut about ten minutes from the original

126 minute length. According to Tony Thomas, the cut footage consists of "some of the dialogue sequences and those portions which had obvious messages for the wartime British" as well as several scenes emphasizing Donald Crisp's role as "Sir John Burleson, advisor to the Queen and friend of the hero . . . including a big scene in which he visits Thorpe in Dover and warns him to be careful in Panama."[8]

We have noted that the swashbuckler normally has a social and political dimension. The villains are usually political tyrants, threatening not only the hero but also the society in which he lives, representing social as well as individual evil. The swashbuckler ends with the hero defeating the villain and freeing the society from his grip. But the exact nature of that freed society's politics and of the hero's own politics has been debated by some of the few critics who have dealt with the swashbuckler. Jean-Loup Bourget, for example, argues that the one film genre which

> almost inevitably acclaims a pattern of social unrest and revolution . . . is the swashbuckler, the pirate film. The most 'democratic' examples include two films by Michael Curtiz, *Captain Blood* (1935) and *The Sea Hawk* (1940). In both an apolitical man is charged with sedition and actually becomes a rebel . . . Both films describe the way a colonial system rests on political oppression, slavery, torture, etc.; they both advocate violent revolution as the only means of destroying such a system.[9]

John Davis agrees, noting that the theme of "justifiable revolution" runs "through all the Flynn-Curtiz adventure films."

> The image of an innocent individual in front of an unjust and corrupt court occurs in *Captain Blood* with Blood before Lord Jeffries and Nuttall before Governor Steed, in *The Adventures of Robin Hood* with Robin before Sir Guy of Gisbourne and Maid Marian before Prince John, in *The Private Lives of Elizabeth and Essex* with Essex before Elizabeth, and in *The Sea Hawk* with Thorpe before the Spanish inquisition.[10]

On the other hand, Jeffrey Richards believes that a set of essentially "conservative, middle class values"[11] including the "defence of established authority"[12] underlies the swashbuckler.

> Subordinate functionaries, wicked princelings, faithless ministers may be removed by individual heroic enterprise or even by limited popular uprising. But the person of the monarch is sacrosanct. His tenure of the throne is determined by strict hereditary succession and, once on the throne, he automatically becomes in that mystical way associated with the crown in medieval political thought, the source of truth and justice. There may be changes in the lower tiers of the structure, but the apex of the structure, the throne and all it implies, is uncorrupt and enduring. With all their fighting, feasting, and love-making, our heroes never seek to subvert the system.[13]

We could resolve this issue by saying the swashbuckler is simply a dramatic structure built on the opposition of hero to villain; the hero's elimination of the villain is part of that structure and whether the hero himself is monarchist or democrat is irrelevant. But this approach evades rather than answers the question.[14] Perhaps the problem arises from trying to generalize about the genre, or even about Curtiz's three films. As a generalization, Richards' remarks are quite accurate. But when we look closely at each of the Curtiz films, we find generalizations less satisfactory, for the political attitudes change from film to film.

Captain Blood's hero is clearly a maverick anarchist. Having escaped enslavement by a corrupt king, he turns his bitterness against all governments, rejects all flags, attacks all ships.[15] The oath of piracy he and his crew swear make his political position unmistakable:

> We, the undersigned, are men without country. Outlaws in our own land, but hopeless outcasts in any other. Desperate men we go to seek a desperate fortune. Therefore we do band ourselves into a brotherhood of buccaneers, to practice piracy on the high seas. We the hunted will now hunt.

At the end of the film, Peter Blood becomes a colonial governor; the only government he can trust is one where he holds high office.

Robin Hood leads what Ernest Callenbach calls one of the earliest guerilla armies.[16] But he is neither anarchist nor revolutionary; he rebels against Prince John's tyranny, but remains loyal to King Richard. He is, in fact, Jeffery Richards' prototypical swashbuckling hero, searching for "justice within the system and not [for] the overthrow of that system."[17] He does criticize the king for giving John the opportunity to seize power by running off to the Crusades and leaving England with only outlaws to protect it. But, as Ina Hark argues, "John's usurpation of power . . . [is] the real revolution. Robin and his men act as determined counter-revolutionaries whose one aim is the restoration of the rightful king."[18]

However, the most patriotic of our heroes is Geoffrey Thorpe. He is not even an outlaw. Nominally a pirate, he is actually a secret agent, as he tells the galley slaves he frees early in the film: "By now you know the purpose of the sea hawks: in our own way, to serve England and the queen." The film's central action is his attempt to steal Spanish gold, not to enrich himself, but to build an English fleet. Unlike Robin Hood and Peter Blood, Thorpe is loyal to the present monarch, not to a once and future king.

At least one pattern emerges from the three films: the hero's patriotism increases as the political stakes increase. *Captain Blood,* while played against a background of upheaval in England, focuses on the changing governorship of one small island colony. *The Adventures of Robin Hood* centers on the English throne itself; the film ends, not with the hero becoming governor, but with him helping the rightful king regain his position. In *The Sea Hawk*, the Spanish tyrant threatens not only England, but the entire world. Its opening scene has King Philip boasting to his counselors:

> ...the riches of the new world are limitless. And the new world is ours. With our ships carrying the Spanish flag to the seven seas, our armies sweeping over Africa, the Near East, and the Far West, invincible, everywhere but on our own doorstep.... We cannot keep Northern Europe in submission until we have a reckoning with England... With England conquered nothing can stand in our way... One day before my death we shall sit here and gaze at this map upon the wall. It will have ceased to be a map of the world. It will be Spain.

As the speech ends, Curtiz slides the camera into a close-up of the map, now covered by Philip's huge shadow.

This pattern no doubt represents the films' responses to the changes in the world situation between 1935 and 1940. Throughout the thirties and forties Warner Brothers was well known as one of Hollywood's most socially conscious studios, filling its films with liberal, pro-Democrat, pro-Roosevelt propaganda.[19] The films it made before 1935, mostly contemporary urban melodramas and musicals, usually recognized the Depression as an inescapable fact of life. *Captain Blood,* as we noted, was something new for the studio, an expensive escapist entertainment set in another time and place. But surely its anarchism is also rooted in the disillusionment of the Depression. Perhaps that is why it seems metaphysical as well as political. The world is out of joint; a whimsical fate rules, whirling Blood through several careers, from doctor to slave to pirate to governor. Although Blood never returns to England, he does act more patriotically when he learns that "James has been kicked out. Good King William rules in his stead." This news "changes the shape of the world" for him, and it is not farfetched to see in it, as John Davis does,[20] a reflection of Warners' own optimistic faith in FDR.

By 1938, while still coping with domestic economic problems, America was beginning to be aware of the dangers from abroad, the threat of international fascism. I would agree with Ina Hark, who finds both concerns reflected in *The Adventures of Robin Hood:*

> On the one hand, Prince John and his supporters foreshadow in their tyranny the atrocities perpetrated by the dictators, and Robin's war against them predicts the struggle of the United States against Germany and her allies....
>
> On the other hand, the root of John's tyranny is so obviously monetary, as he squeezes every last farthing from the Saxon peasantry, that the villains here seem very close to the callous bankers or Wall Street businessmen of countless Depression films.[21]

With so much at stake, there can no longer be any real question of the hero's patriotism, and once again, "FDR and New Deal democracy... lie behind the restoration of social equilibrium promised by King Richard's return."[22]

When *The Sea Hawk* appeared in 1940 isolationism and pacifism may still have been potent forces in America, but there was no doubt about where Warners stood. A year earlier it had released one of the first overtly anti-Nazi films, *Confessions of a Nazi Spy* (directed by Anatole Litvak). Thus the parallel between King Philip's opening speech, with its ominous claim that "the New World is ours," and fascist dreams of world domination was as clear to contemporary audiences as it should be to us today. Throughout the film, Elizabeth's advisors argue over whether appeasement or military action is better. Worried about the Armada, Sir John Burleson urges her to use the money donated by the sea hawks to build a fleet. But Wolfingham, the traitorous fifth columnist, claims the Armada merely protects Spain's empire and poses no threat to England. The Queen agrees that England's safety "lies in diplomacy, not force." Later, publicly chastising Thorpe for attacking the Spanish ship, she asks if he imagines "we are at war with Spain." He answers, "Spain is at war with the world." After Thorpe's capture and Philip's demand that Elizabeth disarm the other sea hawks, she rages that Philip acts as if "the world were a jewel hung around his neck." But only at the end, when Thorpe returns with proof of Philip's plans, does Elizabeth admit the folly of appeasement and isolationism.

According to Tony Thomas, one of the speeches cut from the 1947 re-release print is the queen's final words, while knighting Thorpe, urging her subjects to prepare for a war none of them wants and all tried to avoid. Thomas quotes the lines:

> When the ruthless ambitions of a man threaten to engulf the world, it becomes the solemn obligation of free men, whenever [sic] they may be, to affirm that the earth belongs not to one man, but to all men, and that freedom is the deed and title to the soil on which we exist. Firm in this faith, we shall now make ready to meet the great Armada.[23]

The Sea Hawk's hawkish message is clear. Just as England feels secure from Philip because of the Channel, so America felt secure from fascism because of the ocean; just as the Armada could cross the Channel, so enemy planes could cross the ocean.

I began by asking what sort of society forms around the hero and now an answer begins to take shape. Jeffrey Richards claims that swashbuckling heroes are usually loyal to a benevolent ruler, a "constitutional rather than ... absolute" monarch.[24] But that monarch is usually unseen for most of each film. Within the world of the film, certainly within the world of the Curtiz swashbucklers, the hero himself is the benevolent ruler. Surrounding him are a few close companions, almost his equals, from whom he will accept advice, even criticism. Blood has Jeremy Pitt, Robin has Little John, Will Scarlet, and Friar Tuck, Thorpe has Carl Pitt. All earn their position; Blood assembles his pirate crew from prisoners with naval experience, while Robin's merry men prove their prowess with sword and bow. The hero himself proves that leadership just happens to be among his natural talents.[25]

With all his followers, the hero is friendly and informal, qualities distinguishing him from the cold, arrogant, aristocratic villains. Occasionally he seems to offer them a choice, as when Robin asks his men if they want to keep the king's ransom for themselves or when Blood asks his crew if they want to attack the French at Port Royal. But the crew always agrees, in one voice, with their leader's suggestion. He takes a lot of joking from them, but they remain followers. Much, for example, stops Little John from telling Robin of Friar Tuck's reputation as a swordsman. Nevertheless, born a peasant, he always calls Robin "master." Thorpe's men may mock his shyness with women but in the galleys, although they are all slaves, they still call him "captain," and when he asks them to stop rowing and provoke a fight with the guards, they do so despite the beating they must endure.[26] Whether ship or Sherwood Forest, the hero's world is really rather American in spirit and organization, giving the appearance of equality while maintaining a well-defined social hierarchy.[27]

Thus the politics of the swashbuckler presents us with an apparent paradox; the genre is anti-authoritarian, but pro-authority. We are made to abhor the tyrant, but admire the strong, independent leader.[28] Perhaps we can resolve the problem by turning briefly from politics to psychology. Though I do not want to overstate the case, I would suggest that the hero's conflict with the tyrant-villain often has oedipal overtones. In short, the despot can be seen as a kind of domineering, evil father figure whom the hero must overthrow in order to achieve his own identity; the benevolent monarch, when one appears, represents the father figure with whom the hero identifies rather than competes, the older, wiser role model, who offers the hero advice and aid.[29] Quite often the swashbuckling tyrant is a usurper illegally imposing his will on the mother country. To carry the oedipal interpretation a step further, we could say he occupies the position the hero desires for himself.

At any rate, Ernest Callenbach notes the father-son relationship between Richard and Robin, saying that, at its simplest level, the film is about "the son who fights the evil father (the false king) and is rewarded by the good father."[30] In *Captain Blood* the hero literally supplants the older, overbearing villain; the film ends with Colonel Bishop humbled before Peter Blood, who now sits in the governor's chair he once occupied. The benevolent monarch, "good King William," is never seen, but we could assign his paternal role to his representative, Lord Willoughby. Though hardly a model of heroic action, Willoughby does give Blood the news that enables him to become an Englishman again, and makes Arabella admit she loves him. Bishop, on the other hand, is Arabella's uncle and, like the false fathers of many swashbucklers, tries to keep hero and heroine apart.[31]

The heroine's uncle is also the villain in *The Sea Hawk*. Don Alvarez, diplomatic representative of the tyrant Philip, tries to win Elizabeth's confidence, while the Armada plans its attack. He too plots to keep hero and heroine apart, by arranging for Thorpe's capture. The film has no important positive father figure, but then Don Alvarez himself is the least vicious of the negative ones. Instead of suffering banishment, like Prince John, or humiliation, like Colonel Bishop, he is allowed to slip quietly back to Spain.

None of these tyrant-fathers rivals the hero for the heroine and none of them dies. But each film has a second major villain, a younger man who may or may not be the hero's sexual rival, but who always dies after a climactic duel with him. The pattern here seems to be that as the younger villain's lust for power increases, his lust for women decreases.

We have already discussed two of them. In *Captain Blood* Levasseur's intentions toward Arabella are as obvious as the sword in his hand; in *The Adventures of Robin Hood* Gisbourne, though "desperately in love" with Marian, eventually threatens her life more than her honor. The younger villain in *The Sea Hawk* is Wolfingham; he hardly knows the heroine exists. He never utters a word to or about her and appears with her only in one or two court scenes. His only concern is that there sit on the English throne a "ruler friendly to Spain," himself.[32]

The hero, however, must always be a lover as well as a leader. But Thorpe is not quite as adept as the dashing, self-confident outlaws. Blood kisses Arabella while still her slave; Robin trades insults with Marian at their first meeting. Poor Thorpe, though, is tongue-tied with every woman but Elizabeth. After the Albatross captures Maria and her uncle, a chorus of sailors mocks their heroic captain's helplessness before a "slip of a girl":

First Sailor:	Look at him, willya, he's as tongue-tied as a schoolboy. He's always the same when he has to talk with women.
Second Sailor:	Him what's taken whole fleets of Spanish ships can't trade words with a slip of a girl . . .
Third Sailor:	I hear her majesty's the only woman he could talk to without his knees buckling.
Fourth Sailor:	That's different. Man to man I calls it.[33]

Even before this dialogue, Curtiz suggests Thorpe's comic awkwardness with an equally awkward low angle shot; the side of the ship occupies most of the frame, but towards its upper right corner we see Thorpe on deck, looking puny and insignificant, peering down at Maria, who stares sullenly out of a porthole.

It may be that Thorpe's loyalty interferes with his lovemaking; perhaps he has been too busy talking politics with Elizabeth to learn how to whisper sweet nothings to Maria.[34] But despite his supposed bashfulness, Thorpe has an easier time winning his heroine than either Blood or Robin. We saw how the Beatrice/Benedick pattern of *Captain Blood* is altered in *The Adventures of*

Robin Hood so that Marian admits her love halfway through the film, then actively proves it. Maria admits hers even earlier. Aboard the Albatross she is already struck by Thorpe's concern for the former slaves; by the time she "accidentally" meets him in the queen's garden, she is completely hooked.

One thing unites all of these heroes; no matter how strong their political loyalty, no matter how easily they woo their women, they always contend with forces larger than any single individual. We called this force fate in *Captain Blood,* though it had its human component in the political and moral corruption of King James and his cronies. In *The Adventures of Robin Hood* and *The Sea Hawk,* the force is more clearly man-made, resulting from the political ambitions of Prince John and King Philip. But the hero always prevails. Unlike the tragic hero, swept away by powers he often can neither control nor understand, the comic hero eventually shapes his own destiny, molding society into his own image. We have seen that the swashbuckler is a comic-romantic hero.

Thus, in *The Sea Hawk,* Thorpe's life is changed by the course of history, but he also changes that history. Because he involves himself in the conflict between England and Spain, he suffers in the galleys. But when he escapes, he alters the outcome of that conflict.

The film's structure emphasizes this two-way relationship by alternating scenes of Thorpe on his ship with scenes of Elizabeth in her court, showing the influence of the first on the second. The scene begins aboard the Albatross, as Thorpe captures Don Alvarez and Maria, then dissolves to the court, where Elizabeth and her advisers argue over building a fleet. The argument ends inconclusively but, following another shipboard scene, Thorpe returns to court with stolen Spanish treasure and convinces the queen to support his Panama mission. After the long Panama sequence, ending with Thorpe in chains, we again move back to the court where Elizabeth, weakened by the news of Thorpe's failure, agrees to Don Alvarez's demands for the arrest of the other sea hawks. Thorpe's fate constantly influences England's, and at the end Elizabeth acknowledges this by literally merging court and ship. In the film's final scene, she knights Thorpe aboard a ship at anchor; to honor her champion, she has brought her court to the sea.

It is here, in the film's concern for the individual struggling with large, impersonal forces, that those two directions of social comment and elaborate stylization come together. Curtiz's style makes us share that struggle by forcing us to involve ourselves in and identify with each character's emotions. Curtiz has been called a cynic,[35] but ultimately, if his films make any political statement, it is a highly romantic one, for they imply that no matter how important the events whirling around the hero may be, what is most important is the individual and his emotional life.

We can see this in Curtiz's handling of one of the recurring motifs in his films, the clash between love and duty, private feeling and public need. We recall that in *The Adventures of Robin Hood,* Marian is one of Curtiz's morally divided characters, torn between her Norman background and her love for a Saxon outlaw. In *The Sea Hawk,* Maria faces a similar struggle. A Spaniard, she has fallen in love with the anti-Spanish Thorpe. Learning of her uncle's plans to trap him in Panama, she must decide whether to warn him. It is, perhaps, a minor element in the film, for we know that in a swashbuckler the heroine will join the hero's side. But Curtiz magnifies its importance to us.

As the scene begins, the camera looks at Maria through a stained glass window and moves to imitate her own agitation. She pauses at the window; the camera tracks into a close-up; she turns and walks away from the window; the camera pulls back to a medium shot. Cut from outside the window to inside the room; she asks Emma, her servant, to order her a carriage. She has made her decision; the obstruction to our vision vanishes with the obstruction in her mind. To express her impatience, fear, and excitement, Curtiz fills her race to the docks with close-ups of whirling wagon wheels and pounding hooves. But she arrives too late, and as she stands alone on the dock, watching her lover leave, listening to the town crier's unknowingly ironic cry of "Three o'clock and all's well," the mood becomes mellower. The images are simpler, the editing slower and softer; we cut to a close-up of Maria, then to a longshot of the Albatross, then to a slow pan along its deck into a medium shot of Thorpe. Cut to a full shot of Thorpe; dissolve to a medium close-up of Maria, pulling back slowly to a medium shot of her; dissolve to a medium shot of Thorpe, suggesting that the previous camera movement reflects his imagined vision of her receding as he sails; dissolve to a close-up of Maria; cut to a longshot of the ship; fadeout. As Jeffrey Richards says, the use of large close-ups, a slowly moving camera, and repeated dissolves "establishes the spiritual rapport of the lovers, bridging the gulf of time and space that is opening up between them."[36]

I said that we can usually find in Curtiz's films a central opposition between two metaphoric worlds, which I have called castle and forest, court world and green world. In *The Sea Hawk,* as in *Captain Blood,* they become associated with imprisonment and freedom, and are represented by the contrasting images of a ship's slave galley and top deck.

These images and their emotional implications are introduced quite early in the film. From the opening scene of King Philip at his map, we dissolve to Don Alvarez's boat. On its sunny deck Maria and Martha play a form of tennis; Maria hits the ball and the camera follows it, climbing gracefully to the bridge where stand Captain Lopez (Gilbert Roland) and Don Alvarez. Lopez calls for the quickening of the oars and suddenly we cut to the galley. The camera tracks along a row of slaves, each chained to a giant oar handle, their half-naked bodies glistening with sweat. At one end a barred entrance way allows some light to enter, falling in stripes across the slaves' backs. At the other, a timekeeper beats a

large white drum, marking the beat of the oars like a human metronome.[37] One
shot, dominated by the objects that dominate the slaves' lives, sums up this "hell
below decks."[38] A grotesque closeup of part of the drum fills the lower third of
the screen; above it, stretching deep into the background, are the slaves, dwarfed
by the drum and the stick pounding it. A guard patrols the slaves, whipping
them when he sees fit. All we can hear is a background of low, funereal music,
the steady thump of the drum, the occasional crack of the whip.

Only twice are the associations of upper decks with freedom and galleys
with imprisonment reversed, each time heralding a profound reversal in
Thorpe's life. The first occurs when he returns to the Albatross after being
ambushed in Panama. Many of his men have died; the survivors have struggled
through swamp and jungle to reach the sea. But, after rowing back to the ship,
they find the atmosphere unusually ominous. We hear only some eerie creaking
and foreboding music; the rocking camera gives the boat a ghostly movement.
Suddenly we cut to a high shot looking down at the deck, followed by a slow
leftward pan revealing no signs of life. The unexpected cut and the unfamiliar
angle add to our unease. After a few other brief shots there is a second shock
effect; we see one of Thorpe's men, tangled in the rigging, hanging upside down.
Cut to a close-up reaction shot of Thorpe, a shot of the hanging man's shadow
blackening the deck, and finally to a medium shot of Lopez, emerging from
hiding, announcing that he has captured the Albatross and Thorpe is now his
prisoner.

The second reversal, when Thorpe's men escape and take over a Spanish
ship, transforms the galley into a positive environment. Again the English are
seen at the oars, but now unchained, rowing eagerly for what once enslaved
them now propels them home.

This opposition of galley and deck, imprisonment and freedom, is related
to the larger thematic opposition we just noted between the impersonal force of
history and the individual human life. Here too the film's opening scene makes
the relationship clear. Philip's speech stresses his impatience to achieve Spain's
destiny:

> Philip: The destiny of Spain cannot wait upon the fitness of time. I have but one life and that
> is all too short for me to fulfill that destiny.

It is thus the "destiny of Spain" that causes so many to be in chains. Philip's
shadow on the world map becomes the shadows enshrouding the galley slaves;
the galley itself is a miniature of the world under Spanish domination.

We noted that Thorpe's own imprisonment results from his involvement in
English politics. Again, Curtiz's style underlines the human, emotional consequences of great events by forcing us to share his suffering. Because we know he
is walking into a trap in Panama, we feel that his imprisonment begins there, as

he hacks his way through the jungle, "steamy, swarming, fetid, enervating: a clinging network of plants and branches choking every pathway."[39] Curtiz uses this network as he uses shadows and ship's rigging in *Captain Blood,* to evoke an atmosphere of enclosure and entrapment; by making us look at Thorpe and his men through an impenetrable maze of foliage, he suggests they are already behind bars.

In one shot, a large frond forms an arch across the top of the screen, while others occupy its lower corners; together they form a frame within the frame, encircling the men in the background. Roasting under the merciless sun, tripping over logs, stumbling into puddles, they stagger through the swamps. In another image, the sun is surrounded by an arch of leaves, as if the Spanish had caught it and were using it to torture the British.

Finally the men reach the beach, a bright, empty, open space, stretching to the horizon, a striking contrast to the dense jungle. Curtiz emphasizes the spaciousness and intensifies the sense of sudden freedom by showing the men running to the sea in a medium-long shot, rather than a closer shot.

But that freedom is illusory. Thorpe and his men are arrested, tried, and sentenced to life in the galleys. His trial, similar to Blood's, Robin's, and Marian's but more elaborately staged, begins with the familiar high shot looking down at judge and defendants. A low angle shot of the judge suggests his godly powers, while a crane downward at the end of the scene implies the fall in Thorpe's fortunes.

From the trial we dissolve to a close-up of a hammer pounding a chain into a ship's hull; tilt up to a medium shot of Thorpe, stripped to the waist; the camera pulls back from him, then slowly travels along the row of new slaves. As the captain orders the timekeeper to get the men underway, this whole long sequence that began in the jungles reaches its climax in another of Curtiz's baroque compositions and bravura camera movements. We see the timekeeper looming large in the foreground, solemnly beating his drum while the slaves strain at their oars in the background. Then the camera pulls back, as if abandoning the slaves to the bowels of the galley, finally sliding through a barred window; the visual metaphor of the jungle has become reality; the English are behind bars.

To make us emotionally participate in the slave's escape, Curtiz again uses the moving camera, turning the lens into a searching eye that directs our attention to the significant detail on which the action depends. When Thorpe steals the knife he will use to free himself and his men, the camera moves into a close-up of it, then follows it as it is passed from hand to hand. The actual escape begins with the camera dollying down the left side of the galley, panning across to a medium shot of Thorpe, traveling in for a closeup of him and, after a cutaway close-up of the sleeping timekeeper, tilting down to a close-up of the stolen knife in Thorpe's hand, digging at the chain around his leg.

The elaborate stylization of *The Sea Hawk* involves elements other than Curtiz's visual pyrotechnics, all of which enrich its emotional content. One of these is its gallery of minor characters. Of course minor characters appear in most films, including the other Curtiz swashbucklers. But they usually either advance the main plot or enact a subplot that parallels it. In *The Adventures of Robin Hood,* for example, Much, as Ina Hark notes, resembles Robin "in courage and resourcefulness, but has none of his romanticism or grace. His pragmatic approach to warfare undercuts Flynn's heroics, just as his courtship of Bess, the lady in waiting, comically parallels the love affair between Robin and Marian."[40] But the peasants not only parody the central story, they also become involved in it. When Gisbourne imprisons Marian, Emma replaces her as the merry men's spy in Nottingham Castle, warning Much of the plot against the king. He then kills the would-be assassin and tells Robin of Marian's impending execution.

In *The Sea Hawk,* however, although Carl Pitt and Martha Latham[41] are a comic version of Thorpe and Maria, they do nothing essential to the working out of the main plot. Instead, like the other minor characters, they form their own, self-contained, independent stories, additions to the main plot, which Curtiz uses to focus and intensify the emotions aroused by it. For example, Curtiz ends the scene of Thorpe capturing Don Alvarez and Maria with a sweeping camera movement from a longshot of the Albatross, its deck crowded with ex-slaves anxious for their first glimpse of home, to a close-up of one of them, Tuttle (Clifford Brooke), quietly murmuring, "England." Curtiz concentrates a shipload of emotion onto one face. Later, he concentrates the sailors' sufferings in Panama onto the same face, when Tuttle dies there.

A comic minor character is Eli Matson, who first attracts our attention by swinging from the Albatross to board the galleon without waiting for Thorpe's command. The captain, with a twinkle in his eye, orders him put in irons, but welcomes him back later for the Panama trip, which he survives. Kroner (Francis MacDonald), one of Wolfingham's lackeys, is a minor villain who helps discover Thorpe's secret destination and, at the end of the film, tries to prevent him from reaching the queen. There is even a nonhuman minor character, Thorpe's monkey. The very first shot of the Albatross finds him chattering in the rigging. Brought to the court as a present for the queen, he frightens the ladies and amuses Elizabeth. "He looks like Wolfingham," she says. In one of the film's final images, he grins happily as Elizabeth knights his former master.

Many of these minor characters appear in what I call the film's choral scenes. Scattered throughout *The Sea Hawk,* they consist of the camera tracking along a group of men, stopping at one as he utters a line, continuing to the next as he takes it up, and so on. Usually they function like a Greek chorus, commenting on the hero's actions and personality, implying his importance to

those around him. We noted before, for example, Thorpe's men mocking his
mooning over Maria. In an earlier scene they prepare us for his dramatic
entrance, his first appearance on screen. Their mouths watering at a nearby
Spanish ship, they look forward to fighting her:

> First sailor: The Spaniard mounts forty guns as she mounts one.
> Second sailor: She's loaded down to..
> Third sailor: Maybe she's too big a bite for our teeth, eh, Matson?
> Matson: Did you ever see a Spaniard the captain couldn't swallow whole?
> Fourth sailor: Captain's got the Spaniards bewitched....

As the lines are tossed from man to man, their jaunty rhythm expresses the
pirates' pride in their captain and themselves, their expectations of victory, and
their solidarity that keeps them confident in Thorpe even during their
imprisonment. Finally, Pitt turns to Thorpe, who is off screen, and asks:

> Pitt: ...we can put a draught through their bow pretty quick Captain. What about it?
> Shall we let them have a round?

But Curtiz keeps him off screen as he answers with his first line:

> Thorpe: You'll fire when I give the word, Mr. Pitt.

Only after we have felt the hero as an almost mystical force, a voice and a
presence, is he allowed to assume mere human form, with a cut to him in
medium shot saying, "Suggest they lower their colors."

By slowing the camera movement and speech rhythms, Curtiz creates
quieter, more serious moods. Aboard Captain Lopez's galley at the start of the
film, one of the slaves whispers to a companion that he knows where they are
from the ship's movement, and the camera tracks slowly along the slaves as they
pass the word, "The English Channel." Later, when Thorpe's crew slogs through
the swamps of Panama, their chorus of complaints arouses our own fears. One
worries about "snakes and crocodiles," another about mosquitoes, a third about
"plants with arms like that'll strangle a man if he ain't careful." Of course, the
emotional climax of all these choral effects is the dramatic moment I described
at the beginning of this chapter, when the escaped sailors, urging their ship home
to England, repeat their orders[42] in mounting rhythm, culminating in an
outburst of joyous song.[43]

Probably the most stylized, operatic element of any swashbuckler,
especially *The Sea Hawk*, is its battle sequences. We noted that the swashbuckler externalizes moral conflicts, transforming them into the confrontation
between hero and villain. The battle scene magnifies this confrontation. The
force of good becomes the force of an army of good men, led by the hero; the

force of evil becomes the enemy, an army of men fighting on the wrong side. The battle itself has one simple purpose, to celebrate the victory of what generations of children have rightly recognized as the good guys over the bad guys.[44] Therefore, in the traditional Hollywood swashbuckler, the violence is not only justified,[45] but deliberately made as artificial and painless as possible. In fact, as several critics have noted,[46] battle scenes can be seen as a form of dance, expressing ideas and emotion through movement. The action within every shot, and the editing of these shots, are carefully choreographed and always accompanied by music.

Curtiz's battle scenes are never simply meaningless clashes between armies of extras. He constructs them like miniature narratives, giving each a specific dramatic motivation, which then gives the movement of the battle a strong sense of direction and purpose.[47] In the battle that begins *The Sea Hawk*, the motive is to capture the Spanish galleon and the action moves from the Albatross to the galleon and back. First the Albatross's guns blast the enemy ship as it draws near; Thorpe and his men swing aboard. The action then moves below decks as Thorpe frees the galley slaves and captures Don Alvarez and his party. Finally, Captain Lopez surrenders; Thorpe leads his crew and captives back to the Albatross as the Spanish ship sinks.

During the actual fighting, Curtiz wants us to feel the thrill of battle, not the terrors. Sound and image distance us from the reality of war and death. We hear cannons booming, swords clanging, music swelling, but very few screams. We see decks splinter and burn, masts snap and fall, the galleon's outstretched oars bend and break against the Albatross's hull, but we do not see any blood or mangled bodies. Curtiz's images make us experience the energy, exuberance, and sheer physical joy of heroic action.[48] In one dizzying shot we look straight down to a ship's deck, as seamen shinny down ropes to the melee below; in another, sailors swing directly forward, into the camera; in another, we share a pirate's perspective as we look over his shoulder and along his rifle barrel to a group of Spaniards in the background. We track along the Albatross's hull, passing the comically phallic cannons poking out of the gunports; we stare into the grimy faces of fighting sailors; we watch as the Spanish ship, its sails billowing out around it, slowly slips into the sea.[49]

To keep us involved and prevent the battle scene from becoming a struggle between two abstract, anonymous masses, Curtiz cuts from long shots of large groups, to closer shots focusing on two lone combatants. The enemy in these shots is usually an unknown extra, while the man he fights may be Thorpe, a minor character such as Pitt or Matson, or another unknown. These individual contests become miniature narratives within the larger battle scene, just as the scene itself is a small story within the whole film.

The climax of every swashbuckler is the moment of single combat between good and evil, the duel between hero and villain. As carefully choreographed as battle scenes, film duels are, in Jeffrey Richards' words, "more like a ballet than a real swordfight."[50] They are the most ritualized element of a highly ritualized genre, eagerly awaited in each film and following a rarely altered pattern. Hero faces villain; one taunts the other, who politely allows him to finish, then answers in kind. Their anger bursts; the duel itself begins and continues until, as the music reaches its crescendo, the villain falls dead at the hero's feet.

Curtiz's duels usually follow this pattern, each beginning with some verbal thrusts and parries. Blood and Levasseur argue over ownership of Arabella:

Levasseur: You'll not take her while I live.
Blood: Then I'll take her when you're dead.

Gisbourne and Robin simply argue:

Gisbourne: You've come to Nottingham once too often.
Robin: When this is over, my friend, there'll be no need for me to come again.

Like everything else in *The Sea Hawk,* its duel in dialogue is longer and more elaborate than its predecessors':

Wolfingham: Have you nine lives, Captain Thorpe? Surely by now most of them must be used up. I was expecting you, Captain, but not alone, nor in a Spanish uniform.
Thorpe: You should be wearing one.
Wolfingham: Perhaps I shall, one day. You have some dispatches for me, Captain?
Thorpe: I have some dispatches for the queen.
Wolfingham: I'm afraid I shall have to ask you not to disturb her highness.
Thorpe: It's very thoughtful of you, milord, but I think she'll wish to be disturbed. These dispatches bear the seal of Spain.
Wolfingham: You won't be as lucky this time, as at Panama.

Curtiz's duels, like his battle scenes, are constructed like miniature plots, with a strong sense of movement, direction, and purpose. He lets his characters roam around the set; in effect they chase each other while fighting. Thus, Blood and Levasseur begin their match on the rocky cliffs of Virgen Magra, duel down to the sandy beach and along the water's edge until Levasseur tumbles to the ground and a wave washes over his corpse.[51] The other duels, though staged indoors, are still full of movement. Robin and Gisbourne pursue each other through Nottingham Castle, down the circular stone stairs to a great hall where they duel alone, casting giant shadows on the pillars behind them.[52] Thorpe and Wolfingham start in the latter's chamber, smash through a set of glass doors, struggle down a broad white staircase and end up, like Robin and Gisbourne, in a large, barren hall, casting shadows on its walls.

This shadow shot, as it first appears in *The Adventures of Robin Hood,* is perhaps the most memorable moment of any of the duels (Plate 12). From a high angle we look down at the great hall, where stand three enormous gray stone pillars, bathed in a reddish brown haze. Two tiny figures duel in the foreground, their shadows looming on the column furthest right. The camera follows their movement, tracking right, and as the shadowed column moves to the center of the image, they disappear below the frame. For a moment or two we see only their shadows, huge black forms, dancing around the gigantic pillar. These shadows sum up, as effectively as the explosion of song we began with, the style and spirit of Curtiz's swashbucklers. Hero and villain, though merely insubstantial silhouettes, are still the strongest forces in the visual world they inhabit. They have become literally larger than life, transformed into the figures of myth and legend. Of all Curtiz's talking shadows, their voices are the most welcome, for they speak of the ultimate victory of good over evil.

4

Out West and Other Places: Variations on the Swashbuckler

Before concluding this discussion of Curtiz's swashbucklers, I want to look briefly at a number of films that can be considered related to the swashbuckler. They are: *The Charge of the Light Brigade* (1936), *Dodge City* (1939), *The Santa Fe Trail* (1940), *Virginia City* (1940), and *The Private Lives of Elizabeth and Essex* (1939). The first seems the closest to the traditional swashbuckler, but the hero loses not only the heroine, but his life. The last is the furthest from the swashbuckler; although it is dressed in the period costumes and sets of *The Sea Hawk*, it is basically a romantic tragedy. The other three are all westerns, clearly a separate genre, yet even here style, structure, and characters bear notable resemblances to those of the swashbucklers. All of these films were made between 1935 and 1940. All of them star Errol Flynn, and in all but *Virginia City*, Olivia de Havilland appears. In other words, they are all part of the Errol Flynn adventure cycle that Curtiz made in those years.[1]

With its emphasis on guns, horses, and vast rock-strewn deserts, *The Charge of the Light Brigade* is iconographically closer to the western than to the swashbuckler. But what truly distinguishes it from the swashbuckler is the change in its hero and his relationship to the heroine. The plot has nothing to do with the historical charge, as the opening credits carefully point out:

> This production has its basis in history. The historical basis, however, has been fictionized for the purposes of this picture and the names of many characters, the characters themselves, the story, incidents, and institutions are fictitious. With the exception of known historical characters, whose actual names are herein used, no identification with actual persons, living or dead, is intended or should be inferred.

In the film, the charge is not a military blunder but a planned act of vengeance against a sadistic (and completely fictional) enemy.[2]

The action is set in nineteenth-century India. The British have stopped an annuity to the amir of Suristan, Surat Khan (C. Henry Gordon). Angered, he forms a new alliance with the Russians, then massacres the residents of a British fort on the frontier. A year or so later Surat Khan and his men are fighting with the Russians against the British in the Crimea. The massacre's survivors, led by Geoffrey Vickers (Errol Flynn) are also in the Crimea, hungry for revenge. Deliberately disobeying orders, Geoffrey leads a suicidal charge against Surat Khan, which enables other British troops to conquer Sebastopol.

As in the swashbucklers, Curtiz creates two visually contrasting worlds, the film's castle and forest, the domains of hero and villain. The film begins with the British visiting Surat Khan's palace. A long, slow track left follows Surat Khan and the British as they walk through the palace; on the wall behind them are the whirling shadows of dancing girls; in front of them are musicians playing pipes and drums, servants carrying trays, others squatting and smoking. The conservative British seem distinctly out of place in this exotic, strange, and dangerous realm. The danger is subtly implied when Curtiz dissolves from a close-up of Surat Khan to a close-up of birds in a cage; the camera then tilts down to a medium shot of Geoffrey, and the other British.

On the other hand, the British forts, run by stuffy military men and their silly wives, are quite proper, with a pompous yet homey atmosphere. Curtiz suggests the pomposity by the entrance of the troops into the fort at Chukoti: a series of impressive longshots and high shots of the lines of horsemen approaching the fort which is silhouetted against the sky, of troops opening the fort's huge gates, of the horsemen riding in. He suggests the homeyness with his first shot of the fort at Lohara: a close-up of a piece of needlework with the words "Lohara, India" sewn in it; the camera pulls back to a two shot of Lady Warrington (Spring Byington), wife of the commander, Lord Warrington (Nigel Bruce), and Elsa Campbell (Olivia de Havilland), our heroine.

The swashbucklers are marked by a tripartite structure and, on the surface, *The Charge of the Light Brigade* exhibits a similar structure. The first section introduces hero, heroine, and villain; the second finds the villains ascendant and the hero imprisoned, at least metaphorically; the third section contains the climactic battle between hero and villain and ends with the villain's death.

The metaphoric imprisonment comes during the long, central sequence of the siege and massacre of Chukoti, and Curtiz's visual style here is similar to that in the swashbucklers' imprisonment scenes. British troops are shown covered by shadows, or sitting behind pillars and furniture. Smoke and wreckage clutter the frame. Geoffrey, in close-up, peers through the broken slats of a door; later he and another soldier look through the slats of a window; both shots obviously resemble that first, imprisoning image of Peter Blood and many similar shots throughout the swashbucklers. During a lull in the fighting, Geoffrey talks with Surat Khan about the possibility of surrender. As the interview ends, Geoffrey looks straight out while Surat Khan and an aide stand at either side of him, in profile; they are closer to the camera and therefore larger; Geoffrey is literally surrounded and dominated by his enemies.

However, there is one major element of the swashbuckler's traditional structure that is missing from *The Charge of the Light Brigade:* the third section does not see the union of hero and heroine. What distinguishes Geoffrey from the other adventure heroes is his failure in romance.

The love story in *The Charge of the Light Brigade* is interwoven with its political plot, though not in the same manner as in *The Adventures of Robin Hood* and *The Sea Hawk.* Geoffrey loves and is engaged to Elsa, but she has fallen in love with his brother Perry (Patric Knowles), who returns her love. The audience learns all this in an early expository scene. Soon after, Perry tries to tell Geoffrey, but he refuses to believe him.

Curtiz connects the political and romantic plots with his staging of the scene of the British ball in Calcutta. A waiter walks across the floor; the camera follows him, stopping at Geoffrey who is dancing with an unknown girl. Since the dance involves changing partners, he is soon dancing with Elsa, who looks distinctly upset. Partners change again and Elsa now dances with Perry, who admits he has not yet told Geoffrey about their love. Then we cut to Surat Khan, who enters with his new friend, the Russian ambassador. Cut back to Geoffrey, who stops dancing to tell Sir Charles Masefield (Henry Stephenson), a British diplomat, about the new arrivals. As Masefield and Geoffrey greet Surat Khan, Perry and Elsa dance by and the camera follows them, stopping at Lord and Lady Warrington, who talk with Elsa's father, Colonel Campbell (Donald Crisp). Cut back to Perry and Elsa, who walk onto a balcony where they declare their love for each other. Colonel Campbell overhears them and, in self-righteous wrath, forbids Perry to see Elsa again. Cut back inside, where Surat Khan recites a story that explicitly compares politics and romance:

> I sometimes think, Sir Charles, that a great government resembles a beautiful woman who, intoxicated with the power of her own beauty, is apt to withdraw from a sincere suitor the favors she has always granted, and when she finds this suitor consoles himself with another beauty, regrets her coldness.

The political point is obvious to everyone: Britain is the woman who has withdrawn her love from her old suitor, Suristan, who has a new girl in Russia. But, for the audience, the little tale has a romantic point too: Elsa is the woman who has withdrawn her love from Geoffrey, although he has no other love but the army.

Geoffrey is thus the first hero we have met who is a romantic failure. He is not only a loser, but a stubbornly obtuse one. When Elsa confesses that Perry loves her, he answers smugly, "Yes, he told me, poor chap." He cannot or will not believe that she loves Perry, and never gives her the chance to say so. He seems a bit of a fool, and a hero should not be a fool. On the other hand, his steadfast and unrequited loyalty to Elsa does earn our sympathy, or at least our pity. But a hero should not be pitied. In short, compared to Peter Blood or

Robin Hood or Geoffrey Thorpe, Geoffrey Vickers is a somewhat diminished hero.

The film actually forces us to divide our sympathies between Perry and Geoffrey. We naturally side with Perry when the Colonel orders him not to see Elsa. Campbell has no sense of nor concern for human feelings; while his daughter cries, he dismisses her love for Perry as a "cheap infatuation." Overbearing, autocratic, bound by the rule book, he places propriety above humanity. Therefore, within the love story, Perry, not Geoffrey, is the rebel hero, the "outlaw" who defies authority to win his heroine.

Another way of putting this is to say that in the film, the opposition between hero and villain is less important than the one between authority, tradition, and duty on the one hand—the forces demanding that one follow orders—and human emotion on the other—the urge to defy authority to satisfy one's own desires. This conflict determines both the love plot and the political plot. In the love plot, Geoffrey is on the "wrong" side; that is, he becomes associated with the upholders of tradition. Perry himself makes the association: when Geoffrey screams that he is lying about Elsa loving him, he, equally angry, shouts, "You and Campbell and the whole blasted army can go to blazes."

But in the political plot Geoffrey is the rebel-hero. As John Davis says, the blundering British officials are responsible for almost all the disasters in the film, while Geoffrey constantly and unsuccessfully

> tries...to alert his superiors to inevitable consequences of their actions. He warns a senile English diplomat...about the danger of losing Surat Khan's friendship, but he is ignored; he advises a tradition bound Colonel...against leaving a border outpost undermanned, but the Colonel refuses to disobey orders from another, equally thick-headed officer...[3]

Despite Vickers' desperate pleading, the Colonel agrees to surrender the fort at Chukoti to Surat Khan, leading to the massacre.

Until the end, however, Geoffrey limits his rebelliousness to words. When he does decide to transform those words to action, Curtiz, as usual, uses his camera to involve us in Geoffrey's emotional turmoil. At the British army headquarters at Balaklava, Geoffrey learns that the high command refuses to order his men to fight Surat Khan. As he leaves his superior's office, we see him through the bars of a room divider; he is still trapped by authority. But he walks left, past the divider, then turns around it and heads right, toward his own desk; the camera follows this movement, panning left, then right. As he approaches his desk, the camera slides into a close-up of him; he stops, faces right, then turns and stares straight into the camera, then turns and walks left, finally turns and walks right again, back to his desk; during this entire back-and-forth movement, the camera has held him in close-up. As he sits down behind his desk, he moves out of the close-up; cut to a close-up of his hands holding the hated order to retreat; tilt up to, again, a close-up of his face; superimposed over it are various shots from the massacre sequence. As they disappear, we pull back to a close-medium shot, and Geoffrey begins to write. He is forging the order for his men to advance on Surat Khan. These two shots, lasting about ninety seconds, have taken us inside Geoffrey's mind. Using nothing but camera movement and placement, Curtiz fully describes Geoffrey's mental anguish, the psychic movement that leads to his final decision.

What is most notable, however, is that Geoffrey acts only after he realizes that Elsa does love Perry. The film does not state that Geoffrey's broken heart made him willing to order a suicidal charge, but it certainly implies Elsa's romantic decision makes his moral one easier. Like Perry, he chooses to ignore traditional authority and satisfy his own desire. But unlike Perry and the heroes of the pure swashbucklers, he finds his rebelliousness demands a more serious and complex moral decision and ultimately costs him his life.[4]

We first saw Curtiz's morally divided characters, torn between duty and desire, in *The Adventures of Robin Hood* and *The Sea Hawk*. *The Charge of the Light Brigade* suggests that as this internal conflict becomes more important, the external conflict between hero and villain becomes less so, and the swashbuckler becomes slowly transformed into something else. A brief examination of the Curtiz-Flynn westerns can make this movement clearer.

Many critics have noted resemblances between the western and the swashbuckler. Jeffrey Richards, for example, argues that the western, like the swashbuckler, has its roots in chivalric romances.[5] He sees such traditional outlaw heroes as Jesse James and Cole Younger as "American Robin Hoods" who are romanticized into figures with little relationship to their historical counterparts.[6] He singles out *Dodge City* as an example of a "western chivalric romance."[7]

Richards is right; of the three westerns, *Dodge City* is the closest to the traditional swashbuckler, closer even than *The Charge of the Light Brigade*. One of the western's traditional themes is the "struggle to bring civilization to the wilderness."[8] *Dodge City* is set in the post-Civil War period of westward expansion. An opening title reads:

> Kansas, 1866—the Civil War has ended. Armies disband—the nation turns to the building of the west.

In the only extended study the film has received, David Morse refers to it as a "seminal film in the development of the Western."[9] He is impressed by the "sheer multiplicity... of its thematic and iconographic material,"[10] its attempt to

> incorporate virtually all of the institutions and icons of the cowboy era. We are shown the stage-coach, the steam locomotive, buffalo hunters, a cattle drive, lynchings, saloons and gambling halls, the temperance league, a children's picnic, the covered wagons, a barber's shop, a cattle auction, a funeral at Boot Hill, a pioneer newspaper, a cattle stampede, a bar-room brawl.[11]

But within this multiplicity Morse sees the film's central theme as being the traditional one of "the coming of law and order to the west, the transition from violence and anarchy to stability."[12] In the film stability and civilization are tied to the idea of progress, and *Dodge City* begins with an affirmation of faith in and an image of progress: a race between a train and a stagecoach. Inside the train are Colonel Dodge, for whom the town will be named, and other railroad executives. It is because of the railroad that towns like Dodge City have appeared. As the train pulls ahead of the stagecoach, Dodge proclaims, "...that's a symbol of America's future—iron men and iron horses...."

Colonel Dodge has literally formed a new society around him; the film's hero, Wade Hatton (Errol Flynn) does so metaphorically; when he becomes sheriff of Dodge City he becomes the human agent who brings law and order to the wilderness. By defeating the villains and ridding the town of crime and corruption, he enables the new society to flourish. He is thus clearly in the tradition of the romantic-comic swashbuckling hero.

Hatton's background in fact is remarkably similar to Peter Blood's. Born in Ireland, he has fought in Europe, India, and elsewhere. As Colonel Dodge says, he has been everywhere and done everything. He even has his close companions, Tex (Guinn Williams) and Rusty (Alan Hale), just as Robin Hood had Little John (also Alan Hale) and Will Scarlett.

His most significant difference from the swashbuckler hero is that he is never forced nor chooses to become an outlaw. His moral purity is emphasized in his first appearance. Hatton and his friends had been hired by Colonel Dodge to provide buffalo for the railroad workers; now that the railroad is finished their contract is ended. Rusty and Tex suggest that they grab a few buffalo for themselves, but Hatton not only rejects this idea, but arranges for the arrest of Jeff Surret (Bruce Cabot) and his cohort, Yancey (Victor Jory), who have been killing buffalo illegally.

Hatton's first confrontation with Surret on the western plains may remind us of Robin's initial encounter with Gisbourne in Sherwood Forest. The roles are reversed, that is, Hatton is the authority, Surret the outlaw; but the scene, like the one in *The Adventures of Robin Hood,* identifies hero and villain and promises a series of future meetings which will climax in an inevitable and, for the villain, fatal battle.

Surret eventually becomes the chief force of evil in Dodge City, and the film's plot tells how Hatton joins the fight against him and finally wins it. Surret owns the film's equivalent of Nottingham Castle, the Gay Lady Saloon, and Curtiz introduces this environment with a series of tracking shots similar to those that opened the Nottingham feast scene: the camera pushes its way through a pair of swinging doors into the crowded, smoky, noisy bar; cut to a close-up of a roulette wheel, then tilt up and track past pillars, people, tables, towards the stage; cut to a closer shot of the stage and again track towards it.

The film's two worlds, city and saloon, become associated not merely with good and evil, hero and villain, but with its thematic oppositions between law and anarchy, civilization and wilderness, progress and decay. As David Morse explains, "the school, the chapel, the temperance hall, the women and children, the responsible citizenry, the crusading newspaper" all belong to the world of Dodge City; the "gaming tables, the lynch mobs, the unscrupulous profiteers, the hired gun" all belong to the world of the Gay Lady.[13]

Surret and his men may not be as suave as Gisbourne and Prince John, but they are as arrogant. When an officer tries to arrest them, they run him out of town. When Surret finds a stranger in the town's only bathtub during his regular bathing hour, he summarily orders him out. In fact, *Dodge City* has political overtones similar to those found in the swashbucklers. Like King Philip in *The Sea Hawk,* Surret resembles the fascist dictators who threatened the world in 1939. One of the film's major concerns is the power of a free press to fight such tyrants. Joe Clemens (Frank McHugh), editor of Dodge City's newspaper, leads a crusade against Surret and assembles evidence to convict him. When Surret cannot intimidate him into silence, he has him killed.[14] Hatton's destruction of the Surret gang frees Dodge City from its political and moral tyranny.

Hatton's relationship to the heroine, Abby Irving (Olivia de Havilland), further connects *Dodge City* to the swashbucklers, for it follows the Beatrice/ Benedick pattern found in *Captain Blood* and *The Adventures of Robin Hood.* Hatton and Abby meet on the cattle drive to Dodge City. Hatton leads the drive; Abby and her brother, Lee (William Lundigan), are with the settlers in the accompanying wagon train. They have already started to flirt when Hatton accidentally and indirectly causes Lee's death. Lee's own stupidity and drunkenness are its real cause, but Abby holds Hatton responsible and refuses to speak to him again. Not until Hatton proves his worth to her by becoming Dodge City's sheriff does she soften to him. They then continue to quarrel but with a comic tone. Finally, as in *The Adventures of Robin Hood,* the hero and heroine admit their love for each other and unite to rid their society of its villains.

Critics have noted that the traditional western can have a tragic or elegiac undertone. The western hero may help spread civilization but he himself is often not part of it. Such a hero prefers to be a wanderer, a lonely adventurer who chooses the open range over the quiet homestead, who yearns, like Huck Finn, to light out for the territory.[15] In some westerns, such as *Shane,* the hero may feel some urge to settle down, but he understands that his destiny forbids it.

This tragic possibility is an important difference between the western and the swashbuckler. I have been arguing that the swashbuckler hero is as much comic as romantic. They are never isolated or outside the community and their eventual union with the heroine is central to the themes and structure of their films. Peter Blood, Robin Hood, and Geoffrey Thorpe all return to a re-formed, villainless society with new titles, social roles, and wives. Wade Hatton, as a combination westerner-swashbuckler, gets to have it both ways. At the end of *Dodge City* he is both married and able to light out for the territory. Colonel Dodge offers him the chance to tame a new town further west. He wants the job, but fears Abby expects him to settle down. But she, understanding his character, appears with their bags packed, and the film fades out on a shot of a wagon train rolling westward.

Hatton at first refuses the job of Dodge City's sheriff, saying he is a cowboy, not a lawman. He pins on the badge only after several people he knows are killed. His initial reluctance to join the fight relates him to the hero of the next chapter, Rick in *Casablanca*. But Hatton's moral decision to become involved does not require a great sacrifice, like Rick's, or, for that matter, like Geoffrey Vickers'. Nor does he find himself even momentarily torn between duty and desire, like Marian and Maria. The heroes I will now consider face decisions of some moral complexity and the forms those complexities take reappear in other Curtiz films I will discuss in later chapters.

Santa Fe Trail is set before the Civil War, *Virginia City* during it. Part of their complexity comes from the division of their sympathies between North and South. Like *Dodge City, Santa Fe Trail* concentrates on America's westward expansion. But here the threat to civilization's spread comes not from lawless villains outside society, but from within society itself. That threat is the sectional hatred that arose over the issue of slavery and tore the country apart.

Flynn plays Southern officer J.E.B. (Jeb) Stuart, and the film gives a highly fictional account of his conflicts with abolitionist John Brown (Raymond Massey). The film alters history by making Stuart and several other future famous officers all members of the West Point class of 1854. None other than Jefferson Davis gives the commencement address, stressing the importance of national unity:

> We are not yet a wealthy nation, except in spirit, and that unity of spirit is our greatest strength.... With your unswerving loyalty... our nation shall have no fears for the future.

But America's own citizens are challenging that unity. After graduation, Stuart is assigned to Fort Leavenworth, Kansas. On board the train to Kansas they hear Cyrus Holliday (Henry O'Neill) talk of the troubles facing the nation. Like Colonel Dodge (also played by O'Neill), Holliday is an idealistic railroad builder who dreams of a railroad stretching "clear to Santa Fe." But

> You can't build a railroad over blood soaked ground like Kansas. Decent settlers won't use it.... Kansas is a territory not a state. We're ready to join the Union but the big question is whether we'll go in as a slave state or a free state. On one side is most of Kansas' proslavers, people who come from the South. On the other side are the abolitionists led by John Brown and his sons. Between those two elements they've made Kansas a boiling pot of rebellion and massacres.

Thus, the film's central opposition is not so much between North and South, freedom and slavery, but between statehood and stability, civilization and peace on the one hand, and territoriality and instability, wilderness and war on the other.[16]

However, *Santa Fe Trail* is not a neutral film; it is clearly an apologia for the pre-Civil War South. One of Stuart's first speeches succinctly expresses its attitude:

> I know the truth of this problem [slavery] far better than you [a Northerner] do. The South will settle it in its own time and in its own way.

Later, in a conversation with his fiancee, Kit Carson Holliday (Olivia de Havilland), Stuart expands on this idea of letting the South solve its own problems without outside interference:

> Kit: Can't it [the violence in Kansas] be stopped?
> Stuart: It will be stopped when we hang John Brown. Then the South can settle her own problems without loss of pride of being forced into it by a bunch of fanatics.
> Kit: ...what has pride got to do with human lives?
> Stuart: ...the two things kind of come together down South.

Later, still, Stuart tells Brown himself:

> The people of Virginia have considered the resolution to abolish slavery for a long time. They sense that it is a moral wrong and the rest of the South will follow Virginia's example. All they ask is time!

The film obviously sides with Stuart, its hero. Linda Pepper and John Davis have shown how it twists historical facts and distorts John Brown's character to promote its pro-Southern viewpoint.[17] But it still admits that slavery was a "moral wrong" and no matter what history may say, in the film the issue that divides North and South is slavery and no other. Therefore its villains and heroes are not quite as clear cut, not as purely black and white, as in the swashbucklers. Even the nastiest abolitionist has some strong arguments on his side; even the most heroic Southerner, like Stuart, fights for a lost and immoral cause.

John Brown himself is an equivocal figure. He is wrong, not because he opposes slavery, but because he uses violence to do so. As Kit tells his son Jason, "His reasons may be right, Jason, they may even be great and good reasons. But what your father is doing is wrong, terribly wrong." The film presents Brown not "as a hero or a totally self-seeking villain" but as a "demented religious fanatic."[18] Often he "erupts in violent outbursts, reaching out to slap his son, or ... [shove] his way through his followers, oblivious of them as humans."[19] As

Canham notes, Curtiz emphasizes Brown's nearly insane intensity by "shooting his meetings on hillsides at dusk, or against skylines; Massey is invariably lit in high key, or with a single spot on his face, emphasizing the demoniacal glitter in his eyes, bulging as he intones his biblical prophecies."[20]

Despite the implication of insanity in its portrait of Brown, which Pepper and Davis argue is unfair,[21] the film does allow him some prophetic last words whose accuracy helps to balance our view of him:

> I, John Brown, am now quite certain that the crimes of this guilty land can never be purged away but with blood.

Instead of Brown, the film makes a completely fictitious character, Rader (Van Heflin), the chief villain. He first appears as an abolitionist agitator at West Point, and is thrown out for starting a fight with Stuart. Throughout, his enmity to Stuart is shown to be personal rather than political, and he joins Brown's forces for financial rather than ideological reasons. As a former cadet, he is hired to be the group's military advisor. When Brown has difficulty paying his salary he betrays his plans to Stuart. Loyal to neither side, he is despised by both, and during the climactic attack on Harper's Ferry, Brown realizes his treachery and kills him.

Because he is depicted as such a thoroughgoing villain, we tend to ignore the truth in Rader's sneering attacks on Southern snobbery and slaveholding:

> For fifty years now you've been watering your precious family trees with the sweat of Negro slaves. . . . And anybody who disagrees with you is a lying renegade or a rabble-rousing traitor.

But there is some truth here, and it shines another, less flattering light on Stuart. Although unquestionably the film's hero, Stuart is still limited by his equivocation on slavery. He tells Brown that it is a "moral wrong," but he tells his friend Custer (Ronald Reagan) that "it isn't our job to decide who's right and who's wrong about slavery any more than it is John Brown's." More important, he refuses to see that a moral issue, not a man, lies behind the violence in Kansas. He insists that the violence will end "when we hang John Brown" and believes Custer is wrong in saying that "nothing will ever break Brown's power, not even death." But Stuart is wrong. Custer and Brown and Kit are all right; only blood could wash away "the crimes of this guilty land."

Stuart's position is the reverse of Geoffrey's in *The Charge of the Light Brigade*. Geoffrey is wrong in his private life, right about the political issues. Stuart is wrong politically, though he does win the heroine. But it is an easy victory, with no real competition; in fact, the love story is less important in *The Santa Fe Trail* than in any previous film we have discussed. Therefore the political story becomes more important. Stuart is as smugly self-confident about slavery as Geoffrey is about romance; in both cases our knowledge of the hero's blindness diminishes him in our eyes. However, Stuart's error seems more serious, and *Santa Fe Trail*'s ending more negative, even though Stuart lives while Geoffrey dies. *Santa Fe Trail* ends with Brown's hanging. Kit cries, not for him, but for the country which she feels will soon be torn by war. The scene dissolves to Stuart and Kit's wedding aboard a train heading west. Pepper and Davis claim that "the image of the powerful train . . . drives away the dark fears gathered in the preceding scene,"[22] but I agree with Kingsley Canham, who calls the ending "downbeat."[23] Kit's tears linger in our mind during her wedding, for we know her fears are justified.

Santa Fe Trail is the most disturbing of the westerns, of all the films in this section. The apparently positive terms of our central opposition, the society and stability Stuart strives to protect, are corrupted from within by the sin of slavery. Stuart himself is never in doubt about his moral position, and the audience accepts him as the hero figure, but a more limited one than those in the swashbucklers. In this way *Santa Fe Trail* looks forward to the dark films discussed in the last chapter. In them, the moral conflicts externalized in the swashbuckler occur within the hero. Instead of the purely good hero fighting the purely evil villain, we have a truly morally divided hero, one with some of the lust and greed of a villain, one who contains the means of his own destruction.

In *Virginia City,* however, the love story and the political/moral conflicts are not only of equal importance, but are closely connected to each other. One of the central oppositions in this film is between North and South, but those terms are not associated with positive and negative, good and evil. In fact, *Virginia City* has two heroes, Yankee Kerry Bradford (Errol Flynn) and Confederate Vance Irby (Randolph Scott). Vance's mission is to smuggle Southern gold from Virginia City, a Union stronghold, to a confederate army headquarters. Kerry's mission is to stop him. The film's opening sequences are carefully structured to divide audience sympathy between them, to make us identify first with one, then with the other.

The film begins inside Libby Prison, in Richmond, where Kerry and his familiar sidekicks, Swenson (Alan Hale) and Marblehead (Guinn Williams), are trying to tunnel to freedom. Curtiz uses some of his equally familiar visual techniques to create a claustrophobic atmosphere, including several close shots of the men in the tunnel, each sweaty face covered by a small circle of light, surrounded by dirt and darkness. Vance enters the cell, forces them up from the tunnel, and tells them he has known about their project for several months, but let their own futile labor be their punishment. However, Vance is no sadist. In the next scene, as he talks about the Confederacy's desperate condition, we come to admire his own dedication and nobility.

As in *Santa Fe Trail,* the true villain is a relatively minor figure, despised by both North and South: Murrel, a slimy Mexican bandit (played by Humphrey

Bogart with a silly Mexican accent).[24] Vance reluctantly hires him to divert the soldiers while his gold-laden wagon trails slips out of Virginia City. Naturally, Murrel later attacks the train; in contrast to both Kerry and Vance, he wants the gold for himself, and the two heroes join forces to defeat him.

The heroine, Julia Haynes (Miriam Hopkins), like the audience, is torn between the two heroes and the two sides they stand for. To be more accurate, she is torn between her love for Kerry and loyalty to the South; she may once have loved Vance as a man, but now she sees him only as representing a cause. Marian, a Norman in love with a Saxon, and Maria, a Spaniard in love with an Englishman, face similar problems, but their choices are actually rather easy; both the Normans and the Spaniards are tyrants. Julia's problem is more serious. Both men are heroic; both causes (in the film) just.

The manipulation of the audience by alternating scenes with each hero continues as they each pursue their business in Virginia City. Kerry talks with Union army officials; Vance plans the gold shipment; Kerry interviews a local banker. Finally, the antagonists meet, by accident, at the Sazerac saloon. The Sazerac is as lavish and noisy and smoky as *Dodge City's* Gay Lady, and we enter it with an elaborate camera movement similar to the one by which we entered the other saloon. But it is not *Virginia City's* Nottingham Castle, nor its center of corruption. It is, instead, the neutral yet dangerous territory where opposing forces meet and are held in fragile balance, where pressure builds but is somehow contained. Curtiz uses the crowds and confusion to create a highly charged atmosphere; like Rick's cafe in *Casablanca*, the Sazerac is where spies of all sides gather.

Kerry and Vance face each other for the first time since the one was the other's prisoner. They lie to each other about why they are in Virginia City, but each guesses the other's true purpose. Yet their confrontation ends, not with a fight, but only the promise of one in the future. More important, in the Sazerac Kerry discovers that Julia is not from an aristocratic family, as he thought, but is a saloon singer. Shocked, he treats her like a whore at first, then apologizes, and finally admits he loves her. But she is actually working for Vance, and her love for Kerry creates an intolerable emotional conflict. Ironically, Kerry's own dedication to duty enables her to decide between them. She begs him not to endanger himself by trying to stop Vance. Knowing he is a Northern spy, she asks if the gold means more to him than their love. Not knowing she is a Southern spy, he answers that it "is the only thing that does." So, Mata-Hari-like, she lures him into a trap where he is caught by Vance. Kerry's earlier unjustified sense of sexual betrayal is transformed into a justified sense of political betrayal. In *Casablanca* we will see Rick treat Ilsa like a whore and enact an elaborate variation of this transformation. Moreover, both Kerry and Julia have sacrificed their personal feelings to their sense of moral obligation, which Rick and the other heroes of the next chapter will also do.

But *Virginia City* is still closer to Curtiz's comic swashbucklers than to his tragic romances because of its optimistic conclusion. The problem of the two heroes is solved, as in *The Charge of the Light Brigade,* by one of them dying; Vance is killed in the climactic battle with Murrel. Like Geoffrey Vickers, he who loses his love also loses his life. Before he dies, he asks Kerry not to give the gold to the Union soldiers, who he knows will capture the wagon train. The gold, he says, belongs to the South, and although it is too late to help the Confederacy in the war, it can be used to help rebuild it when peace comes. Kerry agrees and, also like Geoffrey Vickers, becomes a rebel-hero at the end, defying authority by refusing to tell the Union army where he has hidden the gold. The military court sentences him to death, but ultimately his moral decision leads to the comedic reconciliation. His choice has put him and Julia on the same side at last, resolving for both their internal conflicts. Julia pleads with President Lincoln to free Kerry, and he gladly does so. He wants to bind the broken country and he sees in Kerry and Julia the love that can forge that bond. The film ends with them hand in hand; like Robin and Marian's, their marriage joins two formerly warring societies; together they will form a new, reunified society.

The most important opposition in *Virginia City* is between love and duty, private feeling and public responsibility, and it is with these terms, rather than with good and evil that North and South become associated. (Obviously, for Kerry, North represents duty, South love; for Julia the reverse is true.)

As I have suggested, we will see that this opposition is central to *Casablanca.* It is also central to *The Private Lives of Elizabeth and Essex,* which, with its tale of great love doomed by political necessity, can be seen as an earlier variation of *Casablanca.*

Based on Maxwell Anderson's play, *Elizabeth the Queen,* the film has almost as little relation to history as did *The Charge of the Light Brigade.*[25] The aging Elizabeth (Bette Davis) loves Robert Devereux, Earl of Essex (Errol Flynn), but she cannot believe that he loves her; she feels he really wants her royal power rather than her person. Essex does love Elizabeth, but he also loves her throne; he wonders, "Since we're equal in love, why can't we be equal in power as well?" When he tries to seize that power by force, Elizabeth has him beheaded.

In its iconography, its elaborate Elizabethan sets and costumes, its hordes of extras flourishing swords, spears, or trumpets in their roles as soldiers and heralds, its battle with blade and bow between Essex and the Irish rebel, Tyrone (Alan Hale), *The Private Lives of Elizabeth and Essex* does resemble a swashbuckler.[26] It even has its group of courtier-villains, led by Lord Cecil (Henry Daniell[27]), who scheme against the hero. Jealous of his position as Elizabeth's favorite, they goad him into leading the British army against Tyrone, then arrange for his defeat by intercepting his letters to Elizabeth asking for more troops and supplies.

But the film's real "villain," the force that separates hero and heroine, is their own nature and destiny which impel them to put politics ahead of romance. Just as Kerry, in *Virginia City,* says that the gold is the only thing that means more to him than love, so Essex admits that his ambition is stronger than his love. And Elizabeth, like Julia, succumbs to her sense of duty and betrays her lover. Early in the film she says that "the necessities of a queen must transcend those of a woman"; at the end, she acts on that belief.

Ironically, this conflict between public duty and private desire appears even in the story's two titles.[28] Anderson's title, *Elizabeth the Queen,* emphasizes the former; the film's title obviously emphasizes the latter. The dialogue constantly stresses the complex interplay of these two forces within Elizabeth and Essex; almost every one of their speeches slides from one to the other; their private lives are inescapably bound up in their public roles.

As usual, Curtiz suggests this visually; his handling of the opening sequence subtly implies that Essex is already trapped by the demands of public life. Fresh from his military victory at Cadiz, he rides in triumph through London. But we often see him, framed by arches or else in high shots, a small figure surrounded by cheering crowds. He and the procession seem rather stiff and lifeless; throughout the film, court scenes are filled with ritual and convention. Ina Rae Hark writes about the static, symmetrical compositions that characterize the Nottingham Castle scenes in *The Adventures of Robin Hood;*[29] the same could be said of the scenes at Elizabeth's court, with its carefully arranged rows of trumpeters and guards turning human figures into abstract patterns.

Essex's political efforts lead only to further traps. His expedition to Ireland, a result of his own vanity and the intrigues of his enemies, is as disastrous as Geoffrey Thorpe's to Panama and is shot in a similar fashion. Stumbling through steaming swamps and waist-high weeds, Essex and his men become visually and metaphorically imprisoned by the heavy foilage. Eventually, he is literally imprisoned, in the Tower (Plate 13). Elizabeth, however, is as much a political prisoner as he; she moves into an apartment in the tower to await his execution.

Only in their love scenes are Elizabeth and Essex truly free, and then only when they talk love and not politics. The absence of other people turns the public court into a private haven where they can express their mutual love. Alone, they abandon convention, cease posing, smack each other on the rear and fall to the floor laughing. Curtiz charges these scenes with a romanticism reminiscent of Robin and Marian in Sherwood, filling the room with the warm glow of a fireplace, sliding his camera in for huge, intense close-ups of the lovers.

In short, as in his other films, Curtiz here creates two visual worlds which correspond to the terms of the film's central opposition. The worlds of love and politics, private haven and public court, are descendants of the worlds of Sherwood and Nottingham. But in the swashbucklers the two worlds stand for the elemental and external opposition of hero and villain, good and evil; in the end, hero conquers villain, Sherwood absorbs Nottingham. In *The Private Lives of Elizabeth and Essex* the opposition is more complex and more internal and at last destroys hero and heroine. In the swashbuckler the hero is stronger than the public events that invade his life and threaten his society; Robin rescues England from Prince John; Thorpe rescues it from Spain. In *The Private Lives of Elizabeth and Essex,* the force of politics, the demands of public duty overwhelm the individual; to save England, Elizabeth must sacrifice Essex. Thus, the transformation of the swashbuckler, hinted at in *The Charge of the Light Brigade,* developed further in the westerns, is completed in *The Private Lives of Elizabeth and Essex;* the swashbuckler has become a romantic tragedy. In the next chapter we move to *Casablanca,* a complex elaboration of the conflict between love and politics,[30] less tragic, more romantic, and involving one of the screen's most famous heroic sacrifices.

"A Hill of Beans": *Casablanca*

Synopsis of the Film

In December of 1941, Casablanca swarms with refugees desperate for exit visas. Ugarte (Peter Lorre), a petty crook, has murdered two German couriers and stolen the powerful "letters of transit" they carried. He asks Rick (Humphrey Bogart), owner of Rick's Café Américain, to keep them until he can sell them, but Captain Renault (Claude Rains), prefect of police, arrests him under the approving gaze of Nazi official Major Strasser (Conrad Veidt). Rick, unmoved by Ugarte's capture, is upset by the entrance of Victor Laszlo (Paul Henried) and his beautiful companion, Ilsa Lund (Ingrid Bergman). A flashback reveals that Ilsa and Rick were lovers in Paris and planned to leave together when the Germans invaded. But Ilsa stayed in Paris, sending Rick a mysterious note saying she could never see him again. In Casablanca, Laszlo learns from Ferrari (Sydney Greenstreet), a black marketeer, that Rick probably has the stolen letters of transit. But Rick refuses to give them to Laszlo. Later, Ilsa confesses that she still loves Rick, explaining to him that she was married to Victor during their Parisian affair, but thought him dead. The day they were to leave she learned he was alive and therefore had to abandon Rick to help her husband. Rick now agrees to resolve the triangle. He tells Renault to arrest Laszlo when he gives him the letters, but when Renault tries to do so, Rick orders him to take them all to the airport. Rick puts Ilsa on the plane with Laszlo and the letters, and shoots Strasser when he tries to prevent its takeoff. Instead of arresting Rick, Renault decides to leave Casablanca and join a Free French force with him.

Sometimes it seems that every book on American film is required to have a chapter on *Casablanca* (1942).[1] Certainly, it is the best known of Curtiz's films. Critically and commercially successful when first released, it received three academy awards, including Curtiz's only award for best director.[2] Since then it has become a cult object among the Bogart worshippers. Obviously we cannot ignore *Casablanca,* but not because of its popularity—rather because it is so typical of and central to Curtiz's work. In this chapter, after looking briefly at some of the critical perspectives on the film, I want to show how its thematic and structural base, the conflict between love and politics, becomes associated with a number of other oppositions, all contained within its two worlds of Paris and Casablanca.

Considering *Casablanca*'s unusual production history, its success is surprising.[3] Warner Brothers originally announced it would film Murray Burnett and Joan Alison's unproduced play, *Everybody Comes to Rick's* with Ronald Reagan, Ann Sheridan, and Dennis Morgan (in the Bogart, Bergman, and Henried roles), indicating they planned to make it a "B" picture. The studio changed its mind, however, and producer Hal Wallis first put noted screen-writers Philip and Julius Epstein to work on turning the play into a script, then dispatched them to David O. Selznick to convince him to lend his most valuable property, Ingrid Bergman, to the production. They succeeded, even though their script was far from finished. It was still unfinished when shooting started, but the Epsteins left for Washington to work with Frank Capra on the *Why We Fight* series. Howard Koch was called in to complete the script. Working as fast as he could, he often sent pages to the set the day they were to be shot. According to Ingrid Bergman,[4] no one even knew how the film would end. Two possibilities were considered, one where Ilsa leaves Casablanca with Laszlo, and one where she stays with Rick. However, after the first was shot and looked at, everyone agreed that filming the second was no longer necessary. Ronald Haver offers a somewhat different story. He claims that the Epsteins' original ending, derived from the play, had Rick, after letting Ilsa and Laszlo escape, being arrested by Strasser.[5] It dissatisfied Wallis, Curtiz, and Koch but they could not come up with a new one. Finally the Epsteins returned from Washington and invented the one we now have.

Although Koch's self-serving remark that more "articles have been written about it [*Casablanca*] than any other picture"[6] is an exaggeration, and much of what has been written is superficial, nostalgic gush,[7] *Casablanca* has received more serious critical attention than any other Curtiz film. Some of the theories are a bit surprising. William Donelley's "Love and Death in *Casablanca*"[8] argues that the film follows the narrative pattern described by Leslie Fiedler in *Love and Death in the American Novel,* in which the hero rejects mature, heterosexual love for a life of wandering and adventure with another man. In short, "Rick's relationship with Sam and with Captain Renault is a standard case of the repressed homosexuality that underlies most American adventure stories."[9] After all, when finally faced with the possibility of staying with Ilsa, Rick chooses to walk into the night with Renault, and Renault himself has confessed that Rick is the "kind of man that, well, if I were a woman, and I were not around, I should be in love with." While this is an intriguing interpretation, it falters because it seems so irrelevant to our actual experience of the film.[10] Rick and Renault's relationship is, perhaps, the most interesting in the film, but calling them secret lovers simply ignores too many other aspects of the movie, including the obvious reality of Rick's love for Ilsa.

Equally irrelevant is the "allegorical" interpretation which sees Rick as FDR living in the "casa blanca" (Spanish for "white house"), moving from neutrality to active participation in World War II under the urging of Churchill (Laszlo). *Casablanca*'s contemporary political implications are obvious enough (especially in lines like Rick's, "If it's December, 1941 in Casablanca, what time is it in New York . . . I bet they're asleep in New York. I bet they're asleep all over America") without straining for allegorical ones. Moreover, fitting all the minor characters and incidents into an allegorical scheme, besides being rather difficult, reduces the film's complex riches to one casket of political coin.[11]

In *The Movies on Your Mind,* Harvey Greenberg offers an old-fashioned Freudian reading of *Casablanca.* In his view, Rick suffers an Oedipus complex and admits as much when he confesses to a "combination" of the crimes Renault charges him with:

> Renault: I've often speculated on why you don't return to America. Did you abscond with the church funds? Did you run off with the Senator's wife? I'd like to think you killed a man. It's the romantic in me.
> Rick: It was a combination of all three.

For Greenberg, the "stolen treasure" *is* the wife of the murdered, "preeminent older man"; the "essence of the 'combination' of offenses is the child's original desire to kill his father and possess his mother."[12] Ilsa becomes the mother substitute, Laszlo the father figure; Rick would kill him by "withholding the letters of transit unless he can get Ilsa back."[13] Greenberg, a psychoanalyst and film buff, tells us that a man overcomes his Oedipal conflicts when he stops competing with and starts identifying with the father. Rick eventually identifies with Laszlo and "the Cause" and lets him leave Casablanca alive and with Ilsa. Ilsa herself wavers between an older, "idealized, asexual father figure"[14] and the more suitable and sexual Rick. Greenberg argues that Ilsa's infidelities are "explained away" in typical Hollywood fashion by "a twist of plot . . . the fortunes of war" rather than the "vagaries of her unconscious."[15] Unfortunately, Greenberg fails to see that the "twist of plot" is what *Casablanca* is about. As we will later learn, the entire film, like many other Curtiz films, is structured on the relationship between private feelings and public duties. Further, any character exists only within the context of a film; to discuss the character and ignore the context violates that film.

Other critics suggest less unified interpretations, concentrating instead on Casablanca's host of exotic characters. Most have noted, like Richard Corliss, that the minor figures "constitute a dazzling, baroque hall of mirrors that reflect facets and distortions of the leading characters' lives and life-style." Ugarte and

Ferrari, who share Rick's business acumen, "are various corruptions of Rick, as peddler and panderer, respectively"; Sascha, who yearns for Yvonne, is an "unseductive Renault"; Carl, who accompanies Laszlo to the underground meeting, is a "cuddly, less ostentatious Laszlo."[16] For Barry Day, Laszlo "represents another of the possibilities implicit in Rick." He is "Rick with his convictions still intact and his ideals undefiled."[17] Richard Schickel sees Laszlo balanced by Strasser who, unlike "so many movie Nazis . . . is not, apparently, a sadist. Rather, he is an ideologue, a man of action and a fanatic—all qualities present in Laszlo as well."[18] Corliss, on the other hand, calls Strasser a "German version of Renault, a prosaic scientist of war to Renault's master of the boudoir arts, the crazy mirror image of an *Übermensch* as opposed to Renault's *homme moyen sensuel.*"[19]

All of them agree that, next to Rick, Renault is the most important character. Although we remember them fondly, Ferrari and Ugarte are, as Schickel says, wasted;[20] Ugarte is killed twenty minutes into the film and Ferrari appears only two or three times. But *Casablanca* is as much about Renault's conversion to the cause as Rick's. He has the best lines and, by not stopping Laszlo's plane nor arresting Rick, determines the plot's resolution. Certainly, he is as emphatically enigmatic as Rick. When Renault asks Rick, "Have you got those Letters of Transit?" Rick replies, "Louis, are you Pro-Vichy or Free French?" Neither question is answered. A few moments later, Strasser asks Renault, "Are you entirely certain which side you're on?" Renault answers, "I have no convictions if that's what you mean. I blow with the wind. And the prevailing wind happens to be from Vichy." Then, as if to underline his equivocation, he puffs on a cigarette, surrounding himself in a smoky haze (Plate 15).

He and Rick spend most of the film eyeing each other suspiciously. Their relationship, in fact, resembles the Beatrice/Benedick pattern of hero and heroine found in *Captain Blood* and *The Adventures of Robin Hood,* and we can understand how this might inspire a homosexual interpretation. Perfectly balanced, they respect but justifiably distrust each other. Renault fears Rick will help Laszlo escape, which he does; Rick fears Renault will alert Strasser to that escape, which he does. Finally, when their competing loyalties (Ilsa, for Rick, and Strasser, for Renault) leave, they resolve the tension between them and begin their "beautiful friendship." But that tension depends on the strength of those other loyalties. Rick truly wants Ilsa; giving her up is a sacrifice only unselfish idealism could prompt. In place of love, he finds male comradeship, but the trade involves a definite loss.

Nevertheless, Rick's loneliness has a certain appeal to audiences, one which Michael Wood has brilliantly analyzed in his recent *America in the Movies.* The image of Rick waiting for Ilsa, sitting "at a table behind a drink, moodily staring into the middle distance, a glint of self pity in his eyes,"[21] represents "what isolation looks like at its best; proud, bitter, mournful and tremendously attractive."[22] For Wood, that attraction comes from one of the cornerstones of American mythology, the belief that preserving one's individualism means remaining uninvolved, the fear of entangling alliances, be they political or personal, the desire to remain totally self-sufficient, the "dream of freedom from others."[23] I think all this is quite true, yet there may be a further source for Rick's popularity. He is an irresistible identification figure for that urge in all of us for a splendid and noble martyrdom. What could be more satisfying than the image of ourselves sacrificing all that we love for a virtuous ideal, ending up utterly but heroically alone?

Whatever the source of Rick's appeal, he is *Casablanca*'s center, the point around which all the other characters orbit. Each tries to assert his special relationship with him by addressing him in a unique manner: Renault calls him Ricky; Ilsa calls him Richard; Laszlo calls him Monsieur Blaine; Strasser calls him Mr. Blaine; Ugarte and Ferrari call him Rick; Carl calls him Herr Rick; Sam (Dooley Wilson as his black, piano-playing friend) calls him Mr. Rick, Mr. Richard, and Boss. Each of these names, from Strasser's coldly formal "Mr. Blaine" to Renault's possibly gay "Ricky," characterizes its user as much as Rick. But their profusion proves his ambiguity; he is literally different things to different people.

Or is he? Actually Rick is not nearly so ambiguous nor so cynical as he pretends. He is, in fact, as Renault calls him, a "sentimentalist." The first section of the film, from Rick's entrance to Laszlo and Ilsa's first appearance, carefully defines his personality and because of this exposition we never really doubt that his actions in the crisis will be anything less than heroic.

The section consists of a number of encounters between Rick and the other characters and his reaction to each sketches in another feature of his emerging portrait. The first encounter, with the anonymous German banker who demands entrance to his private gambling room, presents the film's major action in miniature. Aggressive and arrogant, the banker represents all the Germans who have invaded Casablanca. Rick's response is equally representative; cooly and firmly he rebuffs the intruder and maintains his cafe's privacy, just as later he resists Strasser's efforts to invade the privacy of his past.

Rick next confronts Ugarte and begins to make his morality anything but ambiguous. He says he does not "mind a parasite...[only] a cut-rate one," but the cynical words fool not even the slimy and obsequious Ugarte. Because he knows Rick despises him for profiting from the refugees' desperation, he recognizes Rick's own integrity and entrusts him with the letters of transit:

Ugarte: You know Rick,...just because you despise me, you are the only one I can trust.

Rick's later refusal to aid Ugarte during his arrest is neither cynical nor unexpected but practical and praiseworthy. Rick really cannot offer any help, and Ugarte would not deserve it if he could.

As Ugarte slides towards the gambling tables, Ferrari enters, full of good humor and dignity. Unlike Ugarte, he approaches Rick as an equal. But underneath his sophisticated charm lies a soul as corrupt as Ugarte's and Rick rejects his morality as well. Ferrari urges him to join in the black market: "In refugees alone we could make a fortune . . . " But Rick refuses: "I don't buy or sell human beings." Ferrari has actually offered to "buy" Sam, so that the relevance of Rick's refusal ranges beyond Casablanca's borders.

Only with Yvonne (Madeleine Le Beau), Rick's next encounter, does he appear genuinely heartless. When the lovestruck girl asks, "Will I see you tonight?" he answers, "I never make plans that far ahead." But anyone ending a one-sided love affair seems somewhat brutal, and Rick at least evidences enough concern for Yvonne to stop her from drinking herself into trouble. Further, the scene is sandwiched between his morally laudable meetings with Ugarte and Ferrari, and his dialogue with Renault, who reveals Rick's politically opprobrious past.

Like Ugarte earlier and Strasser in the next scene, Renault probes into Rick's background. Rick remains wittily evasive, but Renault knows his "record."

Renault: In 1935 you ran guns to Ethiopia. In 1936 you fought in Spain on the Loyalist side.

Rick claims financial motives, but Renault pierces his mask: "The winning side would have paid you much better," he says, pointing up Rick's poorly hidden idealism.

Strasser also knows Rick's record and questions him about it, but Rick outmaneuvers him.

Strasser: Are you one of those people who cannot imagine the Germans in their beloved Paris?
Rick: It's not particularly my beloved Paris.
. . . .
Strasser: How about New York?
Rick: Well, there are certain sections of New York, Major, that I wouldn't advise you to try to invade.

Thus, by the time Ilsa appears, Rick's character has been drawn as clearly as Peter Blood's or those of the other swashbuckling heroes. Just as we never doubt that those "thieves and pirates" are their films' moral centers, so we never really doubt that Rick is *Casablanca*'s moral center. Torn between neutrality and patriotism, cynicism and idealism, he is another of Curtiz's morally divided characters. He faces a more serious decision than Marian, Maria, or any character in the swashbucklers, but his final choice is as unsurprising as theirs. Ultimately, his neutrality is only appearance, his cynicism only words.

In his continuous assertions of self-interest, Rick resembles an earlier, equally popular, and quintessentially American movie hero, Rhett Butler. Despite the differences in the worlds they inhabit, Rhett Butler and Rick Blaine share more than their initials. Like Rick (and many American heroes, including Jay Gatsby), Rhett comes from a mysterious background, is wealthy, sophisticated, and able to control most of the people and events around him. He too has been a gun runner, smuggling arms for the south through Union blockades and when Scarlett praises his belief in the Cause, he laughs back, "I believe in Rhett Butler." (Rick: "I'm the only cause I'm interested in.") He claims he fights only for profit; but when the war, nearing its close, looks most hopeless, his barely submerged better nature surfaces and he joins the Southern army. Rhett measures people not by their social position but by his own standards of moral worth. Thus, he tells Scarlett that Mammy is one of the few people whose respect he craves. Similarly, the only person Rick seems to admire unequivocally is Sam. Until the end, Rhett's spirit remains faithful to one woman, despite her treatment of him, though he occasionally soothes his body with others; his Yvonne is Belle Watling. Finally, both heroes eventually leave their lovers, though for different reasons, and are last seen walking into the fog. In short, as Michael Wood suggests, Rick's pride in his cynicism and isolation, the stoical joy with which he enters that fog, constantly recurs in American movie heroes.[24]

Perhaps the most significant link between *Gone with the Wind* and *Casablanca* is that both films play out a small, intimate love story against a vast background of war and social chaos. Barbara Deming, in her excellent study of films of the forties, *Running Away from Myself*, concentrates her remarks on *Casablanca* on how the film connects love and sexuality to politics. But Deming believes the film blurs that connection, reducing political disillusionment to personal disillusionment. Rick's claim of political neutrality simply shields a broken heart; when he reaffirms his faith in Ilsa, he can also reaffirm his faith in the political struggle. She comments, for example, on the mingling of public and private references in Rick's drunken, pre-flashback speech:

"They grab Ugarte, then she walks in. That's the way it goes. One in and one out. Sam, if it's December 1941 in Casablanca, what time is it in New York ... I bet they're asleep in New York. I bet they're asleep all over America." Look at all the notes that are casually woven together here. "One in and one out" of Ugarte and Ilsa. Ugarte is an opportunist who serves a good cause for a price—as Rick claims to have done. Rick's cold familiarity with this sort of betrayal of a faith here blurs in one split second with his cynicism about love's promises. Note, next, the date ... making this just pre-Pearl Harbor. "I bet they're asleep" ... takes on, automatically, political overtones—and Rick's cynicism about the state of his country too is blurred with the very special cynicism of the jilted lover. Finally, when ... Ilsa appears at the door ... all bitterness can be said to have been focused on her person.[25]

Deming's remarks are quite perceptive but, like Greenberg, she undervalues the complexity of the connection the film makes between politics and romance, the public and the private.[26] Rick is utterly wrong when he says, in his well-known line, "The problems of three little people don't amount to a hill of beans in this crazy world." *Casablanca* is about the "problems of three little people" and their connection to the problems of "this crazy world"; what we remember first about the film is its love story, its tale of love lost, regained, and finally sacrificed, its image of Rick moving from a bitter to a noble loneliness.

Michael Wood, in his description of that loneliness, suggests that Rick and Ilsa "have all the glory of a great love, but they don't have to go on living with it."[27] This insight perhaps explains the continued appeal of what I call the Great Doomed Romance in American popular literature and film. We saw it in the last chapter in Curtiz's *The Private Lives of Elizabeth and Essex*. We see it again in the Ruritanian romances of love between royalty and commoner, such as *Roman Holiday* (1953, directed by William Wyler) and the several versions of *The Student Prince,* and in the many stories of fatally ill lovers, including one of Hollywood's most commercially successful films, *Love Story* (1970, directed by Arthur Hiller). Certainly *Casablanca* is related to films of these genres, but, like *The Private Lives of Elizabeth and Essex,* and unlike its tearjerking cousins, *Casablanca's* lovers are parted, not by the protocol of imaginary monarchies, nor by the unexpected and arbitrary onset of incurable illness, but by a deliberate choice prompted by serious motives. *Casablanca* is a very romantic movie, but it is also a fable of renunciation, and its romanticism is but the melodramatic heightening of an act of renunciation performed by every soldier who leaves his sweetheart for war. As Richard Schickel suggests,

> *Casablanca* . . . was a paradigm for personal commitment that appeared at a moment when many were in the process of making, or trying to make, personal—as opposed to merely political—commitments to the fight against fascism.[28]

In an earlier chapter we noted that the basically simple contrast between court world and green world structured *The Adventures of Robin Hood's* plot, characters, and visual style. In *Casablanca* it is the far more complex connection between political and personal feelings that shapes nearly every situation and every relationship. Renault, for example, ever eager to turn public business into private pleasure, asserts the connection in its bluntest form: to escape political oppression, female refugees must suffer some sexual oppression. Other characters enact subtler variations on the theme. Ilsa's life, even before she met Rick, was molded by politics; in a sense she married Laszlo for political reasons. Young, naive, idealistic, she was overwhelmed by this "great and courageous" activist who "opened up for her a whole beautiful world full of knowledge and thoughts and ideals . . . And she looked up to him, worshipped him with a feeling she supposed was love." After his assumed death, she meets Rick, and her feelings for him are more electric than idealistic. But Laszlo is alive and needs her for his "work," while Rick's own activist record makes her fear his capture if she tells him of her marriage. Events beyond her control force her to leave Rick. As Corliss says, both Rick's and Ilsa's personal love stories "melded into international affairs so imperceptibly and so relentlessly that telling one's confession would sound like a chaotic, personalized history lesson."[29]

Jan (Helmut Dantine) and Annina (Joy Page), the young refugees whom Rick helps, clearly parallel Rick and Ilsa. Political events have created their need to escape Bulgaria and this need endangers their private lives by almost forcing Annina to betray her husband sexually. Rick's "one in and one out" line could also apply to the two couples, for they follow the same route in search of exit visas and constantly appear in the same scenes. As the Laszlos enter Renault's office, Jan and Annina leave in the background; when the Laszlos visit Ferrari, we again see the other two exiting. Finally, both couples ask for and receive help from Rick. However, as Corliss points out, "There is nothing neat about the analogy of plot to subplot here."[30] Annina must sleep with a stranger to save her husband; Ilsa had to abandon her lover for her husband to save both. But each plot does involve the intrusion of public events into private lives.

If Annina's adventures echo Ilsa's, Yvonne reenacts in miniature Rick's progression from abandoned lover to political cynic to active patriot. After Rick jilts her, she reappears on the arm of a German officer, gliding by Rick with a sneer on her face, provoking him to mumble, "So Yvonne's gone over to the enemy." Like Rick, she expresses romantic pain with a political act. Her date with the German, like Rick's calling Ilsa a whore, is a masochistic attempt to hurt a lover by hurting the self. But when Laszlo leads the cafe in "La Marseillaise," Yvonne's shell cracks and she joins the singing, shouting "Vive la France, Vive la démocratie." To make the parallel to Rick's climactic patriotism more explicit, Curtiz shows Rick allowing the singing: when Laszlo asks the bandleader to play "La Marseillaise," we see the bandleader look at Rick followed by a closeup of Rick silently nodding his approval.

Even the most minor characters suggest the problems of the major ones. The Leuchtags, for example, a third refugee couple, appear only once in a tiny scene with Carl, demonstrating their command of broken English. Though basically comic relief, they are one more loving pair whose lives have been disrupted by the war.

Thus, in *Casablanca,* the forest and the castle have become the worlds of romantic involvement and political commitment. From their first moments onscreen, Ilsa is identified with one, Laszlo with the other. As Ilsa walks to her table in Rick's cafe, she shares a moment of shocked recognition with Sam; we know then that she is somehow related to Rick. On the other hand, Laszlo's first words, "I saw no one of Ugarte's description," connect him to the political intrigue that fills the cafe. As the scene continues, Curtiz intercuts these two worlds, private and public, romantic and political, Ilsa and Laszlo. We see a two shot of Strasser and Renault followed by a shot of Laszlo leaving Ilsa to talk with Berger, an underground leader. The camera then tracks into a closeup of Ilsa, followed by a closeup of Sam. Cut to Laszlo talking with Berger; cut back to Ilsa asking a waiter to have "the piano player . . . come over here." Cut back to the bar; Renault joins Laszlo as Berger leaves; cut to Ilsa and Sam reminiscing about the old days. Sam begins playing "As Time Goes By"; Rick comes storming over and collides with his past. But before Rick and Ilsa can exchange a word, Renault and Laszlo enter the frame; the two worlds have joined in one image. Rick, looking at his new guests, sees the conflict that will tear him apart from that moment on.

Of course, Laszlo and Ilsa are not simply personifications of opposing forces. Each, in fact, mingles both forces. Ilsa represents (for Rick) not merely love, but love hounded by political events. He remembers "every detail" of their last meeting, "the day the Germans marched into Paris." He tells Ilsa, "The Germans wore gray; you wore blue." The loss of Paris and the loss of his love are fused in his mind. Laszlo, on the other hand, demands to be thought of as a lover as well as a leader. His penultimate conversation with Rick slides easily from political debate:

> Rick: Don't you sometimes wonder if it's worth all this? I mean, what you're fighting for.
> Laszlo: We might as well question why we breathe. If we stop breathing we'll die. If we stop fighting our enemies the world will die.

to more personal matters:

> Laszlo: I know . . . you're in love with a woman. It is perhaps a strange circumstance that we should both love the same woman.

and he tells Rick:

> Laszlo: Apparently you think of me only as the leader of a cause. Well, I'm also a human being. Yes, I love her that much.

The worlds of romance and politics have their metaphoric homes in the film's twin cities, Paris and Casablanca. Howard Koch reports that Curtiz himself deepened the association between Paris and romance by insisting on inserting the flashback sequence.

> Mike leaned strongly on the romatic elements of the story while I was more interested in the characterizations and the political intrigues with their relevance to the world struggle against fascism . . .
>   One disagreement I remember arose over the flashback sequence in which Rick recalls his Paris love affair with Ilsa. I argued that these could only be conventional scenes with no

dramatic progression until the end shot when Ilsa fails to show up at the railroad station. While they illustrated the cause of Rick's bitterness and cynicism, I felt these were sufficiently exposed in the cafe scene with Ilsa. And I was afraid that the flashback would dissipate the tension that was building in the present.

However, in retrospect I suspect Mike was right. Probably at this point the romantic interlude was a useful retard and relief from tension—and the viewer needed some visual proof of the ardor of the love affair to be convinced of its profound effect on Rick. At any rate, Mike exercised his directorial prerogative and the sequence was written and shot in accordance with his ideas.[31]

The two cities even have their own theme songs. One of the film's best-loved moments is Laszlo leading the singing of "La Marseillaise," a political anthem. Earlier, in an equally well-loved scene, Rick asks Sam to play the film's romantic anthem, "As Time Goes By," echoing Ilsa's request of earlier still. Despite these scenes' popularity, no one seems to have noticed how closely Laszlo's words and actions parallel Rick and Ilsa's:

Ilsa to Sam: Play it, Sam. Play "As Time Goes By."

Rick to Sam: You played it for her, you can play it for me. Play it!

Laszlo to bandleader: Play "La Marseillaise." Play it!

As in his other films, Curtiz expresses the conflict between worlds visually. *Casablanca*'s romanticism appears in its choreography of close-ups and camera movement, which Curtiz uses for his usual purpose of involving us in his characters' emotions. He follows one of the simplest but most effective rules of film grammar: the larger the close-up, the greater its emotional impact. Thus, when Ilsa asks Sam to play "some of the old songs," we see her from the chest up; when she starts humming alone, we cut to an even closer shot and see only her face and shoulders. The Annina-Rick scene begins with the expected medium two shot, Annina and Rick facing each other across a table, followed by alternating over-the-shoulder shots. But as Annina reaches her crucial question, "Will he [Renault] keep his word?" the scene's intensity builds up with a switch to crosscut close-ups. As Annina continues, Rick recognizes the relationship between his situation and hers; we see him listening, in close-up, his cheek quivering. Finally, unable to take anymore, Rick dismisses Annina, "Well, everybody in Casablanca has problems. Yours may work out. You'll excuse me?" and the tension breaks with a cut back to the original two shot.

Similarly, the confrontation between Ilsa and Rick in his apartment begins with a two shot, switches to over-the-shoulder shots and finally to close-ups, but here Curtiz adds camera movement to increase the emotional force. In close-up, Rick taunts Ilsa, then suddenly stops in mid-sentence, staring in surprise. Cut to a waist-high shot of Ilsa, holding a gun; the shot remains long enough for us to see the gun, then the camera slides back into the close-up. Shortly after, when

Ilsa breaks down and confesses her continued love for Rick, the camera again slides from a waist-high two shot into a closeup of their embrace. In both shots the movement draws us into the characters' emotional struggles, forcing us to share their clashing feelings.

Curtiz carefully builds the film's most romantic moment, Rick and Ilsa's climactic parting, with a series of increasingly larger close-ups and sweeping camera movements. Rick asks Renault to fill in the names on the letters of transit; Renault stands in the foreground, seen from the waist up; Rick and Ilsa stand in the background (Plate 18). On Rick's words, "And the names are Mr. and Mrs. Victor Laszlo," we cut to a medium two shot of Ilsa and Rick (Plate 19). Rick urges Ilsa to go:

> Rick: Do you know what you'd have to look forward to if you stayed here? Nine chances out of ten we'd both wind up in a concentration camp. Isn't that true, Louis?

Cut to a waist-high shot of Renault, agreeing, then to a reverse shot, looking at Rick and Ilsa from behind Renault; the camera slides past him into a close two shot (Plate 20). As the dialogue's intensity increases, we cut between alternating over-the-shoulder shots, but closer than any previous ones. Finally, as Rick compares their problems to a hill of beans, we cut to an enormous close up of Ilsa, her face filling the screen. The tension breaks with a sudden cut to Strasser in his car, racing to the airport. This shot acts like a punctuation mark, ending one visual episode but introducing a new tension: the Laszlos must board the plane before Strasser arrives.

Curtiz films the final conversation between Laszlo and Rick in over-the-shoulder shots, similar to earlier ones, not as large as the Rick-Ilsa shots. That episode also ends with a visual punctuation mark, a cut to the plane's propeller starting to spin. As we hear the engine sputter and the music swell, the scene reaches its emotional peak: a series of huge, wordless closeups of Rick, Ilsa, Laszlo, ending with Laszlo asking Ilsa, "Are you ready?" and a closeup of Ilsa answering, "Yes." Cut to a three shot as Ilsa says, "Goodbye Rick," then a close up of her murmuring, "God bless you," then Rick, seen from over Laszlo's shoulder, stoically saying "Hurry up or you'll miss that plane." Cut back to the three shot as the Laszlos turn and shrink into the background. Cut to a waist-high two shot of them; Laszlo walks out of frame while Ilsa walks towards us, into her last, enormous close up; cut back to Rick, in close up, alone.

All this romanticism is set in a dark, fog-drenched airport, a visual expression of the political forces surrounding the lovers. Darkness dominates the other, equally important side of the film's style, associated with the world of Casablanca and politics. Imprisonment, the visual motif that dominates Curtiz's swashbucklers becomes, in *Casablanca,* a metaphor for the power of political events to limit its characters' freedom to control their own destinies.

Curtiz creates this metaphor through his baroque imagery, crowded compositions, and chiaroscuro lighting. Throughout the film, smoke-encircled, shadow-striped figures move through pools of darkness in images similar to and as suggestive as the prison scenes in the swashbucklers. At one point script and camera transform these shadows into two separate metaphors. Ferrari, warning Laszlo that he is being followed, says: "You know that you're being shadowed?" At that moment, Laszlo's body is literally shadowed, and metaphorically caged by the black bars falling across it (Plate 14).

Dozens of similar moments fill the film, from Ugarte's capture, his screaming face dragged into darkness, to Ilsa's return to Rick's after the flashback, the two white-clothed figures isolated beacons surrounded by blackness, unable to reach each other, to Laszlo sneaking to the underground meeting, seen in a high shot, a tiny, vulnerable figure cloaked by the night, to Ilsa herself sneaking back to Rick's, suddenly appearing in his room, her face scarred by the lines of light and shadow from the venetian blinds (Plate 16). Casablanca is a night world, figuratively and literally; except for the flashback, only two scenes take place during the day, outdoors: the prologue and arrival of Strasser, and the market scene, in which Ilsa tells Rick about her marriage.

Casablanca becomes associated with imprisonment in the film's first minute. Over a shot of a spinning globe we hear a narrator say: "With the coming of the second World War, many eyes in imprisoned Europe turned hopefully or desperately toward the freedom of the Americas." The narrator describes the roundabout refugee trail that ends in Casablanca. The fortunate "scurry to Lisbon"; the others "wait in Casablanca and wait and wait and wait." Under these words Curtiz introduces us to the city with his characteristic high shot, looking over the rooftops (actually a miniature); the camera descends to the teeming marketplace (as the model shot imperceptibly cuts to the full-size set).

A brief prologue emphasizes the city's violence, duplicity, and desperation. Police stop a traveller; he panics, runs, and is shot, but all he is found with is a crumpled Free French leaflet. A pickpocket (Curt Bois) warns a tourist of the "vultures, vultures" everywhere, while gently removing his wallet. A plane flies overhead; the crowd stares hungrily up at it. Life is cheap; no one can be trusted; everyone wants to leave.

The prologue successively narrows our focus, moving us from imprisoned Europe to Casablanca to Rick's cafe. It ends with the plane flying over the neon sign spelling Rick's Café Américain, linking the symbol of escape with the symbol of imprisonment. "Everybody comes to Rick's," Renault tells Strasser and, when we enter the cafe, all of imprisoned Europe does seem to be there. Curtiz's camera slides around, picking up snatches of conversation in a babel of accents. The staff, equally international, includes a German math professor turned bookkeeper, Carl (S.Z. Sakall), a Russian sword-swallower turned bartender, Sascha (Leonid Kinskey), and Amsterdam's leading banker turned pastry chef.[32] Refugees all, fate has flung them from their former roles into Rick's.

Casablanca, then, is a physical prison for the political refugees scrambling for exit visas. But it is also an emotional prison for Rick, a romantic refugee who locks his feelings behind a wall of cynicism. The flashback explains why. Perhaps because of *Citizen Kane*'s influence, forties films favored increased use of the flashback as the basis of their narrative structure. The flashback form begins with a complex situation, then explores the events that led up to it. It emphasizes explanations, asking not *what* happens next, but *how* and *why* a known conclusion was reached. It seems especially appropriate to *Casablanca,* where it extends the metaphor of imprisonment by suggesting that Rick is a prisoner of his own past. For him, time is literally out of joint.

The flashback reveals what happened when Rick dared to "stick ... [his] neck out" and give up control of himself by loving someone. Throughout the sequence, Ilsa seems in command. When Rick, violating their pact, asks about her past, she evades him with a kiss. At their last meeting, Rick burbles excitedly about their getting married, but she wears a faraway look on her face, as if locked in some private thought he can neither know nor alter. (Later, of course, we learn what that private thought was.) Curtiz fills his images with premonitions. The scene begins with a long shot of La Belle Aurore Café, the irony of its name heightened by having it written in shadow across the floor. It ends with a romantic close-up of Rick and Ilsa, but as they kiss, the camera tilts down to her hand, which knocks over a champagne glass.

Having had his "insides ... kicked out" in Paris, Rick retreats to Casablanca and becomes absolute master of the little world of his cafe. In fact, Rick's first action in the film is a gesture of control. Curtiz prepares his entrance as elaborately as Geoffrey Thorpe's in *The Sea Hawk.* In a medium shot of the cafe, a waiter crosses left to a small table on which sits a chessboard, champagne glass, and ashtray. From the lower left corner a white jacketed arm reaches out and takes a note from the waiter. Cut to a close up of an IOU; a hand scrawls on it, "OK, RICK." Cut back to the table, a front view of the arm reaching for the cigarette on the ashtray. As it lifts the cigarette, the camera follows it, finally revealing the mysterious Rick. Our first view of him epitomizes his position throughout the film: sitting at a chessboard (whose suggestive overtones need no comment) impassively contemplating his next move. From that moment, through his encounters with Ugarte, Ferrari, Yvonne, Renault, and Strasser, until Ilsa's appearance, Rick controls every situation in his cafe as carefully as he controls himself.

The cafe, in fact, is not only a microcosm of Casablanca, but also an extension of Rick's own psyche, just as the characters who float through it embody warring aspects of his personality. The narrowing movement from the spinning globe and imprisoned Europe to Rick's cafe ends inside Rick himself, and Curtiz visually connects events in the cafe and events within Rick. After Ilsa's entrance shatters Rick's sense of control, we dissolve from the Laszlos leaving to the neon sign snapping off, then to Rick, his face anguished, his impassive facade also snapped off. The camera, imitating Rick's own confident movement, glides easily around the cafe, whose baroque decor and shadowy atmosphere suggest the hidden corners of Rick's mind. During their first onscreen conversation, for example, Rick removes some money from his safe while Renault questions him about his past. At screen left, we see Renault watching Rick; at screen right, we see only the shadows of Rick and his safe (Plate 17). We cannot see the actual safe, where Rick keeps his wealth, just as we never really learn its origin. We cannot even see Rick; his shadow sums up our accumulated uncertainties about his personal and political history. Later, Rick allows the police to ransack his cafe for the letters of transit, just as he allows Renault and Strasser to probe his mind, knowing he can always outwit his inquisitors.

I mentioned earlier that Rick's refusal to let the German banker into his private gambling room parallels his refusal to let anyone into his private self. The Jan/Annina sequence develops this analogy further. The first time we see Rick outside his cafe, in daylight, when he meets Ilsa at the market, he "sees the light" and sustains another attack on his sense of control when she tells him of her marriage. But by night, back in his own world, he regains control and rigs his own roulette wheel to let Jan win. Though Jan does not know it, he gambles not only with money but with his love as well; if he loses, Annina will jeopardize it by sleeping with Renault. Rick also gambled with his love, when he had to leave Paris, but he lost and left alone. Now, in Casablanca, he gambles only when the game is rigged, but he loses something anyway. To arrange Jan and Annina's escape, he must lose some money. To arrange Laszlo and Ilsa's escape, he must lose Ilsa again. But this time he also wins his emotional freedom, his escape from the Casablanca within him.

Rick explains his generosity towards Annina to Renault by saying, "Put it down as a gesture to love." He follows that gesture with the one to the bandleader, permitting the playing of "La Marseillaise," his first indication of political feeling. Strasser then orders Renault to close the cafe and it stays closed for the rest of the film. By the end of that evening Rick is reconciled with Ilsa; the next morning he sells his cafe. He no longer needs it.

The reconciliation scene begins with Rick again refusing Ilsa the letters of transit. She reminds him of how "we once loved each other." She tries insults, tears, finally a gun, but he remains unmoved and taunts her mercilessly. He seems to deserve her scornful attack:

Ilsa: One woman has hurt you and you take your revenge on the rest of the world. You're— you're a weakling and a coward.

What Rick is proving, of course, is the strength of his own feelings and what he wants is an admission of hers. When, at last, she crumbles into his arms, his own shell crumbles, and the Richard of Paris replaces the Rick of Casablanca. No longer "misinformed" about Ilsa, he once more controls his own destiny—controls, in fact, several destinies. Ilsa tells him, "I don't know what's right any longer. You'll have to think for both of us, for all of us." And so he does. From that moment on, he controls the plot, manipulating events until Laszlo leaves with Ilsa, Strasser lies dead and, with Renault's help, he and his friend walk into the foggy future. The scene ends with a shot almost the reverse of that which ended the Belle Aurore scene: again, the two in close up, but now Ilsa swoons, her head on his shoulder while he has the faraway look in his eyes.

One of the things Rick so desperately desires to control is the connection between words and deeds, appearance and reality. Each of Casablanca's citizens uses words to deceive. Ferrari, the "fat hypocrite," feigns distress at Ugarte's death when all he wants are the letters of transit. Renault introduces Strasser as "one of the reasons the Third Reich enjoys the reputation it has today," as deliciously equivocal a compliment as one could muster. Ever the smiling "diplomatist," he wishes Laszlo a "pleasant stay" in Casablanca, while we know he intends to make that stay permanent. Strasser, equally polite, tells Laszlo that meeting him is "a pleasure I've long looked forward to," the warm words barely covering their chilling meaning. Rick stands at the center of this verbal tangle. Once Ilsa's actions proved her loving words, but when she abandoned him, her words on a rain-blurred note became worthless. Now he uses his own cynical words to deny the reality of his political past and his present feelings.

For some people, when the feelings are strong enough, words are unnecessary. Laszlo knows Ilsa's devotion to him is so deep she does not "even have to say it." When he asks her, "Were you lonely in Paris?" and "Is there anything you want to tell me?" she struggles to put into words her love for him, different from her passion for Rick but equally powerful.

> Ilsa: Victor whatever I do, will you believe that I, that I—

But he interrupts her:

> Laszlo: You don't even have to say it. I'll believe.

The film's only unhypocritical character, with his own "reputation for elo- quence" needs no words from others. Just as he trusts the record of Rick's actions rather than his words, he trusts the evidence of Ilsa's feelings. Actually, he knows of her Parisian affair but, as he tells Rick, "I demand no explanations."

In Paris, Rick also needed no explanations. When, at their last meeting, Ilsa said, "Wherever they put you and wherever I'll be, I want you to know that I—," he too interrupts her, not with words, but with a kiss. But in *Casablanca* Rick does need words. He cannot yet understand how events can force people to actions that seem to betray their feelings and belie their words.

He learns this through Annina and her anguished question:

> Annina: If someone loved you very much, so that your happiness was the only thing that she wanted in the world, and she did a bad thing to make certain of it, could you forgive her?

Recognizing a love strong enough to risk itself to save its object, Rick helps Annina. Earlier, Ferrari had been similarly "moved" by Ilsa's refusal to leave Casablanca without Laszlo:

> Ferrari: I observe that you, in one respect, are a very fortunate man.

and offers to help even though it "cannot possibly profit" him. When Annina tries to thank Rick, he brushes her off with words that echo Ferrari's: "He's just a lucky guy."

Ilsa's appearance has stirred up Rick's feelings until they rise to the surface like bubbles in a champagne glass. Curtiz, in fact, visually associates the release of memories and emotions with the uncorking of bottles. When Renault recites Rick's record, the latter opens a brandy bottle. When Ilsa sees Sam and asks a waiter to have him come over, all we see of the waiter is a close-up of his hand uncorking a bottle. The pre-flashback scene finds Rick brooding at a table, pouring himself a drink; as the camera tracks into a close-up of Rick, it passes the bottle, making it also grow in size. The flashback itself suggests the origin of the association, by using champagne drinking to mark the beginning and end of the affair. One of its first images suggests the Ilsa/waiter shot's composition: Ilsa sits in the background while Rick, in foreground, opens a bottle with a loud pop. At their last meeting Rick again opens champagne, but now with only partly comic urgency:

> Rick: Henri wants us to finish this bottle and then three more. He says he'll water his garden with champagne before he'll let the Germans drink it.

Thus, the worlds of Casablanca and Paris become associated with a complex series of oppositions. For both Rick and Ilsa, Paris represents the past, freedom, private feeling, romance. Casablanca means the present, imprisonment, public duty, politics. Moreover, for Rick, Paris means trust, idealism, patriotism; Casablanca means suspicion, cynicism, neutrality. Ilsa discovers the distance between these worlds when Rick rejects her at the cafe and refers to it the next day at the market:

> Ilsa: The Rick I knew in Paris, I could tell him. He'd understand. But the one that looked at
> me with such hatred.... We knew very little about each other when we were in love in
> Paris. If we leave it that way maybe we'll remember those days, not Casablanca....

That evening, at the cafe, Rick acknowledges that same distance when Ilsa requests a table near Sam and he answers,"I suppose he means to you, Paris ... of happier days." When Ilsa finally admits her continued love for Rick she reconnects words and deeds, past and present, Paris and Casablanca. In his reply, Rick replaces his Casablanca motif line, "I stick my neck out for nobody," with his Parisian, "Here's looking at you, kid." Just as Robin Hood unites court and country by becoming Baron of Nottingham and Earl of Sherwood, so Rick merges the night would of Casablanca with the romantic world of Paris. At the airport, he tells Ilsa:

> Rick: We'll always have Paris. We didn't have it, we'd lost it until you came to Casablanca.
> We got it back last night.

Casablanca the prison has become the means of escape. The film began with an image of imprisonment, the plane landing in Casablanca's shadows, bringing Strasser and the Nazi menace. It ends with an image of release, that same plane flying off, taking the Laszlos to freedom.

The refugees escape political prison; Rick escapes emotional prison; all escape manipulation by external forces. If *Casablanca* is about the intrusion of public events into private lives, then, like the swashbucklers, it suggests that the individual hero still retains some ability to shape those events. (Many recent films also use cities or sections of them as metaphors for corruption, but in them the evil overwhelms the helpless hero. In *Chinatown* (1974), for example, the detective hero knows the all-powerful tycoon has murdered the heroine's husband, but no one will believe him.) But in *Casablanca,* Rick not only destroys the villain, but does so in a climactic "duel" as inevitable and ritualized as any ever fought by our swashbuckling heroes. (Strasser, phoning the airport tower to order Laszlo's plane to return, arrogantly ignores Rick's threatening gun. He draws his own, fires, misses, and falls to the ground when Rick shoots back.)

We noted that as the swashbucklers' villains became increasingly political they became decreasingly sexual. Strasser similarly poses a purely political threat. Rick's romantic/sexual adversary is another hero, Laszlo, whose position is strengthened by the political situation. Rick conquers Strasser but cannot, or rather chooses not to, conquer Laszlo. He can manipulate events but cannot always insure his own happiness; he loses the heroine. Unlike the comic swashbuckling heroes, Rick does not form a new society around him nor return to traditional society; he disappears underground to continue attacking it. His band of merry men has been reduced to one, and therein lies the strongest refutation of the homosexual interpretation. Renault functions, not as Rick's lover, but as Little John, his "sidekick." Like Little John, Renault is tested: by refusing to arrest Rick and by giving up his own easy, profitable life in Casablanca, Renault proves he is worthy to join the hero. The darkness he and Rick enter in the film's famous final shot seems altogether appropriate, for they march to a war whose outcome was uncertain when their film was made (Plate 21).

In the Shadows of *Casablanca:* Hawks's *To Have and Have Not* and Curtiz's *Passage to Marseille*

In 1944 Warner Brothers, hoping to repeat *Casablanca*'s commercial success, released two films that resembled it in many details: *To Have and Have Not*, directed by Howard Hawks, and *Passage to Marseille*, directed by Curtiz. Both are set in exotic, French-speaking locales and involve Humphrey Bogart as the would-be neutral drawn unwillingly into the war. During the past few years numerous critics have recognized Howard Hawks as a major auteur, pointing to a number of recurring themes and motifs in his work.[1] They discover this unique signature even though Hawks did not write all his own scripts and did work within various major studios. They have not found such a signature in Curtiz's films. Thus, *To Have and Have Not* is considered a "personal" film, *Passage to Marseille* is not, although both were made at the same studio and inspired by the same earlier film. In this chapter I want to compare these films to each other and to *Casablanca*, to define further the characteristics of Curtiz's own personal signature. Moreover, the comparison should clarify the relationship of the war-melodrama to the swashbuckler.

Beyond its main character's name and occupation, *To Have and Have Not*, scripted by Jules Furthman and William Faulkner, bears little resemblance to the Hemingway novel on which it is based.[2] Harry Morgan (Bogart), owner of a small charter fishing boat in Martinique, is asked by hotel owner Gerard/ Frenchy (Marcel Dalio) to bring Free French leader de Bursac and his wife (Walter Molnar and Dolores Moran) to safety in port. He refuses at first, but changes his mind when he decides he needs money to help Slim (Lauren Bacall) return to America. Shot during the rescue, de Bursac is brought to the hotel where Morgan removes the bullet. Meanwhile, Vichy Captain Renard (Dan Seymour), suspecting that Morgan knows the fugitive de Bursac's whereabouts, arrests his friend Eddie (Walter Brennan). In the climactic confrontation, Morgan forces Renard, at gunpoint, to release Eddie and allow the two of them, plus Slim and the de Bursacs, to sail out of Martinique.

At first glance the similarities to *Casablanca* are striking. Bogart again represents isolationist America, playing the tough, cynical, worldy-wise adventurer determined to keep his private life free from political and romantic involvement. Morgan's dialogue, though written by different men, echoes Rick's. When Renard asks him what his political sympathies are, he answers, "Minding my own business." (Rick: "I stick my neck out for nobody.") When congratulated for joining the Free French, he snaps back, "I'm not. I'm getting paid." (Rick, on being reminded of his gunrunning and fighting in Spain: "I got well paid for it on both occasions.") While eluding Vichy patrol boats he yells to de Bursac, "You save France. I'll save my boat." (Rick: "Your business is politics. Mine is running a saloon.") Robin Wood, one of Hawks' critical champions, notes *To Have and Have Not*'s "obvious debt to *Casablanca*":

> The de Bursacs...are quite blatantly modeled on the Bergman/Henried couple of *Casablanca;* de Bursac even looks rather like Paul Henried. Marcel Dalio is in both films in similar roles, and Dan Seymour, Hawks's unforgettable Captain Renard, has a bit part in *Casablanca*.
>
> To restore the main plot-line of *To Have and Have Not* to that of *Casablanca* all that is necessary is to eliminate the Lauren Bacall character and have Bogart in love with Madame de Bursac.[3]

A superficial look also suggests visual similarities between the Hawks and the Curtiz films. Robin Wood talks of the film's lighting being "easily identifiable as Warners-style" in its "paranoid sense of diffused menace, its emphasis on shadows and surrounding darkness."[4] Frenchy's cafe-hotel is almost as smoky as Rick's, the foggy sea surrounding Morgan's boat as equivocal an avenue of escape as Casablanca's foggy airport.

But a longer look reveals that despite the "Warners-style," the studio lighting and sets, Hawks' visual style, what Schickel calls his "determined plainness,"[5] is quite the opposite of Curtiz's. Where Curtiz chooses the unusual angle, the intense close-up, the all encompassing crane shot, Hawks prefers the medium shot, the camera at waist or eye level. Curtiz strives for subjective effects; Hawks imitates the objective view of the observant bystander. Curtiz keeps his camera fluid; Hawks lets his remain stationary. Curtiz's baroque, complex images often hide his major characters behind objects and other people, smoke and shadows; Hawks' clean, uncluttered compositions allow us to gaze directly at his central figures. In short, Curtiz draws from the UFA style and German expressionism; Hawks' "direct, functional cinema," in Andrew Sarris' words,[6] is "perhaps the most distinctively American cinema of all."

This simplicity of style seems appropriate to *To Have and Have Not*, whose plot, also less dense than *Casablanca*'s, lacks its swarm of minor characters playing variations on the main theme. In fact, Hawks' interests lie beyond its seeming love/duty conflict. The critics who have studied Hawks' films tell us that above all he values professionalism, measuring his heroes by their ability to perform their work well. Usually, that work involves danger and isolates them from ordinary society; Hawks' heroes are hunters, fishermen, racers, pilots, pioneers, soldiers. Ignoring outsiders but intensely loyal to each other, they form close-knit groups bound together by private rituals. As Peter Wollen asserts: "For Hawks, the highest human emotion is the camaraderie of the exclusive, self-sufficient, all male group."[7] His men are creatures of instinct and spontaneous, honest if eccentric emotions. A woman is admitted to the group only after proving herself equal in courage and ability; she must become the hero's buddy as well as bed partner. They follow a "long ritual courtship phased around the offering, lighting and exchange of cigarettes."[8]

To Have and Have Not contains all these Hawksian characteristics. Morgan demonstrates his professionalism in the opening fishing sequence, whose only real function is to contrast his confident expertise with his passenger Johnson's nervous blundering. His skill extends outside his own profession; he removes the bullet from de Bursac as easily as he hooks a marlin. His loyalty extends to the alcoholic Eddie because he "used to be good" and, as a friend, deserves respect. Johnson shows his own weakness by belittling Eddie. Slim, on the other hand, is the only character other than Morgan who correctly answers his ritual question, "Was you ever stung by a dead bee?" Eddie knows this and pays her the supreme compliment: "You're all right lady. She can go with us, Harry."

She passes her other tests as well. Her memorable first meeting with Morgan centers on a cigarette; standing in his doorway, she asks, "Gotta light?" Their courtship continues to involve the "exchange of cigarettes," until the violent climax when Slim, looking for a light for Morgan, discovers in his desk drawer the gun he soon uses against Renard. More important, she proves her competence by assisting in the bullet removing. Madame de Bursac offers to help, but faints at the first sight of blood; Slim immediately takes over, cooly joking during the operation. Later though, the de Bursacs' willingness to admit their own fears yet fight for their cause redeems them and, at the film's end, they leave Martinique with Morgan.

Robin Wood tries to prove the superiority of *To Have and Have Not* to *Casablanca*. He accuses *Casablanca* of being an impersonal, Hollywood movie, lacking an individual, authorial "voice," and claims that the emotions it "expresses and provokes are comparatively generalized and conventional."[9] In contrast, Hawks' characters' feelings arise, not from preconceived notions of "duty" or "patriotism" but from spontaneous impulses. He contrasts the "treatment of the 'commitment' theme—solemn and idealistic in *Casablanca*, casual and personal in Hawks . . . " arguing that only "superficially has Bogart made the same choice in both films: in *To Have and Have Not* his real commitment is not to a cause but to the individuals the Fascists have kicked around."[10]

But, as Michael Wood has suggested, there is nothing especially unconventional about this. Citing films as far apart as *Lives of a Bengal Lancer* (1935, Henry Hathaway) and *Return to Paradise* (1953, Mark Robson), he says:

> The pattern occurs again and again in American movies.... A hero who will not sign up for a cause...joins the fray when a person he cares about (almost always a girl) is hurt or threatened.[11]

Further, Robin Wood accuses *Casablanca* of being impersonal, then attacks everything in it that identifies it as a Curtiz film. For example, he faults the film's "long, nostalgic flashback," its "sentimental-romantic sense of the past," comparing them unfavorably to *To Have and Have Not*'s "spontaneity" and absence of past or future.[12] We know, of course, that Curtiz insisted on the flashback and deliberately created *Casablanca*'s romantic tone. Wood also compares Hawks' film to Sternberg's *Morocco*, because Hawks himself "suggested that the Bacall character in his film is related to the Dietrich character"[13] in *Morocco*. He says that within *Morocco* "we cannot miss hearing just such a personal 'voice'."[14] But "the end effect of a Hawks movie [which] is inevitably optimistic"[15] contrasts with Sternberg's "pessimistic fatality.... Von Sternberg's characters are enmeshed in the intricate visual patterns of light and shadows"; Hawks' simpler style gives his "a freedom of movement...that expresses their inner freedom."[16]

Ironically, Curtiz's style in many ways resembles Sternberg's, his characters similarly enmeshed in a prison of light and shadow. Wood simply doesn't respond to that style. Hawks is cool, reserved, a cinematic Hemingway favoring understated emotions and tight-lipped stoicism. Curtiz is florid, romantic, his cynicism the other side of his lush sentimentality. In short, Hawks can be called a midwestern WASP, Curtiz an East European Jew. Wood's preference for *To Have and Have Not* indicates only his preference for one cinematic style over another.

The significant difference between the films is not quality but dramatic form. Robin Wood unknowingly suggests this when he remarks casually that in *To Have and Have Not* Morgan's interest in the unattached Slim rather than Madame de Bursac "simplifies the issues by removing *Casablanca*'s major love/duty conflict."[17] But this simplification is crucial, for it transforms *To Have and Have Not* from a potential tragedy to a comedy. *Casablanca* entangles Rick's personal and political feelings so that when events reawaken his love, they also rekindle his sense of duty. But this puts him in an excruciating dilemma; he cannot have both Ilsa and his honor. His conflict, as suggested earlier, contains the seeds of tragedy, but he resolves it, at a painful personal price, by sacrificing love for something larger. *Casablanca* therefore becomes not a tragedy but a melodrama, suitably inspiring for wartime.

Hawk's film is lighter, looser, its humor playfully eccentric rather than cynical. Further, Morgan's problems are easier than Rick's. He can act spontaneously because he is not imprisoned by his past; hence, the film needs no flashback. His commitment to Slim, like Rick's to Ilsa, grows with his commitment to the cause, but this creates no conflict. Despite its title, at the film's conclusion Morgan can have and have. He is closer to his swashbuckling ancestors than Rick, for he not only defeats his enemies and asserts control over external forces, but he also forms a new society around him, that heroic group that leaves Martinique together. He tests his followers, just as Robin tested the merry men and Rick tested Renault, but they are not reduced to a single companion. In short, *To Have and Have Not* is closer to comedy than to tragedy or melodrama.[18]

Two years after *Casablanca* (and a few months before *To Have and Have Not*) Warners again assembled Curtiz, Bogart, Rains, Greenstreet, and Lorre for another tale of a reluctant patriot who overcomes his bitterness at past betrayals and joins a good fight. Consistently underrated by contemporary and current critics,[19] *Passage to Marseille* has never been as well known nor as commercially successful as *Casablanca*. *Passage to Marseille* is slow moving and not nearly as emotionally satisfying as *Casablanca*, but visually it does contain some of Curtiz's most effective imagery.

Its plot, though quite simple, has a complex narrative structure resembling a Chinese box of flashbacks. To provide some sense of that structure requires describing it in detail. Like classical epics, *Passage to Marseille* begins *in medias res,* during a nighttime air raid over Germany by Free French fliers. We then fade to their base in England, where Captain Freycinet (Claude Rains) tells Lieutenant Manning (John Loder), a visiting journalist, how he first met some of the airmen. We dissolve to the first flashback, in which an aging tramp steamer, the Ville de Nancy, meets a small boat carrying five men claiming to be shipwrecked goldminers from Venezuela: Renault (Philip Dorn), Marius (Peter Lorre), Matrac (Humphrey Bogart), Petit (George Tobias), and Garou (Helmut Dantine). Alone with Freycinet, they admit that the accusations of another passenger, Major Duval (Sydney Greenstreet), are correct; they are escapees from Devil's Island.

As Renault begins to tell their story, we dissolve to the second flashback. On Devil's Island, Renault, Marius, Petit, and Garou meet Grandpere (Vladimir Sokoloff), an old ex-convict who has saved enough to buy a small boat. If they can find someone to guide them across the ocean and will promise to fight the Fascists in France when they get there, Grandpere will let them escape with him. The convicts agree that Matrac should be their leader and while Renault describes Matrac's histroy to Grandpere, we dissolve to the final flashback.

Matrac, a crusading publisher, denounces the Munich pact of 1938, then finds his newspaper office wrecked by mobs. He and his assistant Paula (Michelle Morgan) flee, marry, and enjoy a brief moment of peace, until Matrac is convicted on trumped-up murder charges and sentenced to fifteen years on Cayenne.

We dissolve back to Devil's Island as Grandpere agrees that Matrac is a "true patriot." Eventually, Matrac joins the others who meet with Grandpere by the water's edge. When they discover the boat will not hold all of them, Grandpere volunteers to stay behind, but makes the others swear to fight for France till they win or die. We dissolve back to the Ville de Nancy; Freycinet promises to tell no one their story. Matrac privately confesses to him that he wants only to return to Paula and will not fight for the country that betrayed him. Soon after wireless reports announce the fall of France, Captain Malo (Victor Francen) confides to Freycinet that, to prevent the Germans from seizing his cargo, he has changed course to England. Duval, a convert to the "new order in Europe," tries to take over the ship, but the convicts, led by Matrac, and the loyal crew defeat him and his followers. Jourdain (Hans Conried), the wireless operator, alerts the Germans of their whereabouts, causing a Nazi plane to attack the ship. Again the convicts and crew repel the attacker, but Marius dies in the battle. Finally we dissolve back to the Free French base, where Petit and Garou are mechanics and Renault pilots the plane on which Matrac is gunner. When it returns, Matrac is dead, still clutching an undelivered letter to Paula and the son he has never seen. At his funeral, Freycinet promises "that letter will be delivered" and the film ends.

Despite its apparent complexity, no one really is confused by *Passage to Marseille*'s structure. Everything that was said about *Casablanca*'s flashback applies trebly here. The entire film, as the title implies, is a passage, a journey through time, first moving us backwards, in slow stages, to its center, Matrac's betrayal, then returning us to our starting point, the airbase, and finally pointing us forward to the war's end. This movement imitates the flight of the Free Frenchmen; the film begins with them leaving the airfield and ends with their return. It also imitates the convicts' laborious struggles to reach freedom; we hack our way through time as they hack through swamp and jungle. Most important, it camouflages the film's lack of plot; we become so involved in that struggle that we never realize how little actually happens. One sentence could summarize the story: a group of convicts escape from Devil's Island to a ship bound for Europe; they fight Vichy officials who attempt to commandeer it and join a Free French unit in England. What requires longer description is the structure, the mechanisms of telling the story.

The characters are equally undeveloped, their relationships not nearly as intricate nor as intriguing as those in *Casablanca*. Telling the story chronologically would mean beginning with Matrac and exploring his relationship with Paula. In the film, this is a mere sketch. In fact, none of the characters is allowed to reveal himself through action; instead they are summed up by a narrator's comments. Freycinet, for example, introduces us to the ship's passengers and crew, clearly naming heroes and villains. He calls Duval a "domineering, narrow-minded martinet," his aide, Lenois (Charles La Torre), "a typical yes man," Jourdain a "treacherous youth." He praises Captain Malo and condemns the chief engineer (Edward Cianelli), who later joins Duval's revolt. Similarly, Renault introduces us to each convict with a sentence or two explaining his crimes. But, aside from Matrac, we never really distinguish them; during the escape and aboard ship, the others blur into a group.

More important, *Passage to Marseille,* like *To Have and Have Not,* lacks *Casablanca*'s central opposition between romance and politics, love and duty. Of course the film does pretend that Matrac's justifiable bitterness may poison his patriotism. We hear him, alone in his cell, railing against "beautiful, decadent France. . . . I hate France." Moreover, when Grandpere makes the convicts swear to fight for France, the camera tracks into a close shot of Matrac, his face fixed into an impassive mask, not uttering a word. Aboard the Ville de Nancy he tells Freycinet, "I don't care about my country. The France you and I loved is dead, Captain. . . . I'm trying to get back to a woman. I never intended to fight." Later, at the news of France's fall, he grins bitterly, and when Duval promises a pardon to those who join him, a close-up shows Matrac momentarily pondering the offer.

But an instant later his doubts, like Morgan's, vanish when "a person he cares about is hurt." The villains strike the messboy for shouting, "Vive la France!" and Matrac immediately strikes back. Despite his surface gestures, we question his commitment to the cause even less than we do Rick's. After all, the film begins with him flying a mission for the Free French. Moreover, Matrac, again like Morgan, need not choose between his woman and his country; Paula and France are on the same side. As Freycinet tells him, "Your wife is waiting for the man who went away, a man who loved his country, a patriot."

This absence of a central conflict between metaphoric worlds is reflected in the visual style Curtiz adopts for the film. In *Passage to Marseille,* the green world disappears; the entire film takes place in the castle. Except for the brief scene of Matrac and Paula's honeymoon, the film has none of *Casablanca*'s romanticism. Almost all the action occurs in three main settings: Devil's Island, the Ville de Nancy, and the airbase. Curtiz turns each of these into a world of darkness and imprisonment.

The Devil's Island flashback begins with Curtiz's familiar crane shot descending through dense vegetation, looking down at a line of half-naked prisoners stumbling through steaming swamp and jungle, in images reminiscent of *The Sea Hawk*'s Panama sequence. While Renault's voice talks of slave laborers "tortured by heat, humidity, mosquitoes, fever," we cut to Petit chopping a tree; he looks down and the camera follows his glance to a man lying in the mud. Renault continues, describing "route zero," a road "under construction for half a century and for that there is exactly 16 miles to show and . . . one dead convict for every yard." We cut to a subjective shot of a steam roller rolling over us, then to several shots of Garou, then to a convict, suddenly gone berserk, running into a swamp. He is shot and collapses into the water, the light reflecting off his bald head. The camera pans right to an alligator who slithers into the water. Cut to the guard who shot the convict, swatting a mosquito on his ear; cut to Garou, his ax angrily splitting a log; dissolve slowly back to the Ville de Nancy to a closeup of Marius' hand whittling a stick with his small knife. The ironic linking of these actions seems to concentrate all of Cayenne's violence into Marius' knife and bring it with him onto the ship.

Curtiz also uses the simplest visual symbol of imprisonment, figures behind bars. We first see Grandpere, a "libré" who has served his sentence but cannot leave the island, outside the prison compound's gate, staring longingly at the French flag fluttering within. A later reverse angle presents a subjective view: we see Grandpere from behind in lower right; bars fill the rest of the frame and through them we see the flag, obviously and aptly implying that France itself is imprisoned. Curtiz uses bars most effectively in the scenes in the "chateau," the isolation cells where "incorrigibles" like Matrac are kept. While Renault describes them, saying "One can go mad in these pits . . . , nothing to see . . . no sound except the heat of one's own pulse . . . " Curtiz dissolves from a long, deep focus shot looking down a black corridor of cells, at the end of which two guards stand silhouetted by a bright backlight, to a high tracking shot, looking down through the bars at the tops of the cage-like cells, onto a man pacing like an animal, and finally, after a shot similar to the first, to one of his most elaborate tracking shots: from another deep focus view of the cell corridor, the camera turns right and tracks into a medium shot, front view, of a single cell, then climbs along the cell up to the guard on the catwalk above, follows him as he walks right and finally tilts down, again looking through the bars at the top of a cell, onto Matrac. Each shot progressively reveals more of the prison's horrors until the last, longest one literally drags us onto a guided tour. When the guards mock Matrac, Curtiz makes us share his suffering by cutting to a low angle shot, the camera in the cell with him, looking up through the bars at his tormentors towering above. Later, he uses another favorite effect to suggest worse punishment: a guard beats Matrac but we see only their shadows twisting on a wall.

The isolated enclosed world of the Ville de Nancy threatens to become, for the convicts at least, as much of a prison as Cayenne. Duval distrusts them immediately, questions them belligerently, guesses their true origin, and demands they be locked up. During the interrogation scene, the unceasing, steady rocking of the poorly lit, smoky cabin, crowded with Duval, Freycinet, Malo, and the convicts, contrasted with the nervous cutting between characters as they eye each other suspiciously, creates an almost palpable tension. As the scene ends we see yet another figure behind bars, a variation of the first shot of Peter Blood: Matrac, peering through the blinds of his cabin door, only his eyes visible, the rest of his face covered by black slats. He closes the last slat and the screen goes black.

Darkness dominates most of the film's imagery; *Passage to Marseille* is more of a night film than *Casablanca*. Almost all its major events, including the opening air raid, many of the shipboard scenes, the escape from the prison barracks and Matrac's return to the airbase at the end, occur at night. Further, the film reverses the traditional moral associations of black and white, light and dark. Most of the prison scenes are shot with dramatic, high contrast lighting, the heroes usually cloaked in darkness, hiding in shadows. Similarly, aboard the Ville de Nancy, when Duval questions the convicts, he wears a bright, white uniform while they wear black and gray striped shirts, blending in with the cabin's dark walls. The Free French airfield, the film's third important setting, is not a prison, but its atmosphere is as somber. These "free" Frenchmen fly only at night, needing darkness to protect them; Manning even mentions their "grim, determined faces" and misses the "laughter...the gay talk" of World War I fliers. Curtiz turns the wartime cliché of the "lights being turned off in Europe" into a visual reality.

In place of *Casablanca's* romanticism, *Passage to Marseille* offers visual embellishments; dramatically simple scenes are lengthened into elaborate sequences by adding a wealth of visual details. For example, Matrac's death moves from the airfield to France and back to the airfield, recapitulating the movement of the whole film. We begin at the airfield; shots of Freycinet and Manning awaiting the air raiders' return are intercut with shots of the control room, the chalkboard listing the planes, close-ups of the loudspeaker announcing each one's arrival, of men running to meet them, worried faces as Matrac's plane fails to appear. Dissolve to the plane; inside we see a crewman dead; cut to Matrac's bloody face, to his hand holding the tube with his letter. Dissolve then to Paula's cottage in France; inside her son eats his birthday cake while she talks of his father's courage. Hearing a plane overhead, they run outside, but no letter tube is dropped. Dissolve back to the airfield as Matrac's plane at last appears. The actual landing is itself extended with shots of ambulances racing to meet the plane, men running, more worried faces. In many of these shots, Curtiz keeps the camera moving, increasing the sequence's energy.

Curtiz similarly expands the film's three major action sequences, the opening air raid, the fight to retake the ship from Duval, and the battle against the attacking German plane. In the first, long shots of planes in formation are cut with closer shots of smaller groups of planes, with shots inside individual planes, focusing on various crewmen, shots on land, showing Germans manning anti-aircraft guns, plus dozens of details in close-up: hands pulling triggers, faces behind gunsights, bomb bay doors opening. One striking image features silhouetted close-ups of German soldiers, backlit by bursting bombs; in another the screen is totally black save for a diagonal slash of light from an anti-aircraft beacon; the camera follows the beacon up, tracking into a single plane.

Thus, *Passage to Marseille* can be seen as an exercise in mood and atmosphere, the mood somber, the atmosphere suffocating. In fact, I believe it is the weakness of the film's love story that makes it less popular than either *Casablanca* or *To Have and Have Not*. What first attracts audiences to *Casablanca* is its highly charged, sentimental love story. What first attracts other audiences to *To Have and Have Not* is its cooly unsentimental love story, its characters warily circling each other until Morgan lets Slim slink into his arms for good. But *Passage to Marseille* has neither *Casablanca's* emotional warmth nor *To Have and Have Not's* comic cool. Since Matrac and Paula are ultimately separated, its tone is closer to the former than the latter. But that separation results from an accidental bullet rather than a necessary decision. The relationship itself is never questioned; Paula, the sketchiest central character, is physically but never emotionally separated from her husband.

However, although Matrac, like Morgan, suffers no potentially tragic internal conflict, *Passage to Marseille* is no comedy. Its ponderousness stems partly from its talky script. Overlong and overliterary, it often makes characters sound as if they are reciting rather than speaking. Freycinet, for instance, begins his narration of the first flashback with a novelist's prose:

> The outbreak of the war brought orders for my return . . . from New Caledonia. I was forced to take passage on the Ville de Nancy, bound for Marseille, with a cargo of nickel ore. The Ville de Nancy was one of those venerable tramps which wallow across the backwaters of the world, year after year. . . .

Worse, the script lacks wit, having neither *Casablanca*'s cynical bite nor the eccentric, shaggy-dog flavor of *To Have and Have Not*. In place of humor it provides each character with a patriotic, sentimental, and sententious speech on the glories of France and his willingness to die for them.

But it is not only the script's humorlessness that separates *Passage to Marseille* from comedy. Like Curtiz's swashbucklers, *Passage to Marseille* suggests that morality has little connection with class, that the most noble and patriotic may be the least socially respectable. Matrac, like the swashbucklers' heroes, leads a band of outlaws against a corrupt, vicious society. But although the situations and imagery are similar, the dramatic tones differ. *Passage to Marseille* does not give us that sense of the inevitability of a comic resolution that identifies the swashbuckler; we are never certain of the hero's final victory and, in fact, Matrac does die at *Passage to Marseille's* end.

One of the reasons for this is the nature of the evil he confronts. In *Casablanca* the Nazi menace seems concentrated in and personified by Strasser; in *To Have and Have Not,* by Renard. *Passage to Marseille,* in contrast, contains no single, powerful villain. Duval, not nearly a strong enough character, is easily overthrown and exerts his influence in only one of the film's several locales. *Casablanca* and *To Have and Have Not* gain dramatic strength by limiting their action to one major setting, a single bar in a single town. *Passage to Marseille* spreads out, and its evil seems all-pervasive. France itself, rather than a single villain-figure, sends Matrac to prison, its own imprisonment by corruption captured in that image of the flag behind bars. Eventually, Matrac becomes but one soldier in a vast army, fighting an impersonal war against an anonymous enemy. Michael Wood says that, at *Casablanca's* conclusion, we "don't see the war film that Bogart and Rains go off to star in."[20] In a sense, *Passage to Marseille* is that war film; and war films, like swashbucklers, feature those huge battle scenes between massive, faceless forces representing good and evil. But the swashbucklers also always have a single, outstanding villain whose defeat in a climactic duel signals the battle's end. *Passage to Marseille* begins and ends with Matrac flying against "the enemy," all of Nazi Germany, and finally one of its bullets ends his life. Matrac does not defeat his enemy, and his death most certainly distinguishes him from Rick and Morgan.

Further, unlike Robin's merry men and Blood and Thorpe's fellow prisoners, Matrac's followers are not all innocently framed victims. Renault is a deserter, Marius a thief, Garou and Petit murderers. Matrac himself shows his own capacity for violence in the film's most ambiguous moment, the end of the air attack on the Ville de Nancy. The plane crashes into the sea, but the crew survives, huddled onto the floating debris. Enraged by the deaths they have caused, Matrac grabs the machine gun and kills them. Horrified, Malo cries that he is murdering helpless men. Matrac has transformed his bitterness against France into a destructive hatred of the Germans. He fights for personal, not political, reasons and he may go too far.

Then again, he may not. Pointing to the dead around him, Matrac answers Malo: "Look around you, Captain, and see who the assassins are." A moment later, the dying messboy tells Matrac, "You finished them—you've shown those dirty Germans. It's great what you did . . . we'll destroy them all . . . drive them out of France." Is Captain Malo the voice of rational humanism lost in war's madness, or of squeamish liberalism too weak for the hard demands of war. War makes easy moral judgments impossible, but perhaps the film makes such a judgment and has Matrac die as penance for the excesses of his outrage. On the other hand, his death may also be the punishment for his brief lapse of faith, his willingness even to consider Duval's offer. Moses-like, he leads his followers out of bondage and across the sea but he, for a sin pardonable in a lesser man, must die without entering his liberated homeland.

One need not accept these possible interpretations. The fact remains that Matrac dies, killed by external forces he cannot control as effectively as Rick, Morgan, and the swashbuckling heroes. Because his death is arbitrary rather than inevitable, *Passage to Marseille* is more melodramatic than tragic. But in its heavy, somber mood, the literal and metaphoric darkness that envelops it, and the death and defeat of its hero, it pushes the wartime adventure-melodrama as close to tragedy as *To Have and Have Not* does to comedy.

Between these two poles stands *Casablanca,* neither tragic nor comic, its final tone as ambiguous as its hero, as uncertain as his fate. Rick manages to conquer both the external enemies and the internal conflicts that threaten him. Nevertheless, the world around him and his own soul are darker and his victories more equivocal than the swashbuckling heroes'. At the end of *Casablanca,* Rick walks not into the sunset, but into the night and fog of *film noir.*

Convicts and Kids: The Art of Heroic Sacrifice

Before entering the world of *film noir* I want to look briefly at a number of Curtiz's films whose heroes, facing moral conflicts similar to Rick's, choose, as he does, to perform an act of romantic self-sacrifice. *20,000 Years in Sing-Sing* (1932) and *Angels with Dirty Faces* (1938) are both about criminals. *Kid Galahad* (1937), although ostensibly about corruption in boxing, has some important parallels to *Four Daughters* (1938) and *Daughters Courageous* (1939), which are family melodramas. Therefore I will discuss it after *Angels with Dirty Faces,* although it was made two years earlier.

The title, *20,000 Years in Sing-Sing,* taken from a book by Sing-Sing's former warden, Lewis E. Lawes, refers to the sum total of all the prisoner's sentences. The film, however, concentrates on one prisoner, Tommy Connors (Spencer Tracy), and his relationship to the warden (given the fictional name Long, and played by Arthur Byron).

Obviously, it is Curtiz's most explicit treatment of imprisonment and by now, without my citing detailed examples, we can imagine how effectively he visually creates a world of oppression and claustrophobia. Jack Shadoian sums up Curtiz's style in this film:

> Almost every image is shot through bars, sometimes two or three layers of bars in perspective, and often, in addition, we get the shadows of bars thrown off as well. The scenes showing Connors in solitary are extremely dark and stifling. Long, deep focus views of the whole cell block with tier upon tier of vertical stripes, the mechanization, army style, of prison routine— these things get to a viewer, disturb and cause discomfort.[1]

Nevertheless, compared to other prisons, the films' Sing-Sing is an enlightened institution. The humane warden seriously tries to rehabilitate the prisoners; he insists that they work and obey the rules, but if they do, he treats them with respect. In effect, the warden tries to create an island of freedom within the prison system. This is not just a metaphor; he actually gives his most trusted prisoners furloughs to visit the outside world, and expects them to return on the honor system.

But the film gives the idea of freedom and imprisonment a more complex meaning, for it is concerned not only with external prisons but also with internal ones. When Connors first arrives at Sing-Sing he is already imprisoned by his own self-image, his pride in his "toughness," which demands that he refuse to cooperate with the warden. His crooked attorney, Joe Finn (Louis Calhern), assures him that, because of their important connections, Tommy will be "taken care of" at Sing-Sing. But he immediately discovers the warden cannot be bought nor intimidated; he must earn the privileges he wants. Slowly Connors comes to respect the warden and to see, as Shadoian says, that he is really

> free only in prison, free to learn what he really is, what his true qualities are. Outside he is at the mercy of crooked politicians, insensitive cops, and copy hungry reporters. . . . he is a creature formed by his environment, an environment which offers him a false and limited choice of options. . . . he lives a life that others, most noticeably the press, have mapped out for him.[2]

Within Sing-Sing, he moves from a state of internal isolation to one of openness to others, most importantly the warden and his girl friend, Fay (Bette Davis).

In keeping with this paradoxical reversal of the expected meanings of freedom and imprisonment, the attempted escape is the film's most nightmarish and imprisoning sequence. "Medium shots of men moving rapidly alternate with extreme long shots of the entire cell block, transforming individual cells into cages within a larger cage. . . . The action is confused and panicky. . . . "[3] Overhead shots looking down on the prisoners trap them still further. Tear gas explodes and fills the screen, blotting out the human figures on it.

Connors proves his new relationship to the warden by refusing to join the escape attempt. In exchange, the warden gives him a furlough to visit Fay, who had been injured fighting off the villainous Finn. The furlough scene gives us our first glimpse of the world outside Sing-Sing, but it proves to be far more dangerous and imprisoning than the one behind bars. As soon as Connors arrives in New York, a detective recognizes him and follows him to Fay's apartment. Fay tells him of Finn's treachery; while he is momentarily out of the room, Finn himself enters and tries to kill Fay. She shoots him; the detective barges in and, with his dying breath, Finn says that Connors shot him. No one within Sing-Sing seems as irredeemably evil as this man from without. Accused of murder, Connors plans to flee the country. While the arrangements are being made, he remains trapped in a sleazy hotel room, pacing like a caged animal.

Because of his commitment to the warden and his system, Connors chooses to return to Sing-Sing. Because of his love for Fay, he refuses to let her admit her guilt. The film ends a few minutes before his execution, as he and the warden wordlessly look at each other with mutual respect. Shadoian and others correctly point out the film's bleak, cynical view of society.[4] Certainly, a brutal irony is at its center: the warden does reform Connors, then the state kills him. But Connors himself, like Rick in *Casablanca,* escapes his internal prison. He moves from cynicism to idealism, from self-enclosed toughness to involvement with and sacrifice for others. His final, Sydney Carton-like gesture, is pure romanticism.

In *Angels with Dirty Faces*, Rocky Sullivan (James Cagney) undergoes the same internal transformation, guided not by a warden but by a priest, Father Jerry Connely (Pat O'Brien). The beginning and end points of this internal movement are suggested externally by the two worlds, the two visual and metaphoric environments through which he moves.

The film opens with a typical Curtiz "environment" shot: a pan across and crane down a city street. Laundry stretches across the buildings; women sit on fire escapes or hang out of windows; the street is packed with pushcarts and people, energy and noise. The crowding, the people's shabby dress, and, most important of all, the laundry, are the familiar visual symbols that define "the slums" in so many films of the thirties that find the roots of crime in urban decay.[5]

We saw that Curtiz often defines his characters through their environment, that for them environment often becomes a form of fate. This seems especially true for Rocky Sullivan. Another pan left across the slum ends with a crane up the side of a building to a fire escape; there sit two products of this environment, Rocky and Jerry. Together they steal from a boxcar; Jerry escapes over a fence but Rocky is caught by the police. A montage follows, showing Rocky in and out of prison, his criminal record growing faster than he.

Finally, as an adult, Rocky returns to the old neighborhood and finds things have not changed much. The camera makes precisely the same elaborate pan and crane as in the first shot. The cars and clothes are new, the background music contemporary jazz. But the streets are still crowded, laundry still waves from the windows, and the unhealthy environment still leads to crime. The new generation of juvenile delinquents, the Dead End Kids,[6] have a basement hideout that visually epitomizes the slums they live in. Littered with old tires, pipes, barrels, and bricks, it looks like the last resting place for the world's unwanted garbage.

While Rocky has become a big-time hoodlum, Jerry has become a priest. Like Sing-Sing's warden, Jerry tries, in Stephen Karpf's words, to create "an island of order, morality, and purpose in a sea of squalor."[7] The second pan/crane shot of the street dissolves from a booming sound truck, its two great speakers staring like blind eyes, to the inside of a church, where a boys' choir sings a quiet hymn. We have entered, if I may again stretch my central metaphor, an aural green world, Father Jerry's idyllic haven from the city's clamor. Jerry, meeting Rocky again after many years, asks him, "Why don't you get a room right here in the parish?" He refuses to see the city in secular terms; for him, it still consists of "parishes."

Jerry tells Rocky about his pet project:

Jerry: Sort of a recreation spot for the kids . . . you'd be surprised how tremendously it helps
         to keep them from becoming . . .
Rocky: . . . hoodlums like me.

But the kids prefer the seedy pool hall to Father Jerry's gym. Rocky himself hangs out in the El Toro Club, a swankier version of the pool hall and another of Curtiz's smoke-filled saloons, as dangerous as Dodge City's Gay Lady and Rick's Café Américain. Thus, the film's two worlds, its moral and visual oppositions, are the pool hall and the gym, church and nightclub, city and parish.

Jerry goes on a one-man crusade against crime, gathering evidence against Mac Keefer (George Bancroft)[8] and James Frazier (Humphrey Bogart), the same men whom Rocky eventually and justifiably kills. As Rocky is about to die in the electric chair, Jerry asks him a last, enormous favor. The kids have come to idolize Rocky for his toughness and ability to bend the law. Jerry wants to destroy their idol to prevent them from following in his footsteps to the death house. He begs Rocky to "die yellow," feign cowardice and go to the chair screaming in fear. At first Rocky refuses, but at the last moment, in one of the screen's most memorable and disturbing death scenes, he starts howling like a terrified animal.

Curtiz increases the scene's horror by forcing us to imagine what Rocky looks like as he dies. We see his shadow struggling with the guards (Plate 22), a close-up of his hands grabbing a rail (Plate 23), a close-up of Jerry, his tear-filled eyes lifted to heaven, but we do not see Rocky's face. The film ends with the kids disillusioned with their hero, following Jerry to church to say a prayer for "a boy who couldn't run as fast as me."

Angels with Dirty Faces is one of several films of the middle to late thirties that try to cover their delight in violence and criminality with an aura of social consciousness. But as serious social criticism it is a sham, inconsistent and self-contradictory. It supposedly argues that slums turn good kids into criminals, but while Rocky and Jerry are both boy thieves, only Rocky graduates to grown-up gangsterdom. Their careers seem to result as much from moral choice as from environmental pressure.[9] If any environment really shapes Rocky, it is the prison system, as suggested by the montage following his first arrest.

Moreover, the force of Rocky and Jerry's own personalities attests to the power of the individual to mold his own destiny. Rocky and Jerry are actually related to our swashbuckling, rebel heroes, for they both fight against authority to alter their society. Jerry defies the mobsters' threats and power, eventually convincing a city newspaper to support his anti-crime campaign. Rocky, aware of his influence over the kids, uses his own death to change their lives. Finally, the film's ending is blatantly hypocritical. By pretending cowardice for the kids, Rocky proves his courage to us. By deliberately destroying his heroic image in their eyes, he ennobles it in ours.[10]

Of course there is the possibility that Rocky really does die yellow. I felt this possibility most strongly when I first saw the film; after other viewings, however, I believe we are meant to see Rocky's fear as an act. But several sources, including Cagney himself,[11] admit the scene was made intentionally ambiguous.

What most concerns us here, however, is the film's relationship to the other Curtiz films we have discussed. Like Rick Blaine and Tommy Connors, Rocky Sullivan faces a serious moral decision, and his final choice leads to a wildly romantic and heroic gesture. Spiritually he moves from the city to the parish, from the night club to the church.[12] Curtiz signals this movement, the painful moment when the morally divided hero makes his choice, as he did in *The Charge of the Light Brigade,* by concentrating on the character's face. As Rocky and Jerry walk to the electric chair, they pass under unseen ceiling lights so their faces are alternately bright and shadowed (Plate 24). The light seems an almost physical force striking Rocky; his face becomes the external sign of his internal struggle. For the sake of something larger than the self, Rick sacrifices his love, Tommy Connors his life, and Rocky "the only thing I have left," his honor.

In *Kid Galahad,* the central opposition is not between city and parish, but between city and small town, the public world of business and the private world of family. Once again these worlds have an external and an internal reality; they are both visual environments and psychic metaphors.

Nick Donati's business, managing prize fighters, is inherently ugly and brutal, and no one seems more aware of this than Nick (Edward G. Robinson) himself. He repeatedly calls fighting "a racket," the people in it "mugs," and insists that "there's no room for feelings in this game." His goal is to create a champion; to reach it he will do whatever seems necessary, including placating gangsters like Turkey Morgan (Humphrey Bogart).

Because of his contempt for everyone in the fight world, including himself, he separates them completely from his family, his mother and sister, who live in a small, upstate New York town. His protectiveness towards them has a neurotically obsessive edge to it; he grows violent when anyone even mentions them:

> Nick: Nobody in this game mentions my family. I keep them out of it.... You know I keep Marie [his sister] away from these mugs who lead this kind of life.... I don't like fellows hanging around them, especially guys in the racket.

Curtiz distinguishes these worlds visually. Early in the film he shows us the decadence and implicit violence of the "racket" in a cynically wild party. The camera travels left across an elegant, crowded, smoky hotel suite, full of party guests drinking, dancing, picking each other up, primping before the mirror, or chattering on the telephone, each absorbed in his own pursuits, arrogantly oblivious to anyone else. The camera movement ends with Nick sitting in a barber chair; the barber tells him he was at a party in this room three days earlier; "same party," laughs Nick. The violence develops when Morgan, an uninvited guest, quarrels with a naive bellboy, Ward Guisenberry (Wayne Morris). In contrast, Nick's family's home is a simple, placid environment, complete with white picket fence, a tree-filled backyard, and plenty of sunshine and open space.

Nick's need to separate these worlds motivates the plot and leads to its unhappy ending. Ward becomes his new contender, but the former farmboy, who obviously belongs with Nick's family more than with his business, falls in love with Marie. His awkward gallantry even earns him the nickname Kid Galahad. He agrees to fight only to earn enough to buy his own farm. But, for Nick, as soon as Ward enters the ring he becomes tainted, a mug unfit for Marie's love. When they continue their romance despite his rage, Nick plots to have Ward killed in the ring.

Nick's mistress, Fluff (Bette Davis), like Nick, has no illusions about herself or the world she inhabits. She warns Ward against joining the fight game:

> Fluff: You'll get thrown into a rotten life that'll knock those clear-cut illusions of yours higher than a kite, get mixed up with a crowd like the one here yesterday. Oh, they may look OK to you, but they're not. And what's more, you'll find yourself in the middle of a war between Nick and Turkey. . . . He'd just as soon kill Nick or me or you as take a drink.

Fluff herself once had ambitions to be a "champion":

> Fluff: I was gonna panic New York with dance and song. So I ended up with feature billing in a Bronx cafe.
> Ward: Where's the Bronx?
> Fluff: From Forty-Second Street it's on the way back to the country.

The Bronx is as close to the country as Fluff has come. Now, she sees Ward as her ticket there, her escape from the world of mugs. She falls in love with him, but he thinks of her as a sister, even asking her advice on courting Marie.

Thus, for the country folk, *Kid Galahad* is a comedy; for the city folk, a tragedy. Ward and Marie are the comic couple; their romance begins in mutual hostility, like the swashbuckling couples', but they end up happily united. Nick and Fluff are the tragic losers. Nick loses both Marie and Fluff to Ward, for Fluff leaves Nick when she realizes her hopeless love for Ward makes it painful for her to be around either. Fluff loses both Ward and Nick to Marie, for in the end Nick decides to save Ward for his sister's sake, and dies doing so. Morgan, assuming the fight was fixed, bets all his money against Ward. When Nick tells Ward how to save himself and win, Morgan kills him.

Nick is obviously a more ambivalent hero than Rick or Connors or Rocky. His own corruption almost destroys his sister's happiness, and does lead to his own death. But his final moral decision, his self-sacrifice for the green-world lovers, clearly relates him to our other self-sacrificing heroes. Moreover, *Kid Galahad's* final image is an early, more negative version of *Casablanca's*: alone, after Ward has won his fight and Marie, while Nick has died, Fluff leaves the ring and walks away from the camera, down a black-shadowed alley, into the darkness of the urban night world.

Four Daughters offers a similar opposition of neurotic city and middle-class suburb. The Lemp sisters (Ann—Priscilla Lane, Kay—Rosemary Lane, Thea—Lola Lane, Emma—Gale Page) also live behind a white picket fence in a small, upstate New York town, where their father, Adam (Claude Rains), is dean of a music conservatory. The film follows their musical and romantic progress, for they each play an instrument and three have men pursuing them.

Ann has two suitors; Felix Deitz (Jeffrey Lynn), the more suitable, is a brash, charming, self-assured young composer. With his all-American looks and humor, he fits into Adam's family as easily as Ward did into Nick's. The other, Mickey Borden (John Garfield), though also a composer, is quite the opposite, a city-bred orphan, a complete stranger to family life. Swathed in cynicism and cigarette smoke, he drifts into the Lemp home like a breath of stale air.

We first see him standing in the doorway, hair dripping from under his battered hat, tie undone, shirt billowing out at the waist, the eternal outsider looking in. He quickly surveys the scene, then cracks, "It's homes like these that are the backbone of the nation." His pessimism clashes with Ann's dewy-eyed optimism. She believes a man creates his own destiny; he believes "the fates, the destinies, whoever they are that decide what we do or don't get" have already decided he will never be a winner.[14]

Opposites attract: halfway through the film, more because of a misplaced mother instinct than from true love, Ann elopes with Mickey. But Mickey really is an outsider in Ann's world, as Curtiz suggests in a number of subtle ways. Mickey is often visually separated from the other characters, locked alone in a static frame, while the others are seen in groups or are joined by panning and traveling shots. For example, when Mickey and Ann return to the Lemp home for Christmas dinner, several shots of Mickey isolated, looking uncomfortable and out of place in the family environment, are intercut with shots of various groups of people. As they all sit listening to Kay's radio broadcast, the camera pans from Adam to several others, but it cuts to Mickey, still alone, smoke veiling his face, then cuts back to another panning shot. Earlier, during Adam's birthday party, we see a large group singing to and encircling Adam, while Mickey sits isolated at the piano.

The Lemp world is constantly associated with energy, movement, and life; Mickey's, with passivity, stasis, and death. Although most of the film takes place inside the Lemp home, the mood there is anything but imprisoning. Scenes burst with rapidly spoken dialogue, music, laughter, and seemingly endless camera movement. The film begins with a longshot of the Lemp home; the camera immediately starts moving forward, past fence and tree, through a window, into the large living room where Adam leads his four daughters in a family musicale. In each of the next four or five shots the camera moves, usually from a close-up of one girl across the room to a close-up of another. Throughout the rest of the film, the camera continues to move around the house, following the girls' own ceaseless activity. Most of these scenes occur in the spring or summer; one of the exterior shots is an elaborate crane down through trees and party decorations, to a group assembled in the backyard.

Mickey's New York City world, though seen only briefly, provides a clear visual contrast. The scenes take place in winter. In one, Mickey and his musician friends huddle together in a cheap luncheonette, wondering how to raise money for a trip to South America. Mickey and Ann's small, cramped, sparsely furnished apartment simply lacks the space needed for the energetic human and camera movement that characterizes the Lemp home.

Eventually Mickey realizes his kind of life will destroy Ann. She can never adjust to his hand-to-mouth existence as a struggling musician in New York, just as he could not adjust to her world of small-town, middle-class families. She belongs with Felix. Like the other heroes of this chapter, he faces a painful moral decision, and like them he chooses the noble, romantic, self-sacrificing gesture, one quite in keeping with his neurotic nature: to free Ann, he commits suicide. Although he fights neither gangster nor political enemy, his sacrifice is still genuine. He dies for the sake of others who belong to a world he never made; the film ends as it began, with a longshot of the Lemp home in spring.

The true sequel to *Four Daughters* is *Daughters Courageous*,[15] which again confronts a middle-class family with a disturbing outsider. This time the conflict is doubled; there are two intruders: Jim Masters (Claude Rains), who returns to his wife, Nan (Fay Bainter), and four daughters (Buff—Priscilla Lane, Tinker—Rosemary Lane, Linda—Lola Lane, Cora—Gale Page) after deserting them twenty years earlier; and Gabriel Lopez (John Garfield), a young troublemaker who falls in love with Buff.

Nan plans to marry Sam Sloane (Donald Crisp), a wealthy, conservative businessman. An early exchange between Nan and Penny, the family cook (May Robson), sums up the personalities of and differences between Jim and Sam:

Nan: Everything Jim wasn't, Sam is.... Jim ran away from responsibilities; Sam revels in them. Jim was flighty; Sam's solid.

Penny: Oh well, marry him. Won't be as exciting as Mr. Masters and there certainly won't be as many laughs around here. But you'll know where he is.... You may not care where he is, but you'll know.

Jim himself understands exactly what Sam is:

Jim: ...at least vice-president of the Chamber of Commerce?
Sam: Secretary.
Jim: ...Shriners, Kiwanis...you're chairman of the membership committee of the country club?
Sam: I founded the country club.

Jim's mocking questions not only establish Sam's middle-class respectability, they separate himself from it.

At first his daughters resent his disrupting presence, but he slowly works his charm on them until their "popular front" against him dissolves. Only Nan tries to resist her ex-husband's warmth and wit, mostly because she believes her children need Sam's material aid more than Jim's late blooming love. Sam has offered to pay for Cora's education and to give Linda's fiancé, George (Frank McHugh), a job. Finally, Nan asks Jim to leave, her reasons a virtual paean to the middle-class values Jim's wanderlust rejects:

Nan: What about the children? What happens to Cora's dream [of drama school] and George—no desk for him....And Linda will wait till he's scraped enough pennies together so they can be married. And you know the one thing she wants more than anything else in the world is her own home with her own paid-up furniture.

So, Jim makes his moral decision and leaves, sacrificing his own happiness for Cora's school and Linda's furniture.

Gabriel's story deliberately parallels Jim's. We first see him when Nan helps keep him out of jail for selling a fragment of Moby Dick's tooth. His cocky disrespect for traditional authority outrages the local judge:[16]

Judge: He may not be a criminal but he's a menace to the community...an affront to the decent.
Gabriel: Wait a minute....You started off by running errands for a ward heeler....You kissed toes and turned the other cheek. Finally some old judge kicked the bucket and they stuck you in his place....And I'm supposed to be the affront to the decent?

Like Rick's, Gabriel's cynicism masks a deeper idealism; he shares Jim's wanderlust but he wants, not merely to travel, but to learn:

Gabriel: Things are happening all around us. Why are they happening? Did you ever see so much hate in one universe? Who sets it off and why?...I'm gonna find out....When I find out I'm gonna do something about it.

Just as Nan has Sam, so Buff has a more respectable admirer in Johnny Hemming (Jeffrey Lynn). Both Felix Dietz in *Four Daughters* and his counterpart here, Johnny, are supposed to be artists (a composer and playwright respectively) but, compared to Mickey and Gabriel, they are tame, domesticated spirits, thoroughly within the middle-class mainstream. Gabriel, a fatalist like Mickey, realizes that for him and Buff "it's not written in the books." Still, for a while, he tries to conform:

> Gabriel: I quit selling whale's teeth for Buff. I wear ties cause of her. I watch my English because of her. Why look, I even went to work because of her.

But in the end he too must leave the one he loves for her own good. As Nan says, "Gabe's not for her...she'll run off with him...and then he'll...break her heart." The unspoken element here is old-fashioned ethnic prejudice. The sons of Spanish-speaking immigrants do not mix with WASPs who found country clubs; Gabriel is not for Buff because a Lopez is not for a Masters.[17]

Jim and Gabriel's sacrifices resemble Rocky Sullivan's more than is at first apparent. Just as Rocky proves his courage by pretending to lack it, so they prove they love Buff by pretending they don't, and leaving her. Their final scene resembles Rick and Renault's in *Casablanca*. They too disappear into the night after forming a "beautiful friendship" between self-sacrificing outcasts:

> Gabriel: It's a big world. Two can travel in it.
> Jim: ...I didn't ask you to tag along after me.... I'm not going to let you do it. It's too lonely a life.
> Gabriel: Not if we're together it isn't.
> Jim: (smiles) Great day for the tramps of the world.

For all the heroes of this chapter, the moral battle has moved inward. Unlike the swashbuckling heroes, they fight, not on the seas or in Sherwood Forest, but within their own psyches.[18] True, three of them do confront and kill an external villain. But their most important struggle is with themselves, the painful moral decisions they must make. Although ultimately they choose rightly, their victories demand immense personal sacrifices, often of their lives. For Mickey Borden, Jim Masters, and Gabriel Lopez there are no villains. The "evil" they destroy, the corruption they banish from their loved ones is themselves.

At least, that is how the small towns they leave see them. Both *Four Daughters* and *Daughters Courageous* seemingly strive to make the world safe for middle-class morality. But from another perspective they implicitly attack the ugliness and emptiness of those same values. Under the surface they have a subversive quality, for they suggest the cruelty of a society that ruthlessly rejects nonconformists, that drives Mickey Borden to suicide and calls Gabriel Lopez "a menace" because he asks too many embarrassing questions.[19] From this viewpoint, Mickey and Jim and Gabriel sacrifice themselves because middle-class morality demands they do so. They can preserve a sense of their own identity only by fleeing the constrictions of a world that doesn't want them.

In the next chapter we move to *Mildred Pierce* (1945) and the *film noir,* where middle-class morality itself is the villain. Everyone is tainted by its greed and hypocrisy. For Mildred, there is only the city; there is no green world, no small town alternative, no escape into the family, nothing to sacrifice oneself for. In the moral battle, there is no victory.

8

Aprons and Minks: *Mildred Pierce*

Synopsis of the Film

When her unemployed husband Bert (Bruce Bennett) leaves her, Mildred Pierce (Joan Crawford) becomes a waitress to support her two daughters, Veda (Ann Blythe) and Kay. Because Veda, "only seventeen and spoiled rotten," considers the job degrading, Mildred opens her own restaurant, buying the property from playboy Monty Beragon (Zachary Scott) and operating it with help from her husband's former partner, Wally Faye (Jack Carson) and her friend Ida (Eve Arden). Mildred has an affair with Monty but ends it when he increasingly lives on "loans" from her. Veda, wanting financial independence, marries a rich boy and then, claiming to be pregnant, demands a $10,000 settlement to dissolve the marriage. Mildred, horrified to hear Veda lied about her being pregnant, throws her out. But, since Kay has died, she cannot forget her only other daughter. To lure her back, she marries the now penniless Monty and buys his family mansion. Veda returns and Mildred again pours money onto her and Monty. Finally, she learns that Monty has driven her to bankruptcy and is having an affair with Veda. Veda screams that Monty will divorce Mildred and marry her, but Monty laughs at the idea, driving Veda to such a rage that she shoots and kills him. At the police station, Mildred claims to be the killer. But Detective Peterson (Moroni Olsen) tricks Veda into confessing. As her daughter is led away, Mildred leaves with Bert.

Early in *Mildred Pierce* (1945) one policeman introduces the title character to another:

> First Policeman: Mrs. Pierce. I mean Beragon.
> Second Policeman: Which is it, Pierce or Beragon?
> Mildred: Mildred Pierce Beragon.

This little identity crisis and its ambiguous resolution neatly sums up the film's central conflicts. Mildred Pierce is a suburban housewife, married to an unemployed realtor, who bakes cakes at home and sells them to the neighbors for extra income. Mildred Beragon is a wealthy business woman, married to an American aristocrat, who buys her daughter fast cars and fancy houses. Mildred Pierce wears aprons; Mildred Beragon wears minks. But they are the same, single woman, one who has moved uneasily from one social class to the other. Her two names represent them; her two husbands personify them, and her wavering relationship to those men reflects her changing attitudes toward those classes.

However, as suggested at the end of the last chapter, the film reveals that neither world deserves our moral approval. Moreover, Mildred herself is at best a morally equivocal character. We have noted how moral issues, externalized in the swashbuckler into conflicts between hero and villain, become internalized in less comic films like *Casablanca* and those of the last chapter. The most important battles are fought within the heroes' psyches, but they always end up making the morally proper decision. Mildred is as morally divided as any of them; the film's central opposition, stated in the simplest terms, is between love and money, human relationships and social/financial ambitions. But Mildred makes the wrong choice; as we will see, her search for material success poisons almost all her relationships.

In this chapter, therefore, I want to show how Curtiz varies the structure and style of his other films to create a work that thematically turns 180 degrees away from the comic swashbucklers. I will begin by discussing the film in the context of *film noir*, then focus on how each character relates to its central opposition, paying particular attention to Mildred's psychology. Finally, I will consider the question, raised by recent critics,[1] of sexism in *Mildred Pierce*.

Inspired by the success of a rival studio's screen version of a James M. Cain novel, Paramount's *Double Indemnity* (1944, directed by Billy Wilder), Warner Brothers producer Jerry Wald decided to launch a production of Cain's *Mildred Pierce*.[2] Although Ranald MacDougall received sole screen credit for the script, five other writers worked on it, including William Faulkner and Catherine Turney; according to Charles Higham, Turney, a noted screenwriter, prepared the first draft.[3]

The final script was sent to Joan Crawford, who, "frustrated by the predictability of the roles offered to her [by MGM] had left Louis B. Mayer's studio in the early forties" and then rejected all parts for "over two years."[4] *Mildred Pierce* became her comeback appearance; a great success, it started her on a new career with a new screen image at Warner Brothers, and earned her her only Academy Award.

Although the film generally follows Cain's novel, there are a few significant changes which make it more melodramatic and more pessimistic than the book. Like *Casablanca* and *Passage to Marseille*, but unlike Cain's novel, *Mildred Pierce* uses a flashback structure. The film begins with Monty's murder. The assailant is unknown, but we are led to believe it is Mildred. A few minutes later, at the police station, Mildred begins telling Peterson her life story. We dissolve to a flashback which, with two returns to the "present" in the police station, forms the bulk of the movie. Once again, this structure makes the story seem at least partly controlled by fate, tragically predestined. We know, no matter what Mildred says, her tale must end in violence and death; no matter how happy her relationship with Monty may seem, it is doomed to failure. The violent opening establishes the film's tone; although the rest of it may be set in bright daylight, it is still infected with the metaphoric darkness of the first scenes.

Not only does the novel not begin with Monty's death, it doesn't even end with it. Instead, Veda discovers that although she will never be the great pianist her mother hoped for, she does have a remarkable singing talent. As in the film, Monty vengefully wrecks Mildred's business and seduces her daughter. But rather than killing him, Veda runs off with him into a career as a "once in a lifetime singer."[5]

The film makes no mention of Veda's voice[6] and gives us the satisfaction of seeing her punished. However, although Veda is punished, her guilt is greater still. In the novel she is merely a monstrous bitch; in the film she is a murderer. Further, in the novel Mildred finally breaks away from Veda of her own free will; on the last page she is able to say "to hell with her." In the movie she prepares to make the ultimate sacrifice by confessing to the murder. Of course she is motivated not only by her desire to save Veda, but also by her recognition and acceptance of her own guilt; she has raised both bitch and murderer. But only after Peterson tricks a confession from Veda and tells Mildred, "This time your daughter pays for her own mistake," does she feel free to leave her.

Mildred Pierce's dark, pessimistic tone, and contemporary setting, with its implied attack on American materialism, connect it to a genre that has recently received much critical attention, the *film noir*. A.M. Karimi, who has attempted a fairly systematic study of *film noir*, notes that French critics, such as Nino Frank and Georges Sadoul, first used the term over twenty-five years ago; it came into prominence in the mid-fifties, when Raymond Borde and Etienne Chaumeton published their *Panorama du film noir américain.*[7] As is not uncommon, it took American critics several years to catch up to French perceptions of American movies.[8]

Admitting that *film noir* is not an easily definable genre,[9] Karimi calls it "a series of crime films which appeared in the forties and whose most representative examples are the private eye films and their variations."[10] The films are characterized by "an ominous and eerie atmosphere, violence, ambiguity in plot and action, ambivalence of characters. . . . "[11] The private eye films, such as *The Maltese Falcon* (1941), *The Glass Key* (1941), *The Big Sleep* (1946), and *Murder My Sweet* (1944) do not focus on a deductive solution of the case, "but rather in the depiction of a corrupt world of crime and violence."[12] Another kind of *film noir*, such as *Double Indemnity* (1944), *Laura* (1944), and *The Strange Love of*

Martha Ivers (1946), does not deal with detectives and professional criminals, but with ordinary people caught in webs of desire and death,

> stories of love triangles, greed, and corruption, committed...by dissatisfied, ambitious housewives, power hungry females, domineering husbands, and psychological or physical "poisoners" of either sex.[13]

Thus, *film noir*'s darkness comes in part from its grim view of American society. It envisions a world where no one and nothing can be trusted. The most attractive characters can be the most deadly, but everyone is tainted by the desire for money and power. Their plots are deliberately complicated, full of frame-ups, fall guys and double crosses, physically and psychically battered characters, hidden motives and twisted relationships.

Karimi traces the *film noir*'s literary origins from "the 'tough guy' literature of the thirties, particularly the works of Dashiell Hammet, Raymond Chandler, and James Cain," back to eighteenth century gothic fiction.[14] He traces its filmic origins back to the horror, gangster, and mystery films of the early thirties.[15] Most important, he notes the strong influence on *film noir*'s visual style of German expressionism, the so-called UFA style, named for the great German studio of the twenties and thirties, and brought to America by European expatriates like Fritz Lang, Otto Preminger, Billy Wilder, and Curtiz himself.[16] Karimi, in fact, argues that style is what is most important about *film noir:*

> The artistic contribution of the American *film noir* is more to a style, rather than the creation of a new genre. Almost all the thematic characteristics of these films had already been established in the literature of the thirties.[17]

Indeed, the *film noir* can be best identified by its visual style, the recurring images that become its trademark, that make it as recognizable as the western.[18] That style is as dark as the films' themes, for their action often occurs literally in the dark, at night or in shadow, in an atmosphere of uncertainty and evil. They are almost always set in a city; their complex plots and ambiguous characters find an appropriate home in a maze of streets and alleys, luxurious mansions and sleazy hotels. The *film noir*'s distinctive iconography arises from this urban landscape, a night world filled with lone figures in trench coats, men in hats and women in spike-heeled shoes, silhouetted against street lamps, looking nervously over their shoulders, walking slowly down dark, rain-spattered streets, past garish, blinking neon signs, into dim, smoke-filled all-night bars. Sooner or later they wander into the police station or detective's office, a cold, sparsely furnished room where the shadows of venetian blinds stripe the bare walls and a naked light bulb and large, slowly turning, four-bladed fan hang from the ceiling.

As Michael Wood observes, the films' plots may not be as intense as their atmosphere; often nothing "that happens in the films quite lives up to the eerie menace contained in the looks of these movies."[19] Nevertheless, that "atmosphere has proved to be the most enduring part of these films."[20] In Higham and Greenberg's words, the *film noir's* "completeness as a genre" comes from its "intensely romantic" imagery which conjures up a unique, self-contained world, as "sealed off from reality as the world of musicals and of...sophisticated comedies, yet in its way more delectable than either."[21]

With its opening sequence, *Mildred Pierce* takes us into the narrative and stylistic darkness of *film noir*. The first image after the credits, words written on rocks, washed away by waves, is yet another of Curtiz's environment-establishing high shots, a night-darkened waterfront street, with a small house facing the beach. The first sound to interrupt the background music is gunshots.

The whole opening sequence, from Monty's murder to the start of the flashback, forms a kind of prologue to the main action. This prologue tells us nothing about the plot, but with remarkable speed it introduces some of its major characteristics, lust, betrayal, greed, and violence. The first thirty seconds contain a murder and a deception. After the establishing high shot of the beach house and the sound of gunshots, we cut to inside; a handsome, elegantly tuxedoed man clutches his gut and crumples to the floor, moaning "Mildred." Later we learn the victim is Monty Beragon and from that moment we assume Mildred murdered him; the entire film is designed to support that assumption. This initial deception of the audience not only mirrors the characters' continued deception and betrayal of each other, but also colors our attitude to Mildred even before we've seen her, helping shape our final judgment that she at least shares her daughter's guilt.

The film's next few minutes do nothing to explain this first scene; Curtiz continues to concentrate on atmosphere. After the murder, we dissolve to a high shot of a waterfront (Plate 25). The camera cranes down, past a neon sign advertising sea food, down to Mildred, walking alone on a dark, wet, foggy boardwalk. She leans against the rail; a low angle shot shows her staring longingly at the water, and we know she is thinking of jumping. So does a cop, who wakes her from her suicidal reverie by banging his nightstick against the rail.

She wanders into Wally's nightclub, a noisy, crowded, smoke-filled room, a strikingly seedier version of Rick's Café Américain. Here are no Arabian arches or exotic decor; instead of Rick's world-weary clientele, there are only drunken sailors.

The scene that follows does not tell us who was killed or why, but it does emphasize those same motifs of violence, greed, and betrayal. It portrays a mutually manipulative relationship between Wally and Mildred, and almost every other relationship in the film resembles it.

Mildred, in her mink, seems out of place in Wally's club and he asks her if she's "slumming." This contrast between setting and character visually defines the class conflict at the heart of *Mildred Pierce*. The same incongruity will be emphasized a few minutes later when Mildred returns to her mansion to find the police waiting for her, and we get a glimpse of the Beragon world.

In his night club, Wally's words reveal the central importance of money and business success, and the casual, impersonal ruthlessness with which it is sought:

> Wally: I hope you're not sore at me about this afternoon. Strictly business, see. I mean, it might just as well have been you selling me out.

The audience does not yet know precisely what Wally refers to, but we do know that he has somehow betrayed her and expects her to accept that betrayal as normal business procedure, with no bearing on their personal relationship. In fact, without missing a beat he switches the subject to sex:

> Mildred: You can talk your way out of anything...
> Wally: Right now I'd like to talk my way into something, know what I mean?
> Mildred: Still trying.

Mildred's response is callous and indifferent, but with a calculation equal to Wally's financial maneuvers, she uses her sexuality to lure Wally to the beach house and frame him for the murder. At the beach house, Wally completes the vicious triangle of sex, murder, and money by verbally associating business with violence.

> Wally: I didn't mean to cut up your business the way I did. I just got started and couldn't stop. I can't help myself. I see an angle and right away I start cutting myself a piece of throat.

Curtiz now shifts his attention from establishing a general atmosphere to exploring Wally's state of mind. Wally has become suspicious; Mildred has never been so friendly to him.

> Wally: All of a sudden—boom—husband gone—soft lights—quiet room—opportunity knocks. Why?

Curtiz uses several of his techniques for subjective narrative to express Wally's growing sense of foreboding. Wally and Mildred enter the beach house on its upper level; as they walk out of frame the camera pans across to Monty's body, then tracks into a close-up of his arm, reminding us of the violence with which the film began. Throughout the scene, the camera follows the characters, moving constantly as if driven by their nervous energy. The house's walls and ceilings are spotted by a weird design of rippling lights and shadows, reflections from the ocean outside.[22]

When he realizes Mildred has left him, Wally begins to panic and Curtiz fills the screen with visual and aural touches which, like the "ripple effect," are the sensuous correlatives of intangible emotions. Wally runs wildly through the house; as he pounds on one door, we see only his shadow, huge but helpless (Plate 26). He tries another door, but an unseen car's wailing horn drowns out the sound. He climbs the circular stairs to the upper level and Curtiz cuts to his most striking effect: a high-angle subjective shot, from Wally's viewpoint, looking down into the whirlpool of the circular stairs (Plate 27); cut to a low angle shot looking up at Wally, a tiny figure trapped within the whirlpool (Plate 28). Finally, he knocks over a floor lamp; the camera follows its fall till it crashes next to Monty's body, and Wally sees at last why he was brought to the beach house.

Curtiz now changes focus within a single shot to illustrate Wally's confusion. He crouches over the body in the background; the foreground is blurred. Suddenly the phone rings; it comes into focus in the foreground while the background blurs. Reaching forward, Wally's arm comes into focus, hesitating over the phone; finally it grabs for the phone wire and impulsively rips it from the wall. As Wally turns back to the body, the camera's focus, like his own, returns to the background.

The prologue's final scene, at the police station, introduces two more major characters, Ida and Bert. Curtiz now concentrates on Mildred's state of mind, her fear and uncertainty. She sits in the center of a large room, bathed in shadows broken by occasional pools of light, reinforcing the visual mood of the earlier scenes. The camera, as if nervous again, roams around the room, coming to rest on Ida. Mildred tries to talk to her, but a cop curtly interrupts: "No talking," he says. Bert enters from another office. Again Mildred tries to speak and again the cop interrupts:

Cop: I said no talking. Know this guy?
Mildred: We were married once.

These short bursts of dialogue are elements of a highly stylized sound track, built on the contrast between an ominous silence and sudden, unexpected, unnaturally loud noises: a pencil being sharpened, a newspaper rattling, a buzzer, footsteps, a few words. Echoing throughout the scene is a clock's hollow ticking. Curtiz uses this sound track, like his camera, to increase the tension, finally broken when the cop tells Mildred:

Cop: He [Detective Peterson] wants you now. Now you can talk.

Mildred then begins to tell her life story to Peterson and, as the flashback begins, we dissolve from the *film noir* atmosphere of the police station to a suburban street on a sunny afternoon. But the prologue's impact is so strong that we feel we are still within the realm of *film noir*.[23] In short, Curtiz has again depicted a world of fear and entrapment; he has shown mid-forties America to be as imprisoning as a medieval castle or a Casablanca nightclub. Only here, there is no alternative, no green world of Sherwood nor even the memory of Paris. *Mildred Pierce*'s visual tone is as stylized as *Casablanca*'s, but not as romantic or noble or sentimental. For the stakes are no longer the fate of the world, but as we will see, merely a chain of restaurants; the enemy is not the Nazis, but some rather ordinary human emotions, lust and greed, shared by all the characters.

With the start of the flashback, the film's central conflict becomes explicit. The script immediately makes clear the tensions between Bert and Mildred. What it deliberately keeps unclear is with whom we are expected to sympathize. As the scene begins, Mildred, in a voice-over narration, expresses her resentment at her middle-class background. She tells us she lived on a street "where all the houses looked alike." As we dissolve from her in the police station, we see, for the first time, not Mildred Beragon but Mildred Pierce, not a woman dressed in mink, standing before the grand stairway of the Beragon mansion, but a woman wearing an apron, working in the ordinary kitchen of the Pierce suburban home.

> Mildred: I was always in the kitchen. I felt as though I'd been born in a kitchen and lived there all my life, except for the few hours it took to get married.

We sympathize with her yearning for a better life and sympathize even more when Bert enters, flops onto the couch, and evades her question about his unemployment:

> Bert: When the time comes I'll get a job.

A moment later, our sympathies shift. Mildred has just bought a dress for Veda, and Bert complains that she has no money because she

> tries to bring up those kids like their old man was a millionaire. No wonder they're so fresh and stuck up. That Veda ... I'm so fed up with the way she high-hats me.... I'm no bargain but I make enough to get by. But no, that's not good enough. Veda has to have piano lessons and fancy dresses so she can sit there smirking her way through a piece any five-year-old with talent could play.... [and Kay] a nice normal little kid who wants to skip rope and play baseball. But she's got to take ballet lessons. She's going to become the ballet dancer so you can feel proud of yourself.

Bert's speech manipulates our attitudes because of a little noted but much used principle of audience response. Unless we know a character to be a liar, we tend to believe what he says.[24] Therefore, although we may feel that Bert is lazy and irresponsible, we have no real reason to doubt his truthfulness and we tend to accept his accusations against Mildred and Veda. Moreover, his self-deprecating honesty about himself (Veda "plays the piano like I shoot pool. . . . I'm no bargain. . . . I'm not smart that way") strengthens our belief in him.

The scene's context supports this belief. We already suspect Mildred of murder and have heard her tell Peterson that she "was wrong" to divorce Bert, who is "too gentle and kind" to kill anyone. We can understand Mildred's desire to "see them [Kay and Veda] amount to something." We may even resent the reverse snobbery in Bert's words, which imply that skipping rope and playing baseball are more "normal" and all-American than high-culture pursuits like music and dance. But Mildred's angry answers to Bert seem excessive:

Mildred: I'll do anything for those kids, do you understand, anything!
Bert: Yeah, well you can't do their crying for them.
Mildred: I'll do that too. They'll never do any crying if I can help it. . . . Those kids come first in this house, before either one of us. Maybe that's right and maybe that's wrong but that's the way it is.

Then, just when we think Bert has won the tug-of-war for our sympathies, the argument takes an unexpected direction. The telephone rings. Maggie Biederhof is calling for Bert, and from his whispered "I can't talk to you now" we realize she is his mistress. We also suspect that the sexual coldness implied in Mildred's belief that the "kids come first . . . before either one of us" may have driven him to adultery. Nevertheless, he loses much of our sympathy and we finally judge the argument a draw.

Curtiz's camera accentuates the scene's manipulation of our attitudes. He shoots most of the quarrel, until the phone call, in one long take, keeping the figures in medium two shot. Mildred, whipping cake batter, bangs her spoon against the bowl with added fury as her anger rises. As John Davis remarks, "The long take seems to stretch the tension,"[25] trapping the figures within the claustrophobic kitchen. But, more important, the refusal to emphasize close-ups of either antagonist prevents us from identifying with one or the other, forcing us to balance our judgment of them. Curtiz, who a few minutes earlier used subjective camerawork to draw us into Wally's and then Mildred's fear, now deliberately holds us uninvolved and objective.

He also keeps the argument unresolved. The rest of *Mildred Pierce* is, in essence, a continuation of that argument. Each major character exhibits a set of attitudes towards the central conflict between human relationships and social ambition. By the film's end we realize these attitudes are not simple oppositions but complex variations, reflections in a distorting mirror.

Most of the characters, in fact, seem willing to sacrifice love for financial or social gain. They form a scale, with Veda and Wally on one end, Mildred in the middle, and Ida at the other end.

Only Ida is motivated always by loyalty, never by ambition. In her unswerving devotion to Mildred she resembles the "sidekick" figures in the swashbuckler, and Sam in Casablanca. Like Sam, she offers no competition in either business or sexual affairs; she works for Mildred (as Sam does for Rick) but would never dream of taking over her business, as Wally does (and as Ferrari does Rick's). But Sam seems like a sexual neuter, as most black men were in forties films. Ida is most definitely a woman, and quite vocal about her sexual frustration:

> Ida: Men!... I never met one that didn't have the instincts of a heel. Sometimes I wish I could get along without them.... When men get around me they get allergic to wedding rings. You know, big sister type. Good old Ida, you can always talk it over with her man to man. I'm getting awfully tired of men talking to me man to man.

Molly Haskell thinks that this portrait of Ida is "heartbreakingly sexist":

> Independent, witty, intelligent, a true friend to her own sex and of all women the most apparently "complete" within herself, she is made to talk constantly and longingly of men, to deprecate her own powers of attraction, to place greater emphasis on sex than all the silly ninny sex objects who have nothing else to live for, in short, constantly to bemoan her "incompleteness." She thus becomes the greatest feather in the cap of male vanity. In what is an obvious contradiction of her true nature—for her relationship with Crawford is close, generous, and satisfying—she confirms the male (and, derivatively, female) idea that a bunch of women together are at best incomplete, if not downright silly.
>
> Even more insidious is her portrayal as being "out of the running" romantically and sexually, while she is the most outspoken and least puritanical of women.[26]

I completely agree with Haskell's remarks, but I think there is another dimension to Ida. By being "out of the running" sexually and financially, she can serve as a kind of Shakespearian clown figure, making bitter, mocking, and reliable comments about the other characters. Like Lear's Fool she warns Mildred against her thankless child; she sees through Monty ("You were probably frightened by a callus at an early age"), Bert (on hearing he's working she says, "The manpower shortage must be worse than we think"), and Wally ("Doesn't sound like Wally—no profit in it"). Ida thus fulfills a specific dramatic function, but the implications of her role make a pessimistic moral point: only the uninvolved can be uncompromised. Because she has no personal stake in anything she can remain untainted by the moral corruption that infects every other character.

Wally, at the other end of the scale, is totally self-serving, shallow in personal relationships, ruthless in business, and verbally violent about both. He talks about "cutting up" Mildred's business, about her and Monty "bleeding [it] dry," and he proposes to her by saying, "I wouldn't drop dead at the idea of marrying you."[27] He's quick to use friends for personal advantage, but he does know how to separate business and pleasure. When Mildred playfully tries to kiss him after he agrees to help her buy the restaurant property, he pushes her away saying "strictly business." Of course his feelings for her aren't really businesslike. He sniffs around her as subtly as a bulldog in heat and later admits "the only reason I helped you was so I could be around when you changed your mind about me." But he warns Mildred against Monty, not only out of jealousy, but also to protect his investment. When she rejects him, he simply accepts it and turns his attention back to money. As we saw in the pre-flashback scene, business and pleasure are again quite separate when he casually refers to his selling her out as also being "strictly business" and then, just as casually, makes yet another pass. He is certainly a villain, but he has none of the style, grace, or exuberance of those in the swashbucklers. Like them, he admits his villainy, but he does so apologetically ("I'm glad you didn't get sore at me . . . I didn't mean to cut up your business"), without their obvious enjoyment of their evil.

But he is somewhat higher on the moral scale than Veda. At least he's willing to help Mildred as long as it doesn't interfere with himself. Veda never lets relationships get in the way of ambition. Colder, crueler than Wally, she is not in the least disturbed by her father's leaving. Her icy, emotionless hauteur breaks only when she hears her new dress has come. She has already learned that sex can be a valuable commodity and she urges her mother to accept Wally's proposal:

Veda:	I heard you and Wally talking. . . . You could marry him if you wanted to.
Mildred:	But I'm not in love with him.
Veda:	But if you married him maybe we could have a maid like we used to and a limousine and maybe a new house. I don't like this house, Mother.
Mildred:	Niether do I, but that's no reason for me to marry a man I'm not in love with.
Veda:	Why not?
Mildred:	Veda, does a new house mean so much to you that you'd trade me for it?
Veda:	I didn't mean it, Mother. I don't care what we have as long as we're together. It's just that there are so many things that I—that we should have and haven't got.
Mildred:	I know, darling. . . . I want you to have nice things. And you will have. . . . I'll get you everything you want. I promise.

Curtiz's direction here suggests that, for Veda, sex is a way of getting money, and money *is* her true sexuality. We see her physical coldness when Mildred leans to kiss her after the dialogue above and she repels her, saying, "I love you too, Mother, but let's not get sticky about it." When she is alone, the camera slides into a profile close-up of Veda; thinking about the riches to come she folds her arms over her head, stretches, and smiles voluptuously.

Veda's money-motivated marriage to Ted Forrester makes the equation clearer. She uses her looks to trap him into marriage, then confesses that she has "made a terrible mistake." She sleeps with him only so she can claim she is pregnant, then uses that claim to squeeze a "settlement" from his family. When she returns home, Curtiz has her throw herself onto a couch and kiss the check. Ten thousand dollars may be a high price, but Veda has made a whore of herself. After Mildred throws her out, she uses her sexuality to earn a living. Scantily dressed, she sings in Wally's nightclub, and the howls of the sailors in the audience show they're more interested in her body than her songs.

In her ruthlessness, Veda resembles Wally, and they are partners in the Forrester blackmail scheme. But the violence that is only implicit in Wally's words becomes explicit in her actions. When Mildred demands the check, she screams, "Not on your life!"; when Mildred grabs it, she smacks her mother's face; when Monty won't marry her, as the audience finally learns, she shoots him. What is most frightening about Veda is her refusal to accept responsibility, to see her own guilt. When she describes Monty's killing, she is strangely detached, saying "the gun kept going off over and over" as if it had a will of its own.

Veda's irresponsibility resembles Monty's, and it is Monty she most wants to emulate. Unlike Wally, she does not want money for its own sake. What she really wants is "the kind of life Monty taught me," a life of polo, parties, and social position, and she has always thought that money buys the ticket to that life:

> Veda: With this money I can get away from you, from you and your chickens and your pies and your kitchens and everything that smells of grease.[28] I can get away from this shack with its cheap furniture and this town and its dollar days and its women that wear uniforms and its men that wear overalls. ... With this money I can get away from every rotten stinking thing that makes me think of this place or you.

Michael Wood has suggested that the "experience of class, the sense of America, proverbially open and unsnobbish, as a place of high walls and closed doors" is "the real, hidden, half focused subject of the *film noir*."[29] He finds, in *Mildred Pierce*, "a rather disturbing portrait of genuine snobbery, of an almost Victorian concern for social origins ...," an image of "the authentic monster of social class: a girl who found she could not escape her station in life, a daughter who thought her mother would never be good enough for her and a mother who couldn't really say that her daughter was wrong."[30]

Wood is right. Mildred cannot say her daughter is wrong, for she has indulged Veda's desires. She too resents living on a middle-class street where "all the houses look alike." Curtiz makes us see Mildred's initial attraction to Monty as an attraction to his social class. His beach house, with its large, comforting fireplace, its glass doors opening onto the ocean, its air of casual elegance, is a world far removed from Mildred's suburban kitchen.

Monty is equally elegant, quick with clever lines about his habits ("I loaf in a decorative and highly charming manner"), and his background ("We Beragons come from a long line of teacup readers"). His attitude to both sex and money is as careless as Mildred's and Wally's is energetic; he is used to having both without working for either. An old hand at seduction, with a closet full of swimsuits for his "sisters," his charm is only surface, his lines simply lines, to be pulled out when occasion demands (as when he uses the same "teacup" routine on Veda he had earlier used on Mildred).

Mildred sees this; when Monty tells her, "You're very beautiful..." she answers, "I bet you tell that to all your sisters." But she falls for it anyway. Like Veda, she is seduced not by the man but by the flickering firelight and soft music, the romantic and expensive atmosphere. Actually, Monty's lovemaking has an edge of almost comic exaggeration. It's difficult for us not to squirm when he looks deeply at Mildred and says:

> Monty: When I'm close to you like this there's a sound in the air like the beating of
> wings...the sound of my heart, beating like a schoolboy's.

Contemporary audiences might find this heavy-handed, melodramatic dialogue typical of the forties. But I think we are meant to hear it as insincere and corny; its falsity indicates both the hollowness of Monty's charm and the blindness of Mildred's reaction to it.

In fact, although Monty's words are more elegant, his gestures do not differ significantly from Wally's. As Mildred passes Monty in the beach house, he yanks on her bathrobe string, pulling it off, revealing her in her bathing suit; when Wally visits her the night after Bert leaves, he also tries to yank on her bathrobe string. Monty tells her, "You take my breath away"; Wally says, "You make me shiver." Mildred takes it from Monty but rejects it from Wally because Wally does not have Monty's class, which is simply another way of saying he isn't *from* Monty's class.

Kay's death immediately follows Mildred's night with Monty. While some critics may see it as a moralistic and sexist punishment for Mildred's becoming Monty's lover,[31] I think it also represents what that action implies for her: a final separation from the Pierce world. Certainly the film's structure suggests this. Kay's death is placed between Mildred's introduction to the Beragon world (the love scene) and her apparent entrance into it (the restaurant's financial triumph). Moreover, Kay is constantly associated with the Pierce world's positive values. From the start, her loving nature is contrasted with Veda's venality. She is the "nice normal little kid who wants to skip rope and play baseball"; she cries when her father leaves while Veda remains arrogantly impassive; she mocks her sister's displeasure with her dress ("Want it inlaid with gold?"). When Bert says, "Kay is twice the girl Veda is.... She thinks you're wonderful," Mildred admits, "Maybe that's why I keep trying to please Veda." We can't call Kay's death Mildred's conscious rejection of all she stands for, but it does sever her ties to it. Without Kay, Mildred is left with Veda and Monty.

But truly entering the Beragon world requires more than money. It takes a family name to become part of the aristocracy. Money can sometimes buy a name, however, and with it Mildred buys the Beragon name.

Curtiz fills the "proposal" scene with sharp emotional shocks, turning it into one of the film's coldest, cruelest sequences. It begins with a long shot of the Beragon mansion; in the foreground, appropriately enough, is a sign saying "For Sale (Owner on Premises)." Mildred wants both to buy the house and to marry Monty. He seems at first warm and sympathetic. He understands that Mildred's "reason for doing anything is usually Veda." He remembers how she once loved him and wants her to again. As he says:

> Monty: . . . love me again the way you did then. I need that more than anything. . . . I loved
> you then, Mildred, and I love you now.

Then comes the punch line. Monty "can't afford" Mildred, but "if I owned a share in your business . . . " Mildred gets the point, and Monty gets his one third share; she closes the deal with a bitter, "Sold. One Beragon." Ironically, Monty had begun his proposal by saying, "All I have is pride and a name and I can't sell either."

However, it is a two-way sale. Mildred has done exactly what Veda did with Ted Forrester, exactly what she accused Veda of wanting her to do with Wally; she has sold herself for a new house.

But also for Veda. Neurotic, obsessive, and self-destructive as it is, her unrequited love for Veda is what distinguishes her from her daughter and the other major characters. Only Mildred seems possessed of both personal ambition and the ability to love; she does belong in the middle of our scale. She clearly contrasts with the film's two other "mother" figures, Maggie Biederhof and Mrs. Forrester. Instead of the siren-like "other woman" we might expect, Maggie Biederhof turns out to be a kindly, maternal type, with apparently few aggressive instincts, who cares for Kay in her fatal illness. Mrs. Forrester, on the other hand, is all arrogance and social ambition, who dominates rather than loves her son. She, more than Mildred, is the image of Veda as an adult.

Even Detective Peterson fits into this scale. His ambition is not to rise socially or financially, but simply to solve a murder. In pursuing it, however, he is as ruthless and manipulative as Wally and Veda. Sliding between roles, first playing protector, then prosecutor, he uses his oily, sing-song voice alternately to comfort and cajole Mildred. He first assures her that "detectives have souls, same as anyone else," then says he doesn't need to talk to her because "we got him [the killer] . . . you're in the clear . . . you can go now." Underneath the friendly fatherliness, he's playing an almost sadistic psychological game; he does not tell her who the suspect is, and he pretends to be unaware that she desperately wants to know. The games continue when we return to his office after the first flashback. He glibly traps Mildred into revealing that she knows more about the murder than she has admitted:

Peterson: Why did you take him [Wally] to the beach house? Did you know that Beragon
            was lying there dead?
Mildred: No.
Peterson: Then you were at the beach house this evening. Why didn't you tell us that before?
            And why did you run away from the house? Wasn't it because you knew Beragon
            was there dead? And if you did know, why were you trying to pin the murder onto
            Faye? I think you better tell us the truth now.

Now playing the probing policeman, Peterson says this last line very slowly, deliberately, accenting each separate word, in a manner reminiscent of Baron Jeffries, who prosecuted Blood. After Mildred finishes her story, he calmly admits to manipulating her, calling her "the key" to the crime that had to be pressured. Having satisfied his ambition by solving the crime, he can then return to his patronizing paternal role, pulling up the shades in his office, while saying, "We need some fresh air in here," as if his words were enough to enable Mildred to ignore what she has suffered.

Earlier I said that Mildred, unlike the swashbuckler heroes, internalizes the film's central conflict. But violence, verbal and physical, is as important to the *film noir* as to the swashbuckler. Mildred's internal conflicts become external in a series of arguments with the other characters. These arguments form a distinct, though complex, pattern, in which Mildred first rejects, then seeks out each character.[32] Each of the film's dramatic sections is ended by one of these arguments, usually followed by a change in Mildred's financial and social status.

During the film's first half, the quarrels are associated with a rise in that status. Thus, Mildred's initial argument with Bert forces her to find a job; the break in her personal life leads to her first step towards financial independence. The next movement ends with Mildred's fight with Veda. Veda accuses her mother of degrading the family by becoming a waitress; Mildred slaps her, then apologizes, explaining:

Mildred: I wanted to learn the business the best way possible. . . . I'm planning on opening a
            place of my own.

Actually, she had no such plans, but she now acts as if she did; the violent argument leads to her decision to become a businesswoman. While seeking a site for her restaurant, she also finds and falls in love with Monty. Their sexual encounter is followed by a scene of at least metaphoric violence, Kay's death, which is itself followed by Mildred's next financial success, the triumphant opening of her restaurant. Though not a quarrel, Kay's death does imply, as mentioned earlier, Mildred's neglect of the middle-class Pierce world and the personal cost of that neglect. This becomes explicit with the fight between Bert and Monty that follows the restaurant's opening and ends the first flashback. Bert, angered by Monty's insensitive remark that Mildred's success is "one man's meat . . . another man's poison," throws his drink in Monty's face. Mildred may be only an onlooker here, but she has chosen the upper-class Beragon over the middle-class Pierce.

Back at the police station, Mildred confesses to the film's most violent confrontation, Monty's murder. The second flashback then begins with a description of Mildred reaching her financial peak:

> Mildred: In a few months I opened another place. And then I started a chain. In three years I'd built up five restaurants. . . . They made money. Everything I touched turned into money . . .

Her fortune at its summit, she discovers the emptiness of her relationships; the second flashback's first half includes three confrontations. Mildred first quarrels with Wally; when he warns her against Monty she sends him away by saying, falsely, that she loves him. Soon after, she accuses Monty of sponging off her, and he leaves. Finally, she throws Veda out when she learns the truth about her marriage to Ted Forrester.

The film's final section reverses the pattern; Mildred reconciles herself with each character while her fortune crumbles. She seeks out Veda but is herself rejected; then she finds and marries Monty and regains Veda, but at the cost of giving Monty one third of her business. Finally, after her business has been stolen and her daughter has become a murderer, she returns to where she started by rejoining Bert.

This pattern of association between financial affairs and violent disruptions in personal relations suggests that Mildred must choose between business success and personal success; it seems as if she can achieve one only at the cost of the other. Actually, Mildred's choice is not so simple.

I said that *Casablanca*'s central opposition of love and politics was related to a whole series of oppositions all gathered under the general headings of "Paris" and "Casablanca." Simply stated, Paris becomes associated with love and personal feelings, Casablanca with politics, public responsibility. *Mildred Pierce* also has a central opposition, love and money, and two metaphoric "worlds," Pierce and Beragon, middle and upper class, aprons and minks. But we cannot equate these two pairs; we cannot identify the Pierce world with love, or call it a true moral alternative to the Beragon world. We saw that Kay represents the Pierce world's positive values, but that world also has negative characters like Wally and Bert, and Kay herself dies.

Towards the end of the film, Curtiz sets up a complex shot that subtly suggests Mildred's growing disenchantment with the Beragon world, her movement back to her only alternative, Bert. Bert brings Veda to Mildred, who now lives in the Beragon mansion. Mother and daughter stand in the left foreground, Bert in the right background; then, Mildred walks toward Bert (in the background) while the camera follows her, panning right and leaving Veda offscreen. Monty then enters the frame in the right foreground, walks left, towards Veda, across and finally off the screen, while Mildred and Bert remain visible in the background. The composition and camera movement separate the characters associated with each world; Mildred's physical movement from Veda to Bert implies an emotional one as well; and Monty and Veda's off-screen conversation hints at their developing offscreen romance.

At this point, Bert may seem like a positive alternative to Monty. He has finally found a job and given up his mistress. (Actually, she has given him up by getting married.) But throughout most of the film Bert and Monty are really quite similar. Bert, too lazy to work for either love or money, settles for sex with Maggie Biederhof. Monty, equally indolent, uses his charm to borrow both from whatever woman passes by. Both John Davis and Joyce Nelson have noticed how much Mildred's men have in common. Davis says:

> Both [Monty and Bert] are unrealistic weaklings much more concerned with putting up a good "front" than with working. Their major difference is that Bert comes to respect Mildred's ability, while Monte [sic]... can only snobbishly despise it.[33]

Nelson adds:

> Both have other women besides Mildred in their lives: Monte's [sic] "sisters" and then Veda, Bert's Mrs. Beiderhoff [sic]. Each is connected with selling real estate: Bert's former job and Monte's means of support, selling off property bit by bit. ... The differences between the two husbands are class differences.... Monte's leisure is characterized by... playing polo... while Bert plays gin rummy with Mrs. Biederhoff.[34]

Mildred thus has no escape from the *film noir* darkness of mid-forties America. More important, Mildred can do nothing to brighten that darkness. We noted that the swashbuckler heroes have the power to alter their environments. The hero's triumph reforms his society in both senses, making it new and making it better. Mildred, like other *film noir* heroes, reforms nothing. American society is too strong for her. She is its child, not its challenger; the materialism it breeds in her poisons her human relationships.

But the reverse is also true; her relationships help destroy her business. She drains its resources to let Veda live in style, while Monty, angry at her rejecting him, revenges himself by forcing her to sell it. Wally agrees with this scheme, basically to make more money, but also because he too is a rejected lover and yearns to see Mildred's icy independence melt.

I called the swashbuckler a combination of romance and comedy. I also think the *film noir* is a form of melodramatic tragedy. Certainly, Mildred is a tragic figure, destroyed by both her character and her circumstances, her own inner drives and external, fate-driven forces.

One of Mildred's internal struggles is fought between her emotional need for Veda's love and approval and her moral outrage at her actions. Until the end, Mildred succumbs to those emotional demands. But, like all tragic figures, she must come to recognize the consequences of her choice; she must undergo a moral education.

Mildred's education is one of the film's subthemes. Wally refers to it explicitly when he visits Mildred the night after Bert leaves and says, "You gotta be educated, Mildred." In particular, he is speaking of her nondrinking, a lesson she learns quickly enough. After Mildred has thrown Veda out, Ida notices that she "never used to drink during the day" and she answers, "I never used to drink at all. Just a little habit I picked up from men." Wally notices it too: "You never used to drink it straight like that," he says. She answers, "I've learned how these last few months. I've learned a lot of things."

So she has. Rather quickly, she learns waitressing and the restaurant business. She learns how business concerns can control personal affairs; because of California's community property law she must divorce Bert before opening her restaurant. Most important, she learns to see through people, through Wally and Monty and finally Veda.

Her education is very much a matter of "seeing clearly." The dialogue uses the metaphor consistently. As Mildred fights with Veda over the Forrester affair, she says, "I think I'm really seeing you for the first time." When she realizes Monty's price for his name is one third of her business, she mutters, "I see." Curtiz fills the film with images of looking and seeing, of characters glimpsed incompletely, covered in shadows, reflected in mirrors and half-seen through windows. For example, we see both Monty's murder and the beach house love scene between Monty and Mildred as reflections in a mirror. Mildred sees Veda framed by a window on several occasions, such as when she returns to Mildred at the Beragon estate; Mildred also sees Bert leave her through their kitchen window. Taken together, these images become metaphors for a limitation of vision, an inability to see things wholly and clearly, to perceive the truth below surface appearances.[35]

Perhaps the most significant instances of this imagery occur towards the beginning and ending of Mildred's relationship with Veda. In the early scene in which Veda urges Mildred to marry Wally, Mildred stares, not at her daughter, but into the distance; she literally cannot see Veda. Even when she later says, "I'm really seeing you for the first time," Mildred is not seeing Veda fully. Only when she finds her in Monty's arms does she "see the light," and Curtiz makes the metaphor literal: Mildred walks down the beach house's circular stairs; we see her first in silhouette, through the translucent wall surrounding it; she steps forward, and the shadow across her face lifts (Plates 29-31); cut to a medium shot of the bar, with Veda's back against it and Monty bent over her (Plate 32); they both lean back, their faces pass from shadow to light; cut back to a close-up of Mildred, who walks forward, her face moving from light to shadow to light again, suggesting the emotions moving within her; cut back to the bar, a subjective shot from Mildred's viewpoint, the camera slowly tracking towards the two figures, who turn to face their discoverer.

Mildred's movement into light, out of the shadows that covered her face, the darkness of being deceived, means she recognizes the dual betrayal she has suffered. She has been robbed of both love and money. Monty has stolen her business and her daughter's love; Veda has stolen her husband, if not his love then his body (and this incestuous sexual betrayal may be the most horrifying). It is both inevitable and poetically apt that these two who, as noted, so resemble each other, should come together to bring her down.

Nevertheless, before her education is complete, Mildred must see one thing more, her own guilt. Hearing gunshots, Mildred returns to the beach house to find Veda standing over Monty's corpse. She starts to call the police despite Veda's hysterical tears and stops only when Veda says:

Veda: It's your fault as much as mine.... It's your fault I'm the way I am.

Until this moment Mildred was blind to her own responsibility. She had told Monty that Veda is "spoiled rotten.... I blame it on the way she's been living. I blame it on you." Now she knows she must blame it on herself.

In fact, we can even blame Monty's murder on her, taking his dying word "Mildred" to mean that Veda is really her alter ego. Parker Tyler adopts this view, claiming that Mildred "fundamentally if not actually pulled the trigger of the death weapon."[36] He says that Mildred "as a betrayed mother and wife... would have killed her husband... and not Veda.... If Mildred seeks to protect Veda, it is because Veda is a form of herself."[37] We could answer this by saying that if Veda is a projection of her mother, she is a projection of only her worst features, her ambition without her willingness to work, her snobbery without her skill.

But Tyler's argument is more complicated. He thinks the deepest betrayal Mildred suffers is the dual sexual one, as "mother and wife." A self-proclaimed "psychoanalytic-mythological" critic,[38] whose insights are often as brilliant as his prose is irritating, he finds the true source of Mildred's guilt in an unresolved Electra complex. Veda is her "scapegoat." Mildred displaces her complex onto Veda and purges her psychic guilt with Veda's capture. In Tyler's words:

The passionate desire to give Veda everything, to see her grow up happy and successful in every way, is an ordinary case of displacement; paradoxically Mildred wants to give her every charm and chance to accomplish that which *she* was prevented from accomplishing, union with her father. But the desertion of Mildred by Pierce, Veda's father, lends extra neurotic energy to Mildred's aim, and it is not till late that she realizes she must supply Veda with another "father" to complete her own (Mildred's) incest pattern. This she does by marrying Berargon [sic]; sure enough, this brings Veda and Berargon together, and Mildred duly surprises them in an incestuous embrace. But in the shock of the moment Mildred wakes up, so to speak, from her complex and objectifies her own guilt as a daughter, identifies Veda as her own past, and changes at this moment into the outraged mother that her own mother would have been had she caught her (Mildred) in the arms of her own father.... [39]

Tyler's thesis is an acceptable reading of *Mildred Pierce*. But the Electra complex seems to be only one element of Mildred's highly complex psychology. As Molly Haskell, using the perspective of feminist criticism, observes, Mildred's conflicts come from the traditional "woman's roles" society imposes on her. At first, one might think Mildred a very untraditional character, since she successfully runs her own business. But, as Haskell says, Mildred's business is "not a sign of independence sought for its own sake, but of initiative in the service of family.... Mildred's ambitions are for some 'higher purpose' than self-fulfillment."[40] That "higher purpose" is woman's most traditional role, motherhood, and her business, a restaurant chain, is simply an extension of her own kitchen.

Haskell discusses *Mildred Pierce* not in the context of the *film noir*, but as an example of the "woman's film," which she rightly calls a genre "as popular as the crime melodrama or the Western"[41] throughout the thirties and forties. The woman's films of the thirties, designed to appeal to the housewife's escapist fantasies, were usually sentimental tales of romantic suffering (such as *Back Street*, 1932; *Love Affair*, 1939; *Madame X*, 1937). During World War II, however, when so many women whose husbands were overseas became both breadwinner and single parent, the genre grew to include celebrations of woman's new strength and self-reliance[42] (in films like *Swing Shift Maisie*, 1943; *So Proudly We Hail*, 1943; *Mrs. Miniver*, 1942). But motherhood remained an important preoccupation, and the "sacrificing mother" was a familiar figure even in the films of the forties.

Haskell psychoanalyzes this recurring character with as much ingenuity and perception as Tyler. She writes that Mildred's obsessive love of Veda is a "veiled expression of self-love,"[43] the socially approved sublimation of her own desires and ambitions. But, more important,

[it] betrays a fear of its opposite, of a hatred so intense it must be disguised as love.... In the materialism with which mothers like... Mildred Pierce smother their children... in pushing them to want "more," they are creating monsters who will reject and be "ashamed" of them.[44]

Everything that Mildred does serves contradictory purposes; she works for both herself and Veda. In turning herself into a businesswoman and her daughter into a snob, she simultaneously draws her closer and pushes her away, by assuring that Veda will push *her* away.

Certainly, Mildred's suppressed guilt for her "deep, inadmissible feelings of not wanting children"[45] helps explain the implicit masochism of her relationship with Veda. Mildred continually turns the violence she feels towards Veda against herself. When, for example, Veda accuses Mildred of degrading the family by becoming a waitress, Mildred slaps her, but immediately apologizes saying, "I'm sorry,... I'd have rather cut off my hand." Mildred schemes to get her daughter back, although she knows Veda hates her, and finally Veda drives her to contemplate suicide.

But the films of the forties not only cheered woman's new independence, they also expressed men's fear of it. These fears appear in oblique form in the "fatal woman" character, the desirable but deadly creature who leads the hero into the tangled murder plots characteristic of *film noirs* (like *The Maltese Falcon*, 1941; *The Killers*, 1946; and *Lady from Shanghai*, 1949).

At first, Mildred seems like one herself, as she lures Wally to the Beragon mansion. But as she begins her story to Peterson, we realize she is more a sacrificing mother than a fatal woman,[46] just as *Mildred Pierce* is both a woman's film and a *film noir*.

Mildred's only real "crime" seems to be leaving her children while she goes to work. But one can say the film *does* consider this a crime, that Mildred brings her troubles on herself by abandoning the traditional roles and entering the "man's world" of cutthroat commercial competition. In short, one can call *Mildred Pierce* sexist, and see it as warning women against neglecting home and family, instilling ambition in their daughters and having too much themselves, lest their husbands leave them and their children turn into Veda-like monsters.

June Sochen presents this view in its simplest form:

> ...Mildred...was blamed implicitly (and blamed herself) for her children's behavior.[47]
> ...[She] had been humbled by her hubris, by her overarching ambition for herself and Veda.
> ...*Mildred Pierce* appeared as the ultimate message to all strong independent women.
> ...Women's strength inevitably destroyed others as well as themselves.[48]

Joyce Nelson adopts it in far more complex form. She attacks the film for its ideology, but she must twist it to make it fit that ideology. I accept her first premise, that the flashbacks are the film's most important sections because they create the context within which we can understand Monty's murder. The story Mildred tells, her "discourse," emphasizes the "gradual changes within her life."

> ...For Mildred the Beragon murder is not a discrete moment which can be...considered in isolation.... Her discourse unfolds a series of complex familial and business relationships within which a series of crimes occur, all having to do with the present Beragon murder.[49]

But I cannot accept Nelson's claim that the film "asks us to deny our own feelings that Mildred's discourse is the primary one" and insists that "what should really concern us is the murder."[50] She argues that the film's "temporal structure" gives the murder "privileged status through repetition"[51] (because we see it at both the beginning and the end of the film). Furthermore, according to Nelson, each flashback culminates in "a return to the present with the chief detective invalidating her narration. He demands that she "now tell us the truth—that is, stay with the 'facts' of the Beragon murder only."[52]

I believe the film cannot make us "deny our own feelings" about the importance of Mildred's story because it creates those feelings. Nelson misreads the role of the chief detective, Peterson. His insistence that Mildred "stay with the facts" indicates the limitations of his own personality, which we noted earlier. He invalidates her discourse for himself, but not for us.

Nelson uses a complex, jargon-filled argument to deny the film's own complexity. She says, for example, that although Wally is clearly an unlikable character, the "order in which information is given us in the film makes us read his character in a more sympathetic light than he deserves."[53] For proof, she cites the scene of Mildred trapping Wally in the beach house while he blithely apologizes for stealing her business. Nelson claims that in a way "we treat his words as noise at this point, since the film asks us to concentrate on Mildred as the probable murderer, the corpse in the next room, the fact that she is framing him."[54] I suggest we do not "treat his words as noise"; we are meant to be aware of both his guilt and his gullibility; we simultaneously dislike him for his selfishness and sympathize with him in his danger, and this conflict within our own responses gives the scene its remarkable tension. This is precisely the kind of audience manipulation Curtiz excels at, but Nelson overlooks this.

Moreover, although she notices the similarities between Mildred and Veda, she argues that "the film attempts to obscure the very real differences between them."[55] Again, the film is more ambiguous than she admits; as we have seen, it emphasizes rather than obscures the complex set of similarities and differences between the characters.

Nelson's aim is to expose the film's "ideological work,"[56] which asks us "to read the character of Mildred as a castrating bitch, within the same paradigm as the murderer"[57] rather than as a "competent, compassionate businesswoman worthy of her position."[58] It is true that the film's men, as John Davis notes, are dominated by its women. This includes "minor characters like the bald-headed accountant almost frightened to death by Ida's comic sexual assertiveness and Ted Forrester, the rich mama's boy. . . ."[59] Perhaps most dominated is Ted's father, who simply never appears at all.

But the film does not condemn this domination as a violation of the traditional sexist social order. Rather, it results from the men's own weakness and corruption. Mildred's suitors, Bert, Wally, and Monty, are simply worthless. More interested in her business than her body, they deserve and receive both the audience's condemnation and Mildred's rejection. Wally, never a serious contender, gets wrapped in an apron the night Mildred's restaurant opens; Monty and Bert can only protect their pride by walking out on Mildred before she throws them out.

Nor does *Mildred Pierce*'s obligatory happy ending erase all that has preceded it. I agree, as Nelson notes, that "we are asked to read the final image of *Mildred Pierce* as a positive resolution."[60] Mildred leaves the police station with Bert; they walk from the doorway's darkness into the dawn's early light, while church bells chime and the music surges to an inspiring climax. But Mildred's final acceptance of Bert does not mean she was wrong in their initial argument. Even at the end, although he has changed, he is still not really worthy of her. At the beginning he had been lazy and unemployed, unable to support his family; Mildred had become a businesswoman because she had to.[61]

Leaving her children is not Mildred's crime; not loving them enough is. She ignores Kay and her love for Veda is more neurotic than nurturing; she spoils her more than loves her. What is condemned in Mildred and Veda is also condemned in Monty and Wally, not simple ambition but the ambition and avarice that destroys human relationships.

Mildred is finally a tragic figure, sinned against as well as sinning. According to David Thompson, *Mildred Pierce* was one of Hollywood's first films set in suburbia,[62] and its picture of that setting is not a pretty one. It shows a people deformed by their belief in the sacredness of the dollar, a society that urges one to run down the road to riches, even though the road leads to murder and the riches are worthless. Mildred's only real sin is believing in the American dream of success, the myth of moving from aprons to minks.

Artists, Athletes, and Tycoons: Ambition as Self-Destruction

In 1950 and 1951 Curtiz directed five complex, pessimistic films which, although they are not true *films noirs,* do deal with the corrosive effects of ambition and greed. In this chapter I will discuss three of them, *Bright Leaf* (1950), *Young Man with a Horn* (1950) and *Jim Thorpe: All-American* (1951).[1] Like *Mildred Pierce,* each one details its central character's rise and fall. Although they act in different fields (the hero of *Bright Leaf* is a businessman, of *Young Man with a Horn* a musician, of *Jim Thorpe: All-American* an athlete), the pattern of their lives is noticeably similar. In addition, I will look at *The Helen Morgan Story* (1957), also about a musician's rise and fall, the only film Curtiz made at Warners after he became a free-lance director in 1954. Inferior in some ways to the others, the film still has important thematic and structural similarities to them. Finally, I will very briefly discuss a number of Curtiz's musicals which, in their own somewhat different manner, also deal with ambition.[2]

One of *Bright Leaf's* most striking qualities is its ability to prevent us from holding a simple, consistent attitude towards its characters. It is full of confrontation scenes which, like the argument between Bert and Mildred that begins *Mildred Pierce,* force us continually to shift our sympathies between the characters. Set in the 1890s, it begins with Brant Royle (Gary Cooper) riding into Kingsmount, "Home of the Singleton Tobacco Company." Years earlier, James Singleton (Donald Crisp, playing the same kind of self-righteous, arrogant aristocrat he had played in *Charge of the Light Brigade* fifteen years earlier) had driven the Royles out of town. We never really learn why, except that they are the "common white trash" Singleton hates. Now Brant returns to the only thing he has left, a small cigarette factory left him by an uncle.

The film's social conflicts are clear: rich versus poor, landed gentry versus landless upstarts. Its moral conflicts are equally clear: ruthless ambition against human feeling, power against love, vengeance against forgiveness. But, as in *Mildred Pierce, Bright Leaf's* moral oppositions cannot be equated with its social oppositions, its conflicting worlds. Singleton, essentially an unsympathetic character, still has sympathetic scenes; Brant, though clearly the film's hero, ends up acting more like its villain.

At first, however, we have no questions about where our sympathies lie. When Singleton, seeming as tyrannical as Prince John, orders Brant to leave Kingsmount "as quickly as possible," we naturally cheer Brant's rebellious reply, "I leave . . . when I'm ready and not a day before."

Brant forms a group to fight Singleton, and like Robin's merry men, they are all outcasts from the traditional society. Chris Malley (Jack Carson) is a con man, first seen running from the police after trying to sell some of "Dr. Monaco's Miracle Medicine." Sonia Kovac (Lauren Bacall) is the local madam, and her name suggests her non-WASP ethnic origins. James Barton (Jeff Corey) is the most outcast of all; he is a Northerner. He is also an inventor, and his machine becomes the group's chief weapon, for it can produce and package cigarettes in quantity, making smoking "the cheapest habit in America." Within a few years, Brant's factory has grown into the area's most powerful business, swallowing up its competition, including the Singleton Company.

But in the process Brant changes, becoming hard, ruthless, insensitive, alienating those closest to him. Barton finally quits; Sonia's love for him turns to bitterness as she watches his "heart [get] all choked up with nothing but money." Chris calls him "a man with a sickness," and warns him about the "little fund of hatred" created by "everything you've done to get where you are."

Brant's problem is that he wants more than Singleton's power; he wants his daughter. *Bright Leaf*'s two heroines personify its moral worlds, represent Brant's moral choices, and Brant chooses wrong. If Sonia is the proverbial whore with the heart of gold, Margaret Singleton (Patricia Neal) is the lady with the heart of steel. Brant is drawn to her for the same complex of reasons that Mildred is drawn to Monty; she is beautiful and she is an aristocrat. To possess her is to live a sexual and a social dream; she incarnates the bitch goddess Success. Just as Mildred sees through Monty, Brant sees through Margaret's seductiveness, but he lets himself be seduced anyway:

> Brant: May I call on you?
> Margaret: I don't want you to disturb Miss What's-her-name [Sonia].
> Brant: Oh, yes you do!
> Margaret: Eight o'clock.
> Brant: I'll be looking forward to it.

He sees the goddess, but he doesn't see the bitch.

Margaret's teasing, arrogant eroticism contrasts with Sonia's honest, healthy sexuality. There is even something of the neurotic voyeur in Margaret, as she asks Brant how he makes love to Sonia:

Margaret: Do you apologize to her for kissing her?... You do kiss her, don't you? And she kisses you?... Are you rough with her? Yes, I think you are.... And then you touch her....

Worse, Margaret uses sex as her weapon against Brant. Knowing he will soon take over Singleton Tobacco, anxious to secure her own future, she plans to marry him, despite her father's pleas. It is at this moment that Singleton appears most sympathetic:

Margaret: What about me? What am I supposed to do when all this is gone? You made me a Singleton. It's all I'm good for...
Singleton: No Singleton ever were the like of you.

Distraught over Brant's commercial triumph and the dissolution of his own empire, Singleton kills himself. Now it becomes Margaret's turn to seek vengeance against Brant. She marries him, then destroys him, by keeping him out of her bed and by draining his company of millions, as Monty drained Mildred's. Brant's final confrontation with Margaret is one of Curtiz's most emotionally brutal scenes.[3] He realizes at last the extent of Margaret's treachery, and the meaning of Chris's warning:

Brant: I've never seen you before, the way you really are.... Now get out.
Margaret: I will. But you'll never forget me.... There won't be a day or an hour that you'll get me out of your mind.
Brant: You're insane like your father. You're out of your mind with pride and arrogance.
Margaret: You'd like to believe that.... You'd like to comfort yourself thinking that anybody with the nerve to stand up to the high and mighty Brant Royle is crazy mad. I knew exactly what I was doing all this time... You know what kept me going?... I was thinking of this moment, the look on your face.... I'll forget it. See if you can.

Even more than *Mildred Pierce*, *Bright Leaf* is an essay on the excesses of capitalism,[4] a tale of the individual entrepreneur who builds a vast fortune, but loses his soul along the way. In his zeal to conquer Singleton, Brant has become the image of his enemy. With Margaret gone, he is at last ready to leave Kingsmount; his business survives because it is "so big now it doesn't even need me," but Brant himself rides out of town as alone as when he came. Not even Sonia comes to comfort him; like Mildred, Brant has let his ambition crush all his human relationships.

Young Man with a Horn also centers on a hero destroyed by ambition, but here the ambition is not financial but artistic. Rick Martin (Kirk Douglas), a jazz trumpeter, dreams of doing "things with this trumpet nobody's ever thought of doing. I'm gonna hit a note that nobody ever heard before."

We first see Rick as a lonely, unhappy orphan, living with a sister too busy to care for him. Music becomes the only thing he lives for, his obsession, his salvation. The film gives the salvation metaphor a literal basis, for Rick discovers music by listening to, then imitating, a church pianist, while the narrator, Smoke (Hoagy Carmichael), one of Rick's jazzman friends, says that Rick "was cut out to be a jazzman the way the righteous are chosen for the church."

Jazz also makes Rick a rebel, defying the musical authorities who surround him. He quarrels with commercial hacks who "want every number played the way it's written" and discovers he must play two ways, "one way for money . . . and one way for himself." In one exemplary scene, while working for a dance band, he convinces some of "the boys" to play a few tunes "our way," and gets himself fired. Rick's attitude obviously aligns him with Curtiz's other anti-authoritarian heroes. But unlike the swashbucklers', Rick's rebellion is as much internal as external. He struggles against his own natural human limitations. His ambition to find that new note is a demand he puts on himself; he tests himself, not against external values, but against a scale he creates himself.

The danger, of course, is that such internal contests often cannot be won. Throughout the film's first half, various characters warn Rick of the psychic risks he runs, saying things like:

> You got to have some other interest or you'll go off your rocker.

> You're kind of locked up inside yourself. You're like a bird trying to fly on one wing. You'll stay up for a while; then you're going to fall.

Rick is "locked up inside"; music is "his way of talking," his only outlet for his pent-up emotions.

His inability to handle his feelings is reflected in his choice of women. Like *Bright Leaf, Young Man with a Horn* uses two women to represent the conflicting directions its hero can follow, the alternatives from which he can choose.[5] Here, they are not so much moral alternatives as psychic/emotional ones. Jo Jordan (Doris Day) is as uncomplicated, healthy, and direct in her feelings as Sonia. Rick recognizes her singing talent, but she does not need her music the way Rick needs his. She does not let her talent or ambition overwhelm her emotional life; she knows how to be "a human being first and an artist second."

But Rick is more attracted to Amy North (Lauren Bacall). Neurotic, insecure, she is as emotionally confused and pent up as Rick, but she has no single ability through which she can express herself. She describes herself as an "intellectual mountain goat, leaping from crag to crag," who has tried writing, singing, and interior decorating with equal lack of satisfaction. As cold as her name implies, she analyzes but cannot feel, and makes herself an observer rather than a participant.

Rick: I don't do much thinking about it [jazz]. I just like to play it. If you listen to it enough—

Amy: I didn't come here to listen to it. I came to study the people, to watch their faces....

Rick's passion for the impossible Amy is analogous to and as destructive as his search for his new note. At one point, he explicitly compares the two:

Rick: I thought you were class, like a real high note you hit once in a lifetime.

He marries her, but soon discovers their incompatibility. She keeps him out of her bed;[6] he starts drinking and stops playing. He finally breaks up with Amy, but it is too late; he descends into alcoholism and ends up in a sanatorium, delirious with pneumonia.

Throughout the film, along with his other visual techniques, Curtiz repeatedly uses two devices to help tell his story. One is deep focus photography which, by allowing foreground and background to remain equally in focus, suggests relationships of cause and effect, dominance, and so on, between elements within the image. For example, when Rick, as a child, first learns about music from the church pianist, we see the piano in the foreground, the wide-eyed Rick in the background. When Amy pours Rick his first drink, a close-up of her hand holding it dominates the foreground, while Rick again stands in the background. Later, during one of Rick and Amy's worst fights, she again occupies the foreground, while he argues from a visually less forceful position in the background.

Perhaps the most striking effect of this kind of composition is its ability to comment wordlessly on the changing relationship between Rick and his father figure/trumpet teacher, Art "Pops" Hazzard (Juano Hernandez). Early in the film, when they first meet in a jazz nightclub, we see Hazzard in profile, in the foreground, playing his trumpet, and Rick in the background, listening intently. Later, they meet again after several years; Hazzard can no longer play "like he used to," but Rick, now an adult, has a growing reputation. As Hazzard listens to Rick, the image, like the relationship, is reversed; Rick, in profile, in the foreground, plays his trumpet; Hazzard, in the background, listens admiringly to his former pupil. Finally, at Hazzard's funeral, the positions are reversed again, but with a difference. Rick plays in the background; the coffin lies in the foreground. The dead man dominates the image as he dominated Rick's life; without his training, Rick would never have found success. His loss is one more blow that smashes up Rick's life.

The other repeated device is the use of windows and mirrors.[7] Curtiz constantly stresses Rick's emotional alienation, his position as an outsider, by having him look at the things he wants from a distance, through a window. One of the film's first scenes is the funeral of one of Rick's parents; its final image is the child Rick, staring at the grave through a back seat car window, crying as the car pulls away and his face disappears in the distance. Later we see Rick peering through a pawn shop window at a trumpet he wants, looking through a transom at the nightclub where Hazzard plays, and glancing at a store window full of Jo's records. Curtiz suggests the division between Rick's woman and his music by showing him dancing with Amy while staring longingly at a trumpeter's reflection in a mirror. Finally, toward the end of the film, we again see Rick looking at a trumpet, only now he is drunk, unshaven, and on his way down.

Young Man with a Horn moves in an unmistakable direction; everything seems to be leading it to a tragic conclusion. The film even includes what appears to be Rick's death scene. As Jo visits him in the sanatorium, he hears a siren. Hair matted with sweat, eyes bulging, he sits up in his bed and tells Jo that that is the note he has searched for: "You said I tried for something that didn't exist.... Hear that note, Jo? It's clean and sweet." He begins to sink back to his pillow, but precisely at that moment we dissolve to Smoke, sitting at his piano, telling us that Rick recovered, learned his lesson, and went on to be a successful, though tamed, artist. All this suggests that the happy ending was added after the film was completed, probably after a preview audience rejected the original one.[8] Awkward, unexpected, and unconvincing, the ending we have now clearly violates the spirit and intent of what has preceded it, and simply does not belong. *Young Man with a Horn* makes sense only as another study of ambition and defeat.

Though not nearly as complex nor as rich as *Bright Leaf* and *Young Man with a Horn, Jim Thorpe: All-American* does concentrate, like the others, on a hero's early success and subsequent self-destruction. At first, Jim's life might seem different from the others'. His defeats seem to come from external forces, such as ethnic prejudice (he is a full-blooded Indian) and arbitrary fate (such as the death of his son) rather than from his own moral choices. However, while this is partly true, there is a continual interplay between his external and internal battles; as he starts losing one, he also loses the other.

His first battle is to find a place for himself at Carlisle College. Hostile, unsure of himself, not a particularly good student, he (Burt Lancaster) crawls into an emotional shell; like Rick Martin, he is locked up inside himself. His only outlet, the "sheer physical joy of running," becomes his means of victory. When Coach "Pop" Warner (Charles Bickford) spots Jim's athletic ability and puts him on the track and football teams, Jim can allow his shell to dissolve. He too tests himself, mentally with his studies, physically on the field, and he passes both tests.

His other early struggle is with ethnic prejudice, both within himself and in the world at large. He wins the first but not the second. At Carlisle he falls in love with Margaret Miller (Phyllis Thaxter). He believes she is also an Indian and that without that common heritage they "would be strangers." But when he learns she is not an Indian, his love conquers his fears, and they marry anyway.

Unfortunately, the rest of the world is not so open-minded; after graduation, Jim loses an important coaching job to a white athlete.

This setback only inspires him to further contests. He enters the 1912 Olympic track and field events, determined to set as many records as possible to insure another job. He does return with an armload of gold medals, but again closed minds defeat him. Because he once earned money playing with a small town baseball team, the American Olympic Committee calls him a professional, strips him of his medals and strikes his name from the records; again he loses his job.

Jim turns professional, and is successful on the field. His real decay begins after his son dies and, as Warner the narrator says, he crawls back into his shell. He drifts aimlessly from team to team, starts drinking, which interferes with his playing, and finally so alienates Margaret that she leaves him. Thus, the emotional alternatives facing Jim, openness and closedness, expression and repression, are similar to those facing Rick. What defeats him is a combination of his own and the world's weakness.

Curtiz visualizes this conflict by again using deep focus photography. Jim is most open, most expressive, on the field, where Curtiz's images celebrate Jim's athleticism. Composition in depth can be more dynamic than flat compositions stretched out across the frame; here, the depth of field allows an uninterrupted view of Jim's physical grace as he moves forward from the background. For example, we see the bar over which Jim will jump, or the football he will kick, in close-up in the foreground, and Jim himself a small but sharply focused figure in the background. As he runs forward, growing larger, finally reaching his goal, the deep perspective seems to emphasize the unity of man and object.

On the other hand, as Jim begins to drink and close himself off from others, Curtiz emphasizes dark, interior shots, using his familiar bars and shadows in one crucial scene. Hung over and groggy, Jim wakes in a small, sleazy motel room and finds Margaret gone; Curtiz shoots through the bars of the bed's headboard, imprisoning Jim in his alcoholic, self-pitying world.

The flashback structure, used in *Mildred Pierce* to give the film a tragic inevitability, a sense that things must end badly, is here used with the opposite intent. The film begins with a testimonial dinner honoring Jim's early successes, then tells his story in flashback, and finally returns to the dinner. Jim's moment of triumph literally surrounds his story; we are meant to feel that no matter what happens to him, he will eventually reach this moment of public praise. Certainly this film was planned with the optimistic end in mind, perhaps because its subject was a living man.[9] But, like *Young Man with a Horn*'s ending, the dinner seems artificial and out of place. The film's final third concentrates on Jim's decline; in its penultimate scene Jim, now working as a truck driver, meets a group of boys playing football and offers to be their unofficial coach. Pop Warner's words assure us that Jim had once again found "the bright path," but we never see this, and the words remain suspect. The film derives its true emotional impact from its portrait of a talented man's slow decay.

The Helen Morgan Story is also a biographical drama that begins with its subject's early triumphs, here as a nightclub singer and Broadway star in the 1920s, then focuses on her descent into drunkenness and defeat. Helen (Ann Blythe) would like to combine the worlds of show business and romance, join her public success to some private happiness, but again a combination of fate and her own failures do not allow this. She has a choice of two men, apparently representing two worlds, one of lower-class criminality, the other of upper-class respectability. However, Helen's choice is in reality less like Brant's or Rick Martin's and more like Mildred's; neither man is any good for her.

Larry Maddox (Paul Newman), a con man, bootlegger, and thief, seduces Helen at the film's start and continues to haunt her until its end. He drags her into his many schemes, of which most backfire and at least one lands her in jail. His constant feud with a rival racketeer first gets her fired from a singing job, later leaves her stranded in a speakeasy that gets raided, and finally causes her own night club to be raided. Every time she seems over him, he reinvades her life; the final blow for Helen seems to be when he is severely wounded in a warehouse robbery. Realizing Larry will never change, unable to forget him or her other romantic failures, Helen, like Rick and Jim, begins drinking and soon slides from show business success into alcoholism and obscurity.

But Larry is not merely an external cause of Helen's troubles; he also represents many of her own internal drives and determinations. Most important, his ambition mirrors her own. Early on, when a theatrical agent warns Helen about her slim chances for success, she answers grimly, "I'm not giving up and I'm not going home." A few scenes later, Larry admits his own ambition. Standing on a balcony, looking down at the tiny people below, he says, "You see that down there. That's nothing but a sewer filled with a bunch of rats. . . . From now on I'm looking out for myself, Larry Maddox." Larry recognizes that Helen's own ambitions are not so different from his: "I know what's eating you. You wanna see your name in lights. Well, I got a hunch you're gonna be a big star." In a later scene, Larry talks about the two of them being "hooked" on one another, being "inside" each other. In their specific context, the words have an obviously sexual connotation, but they also metaphorically imply that Larry reflects Helen's psychological "inside."

The other man, Russell Wade (Richard Carlson), seems to offer Helen everything Larry cannot. He rescues her from jail and introduces her to a higher kind of life and a fancier set of people. He is wealthy, respected, a prominent attorney with a promising political future. Unfortunately, he is also married. Moreover, his respectability is only the pleasant façade covering his own ambition and desire. He too uses Helen financially and physically. He backs Helen's nightclub (which serves illegal alcohol) as long as his name "is kept out of it." Like Larry he is hooked on Helen sexually, but he can't, or won't, give up his chosen life style to marry her. For all their surface differences, Larry and Wade are equally destructive to Helen.

In one sense, Helen's problem reverses Rick Blaine's and those other characters' who found their private lives disturbed by public events. Helen has public success, but it is poisoned by the chaos of her personal life. Her story is full of forebodings of disaster. Early in the film a young girl commits suicide at a party when her boyfriend appears with another date. The scene is, in effect, a miniature of Helen's life, a glittering show hiding a deadly private failure. In the same scene, Helen tells Larry of her own sense of being doomed:

> I'm in a hole that only gets deeper. . . . I feel haunted. Not just because of what Sue [the suicide] did tonight. It's been like that ever since I was a kid.

Throughout the film, Curtiz's camerawork, appropriately dark, gloomy and imprisoning, with few exteriors or daylight shots, underlines this sense of inescapable disaster. Some critics consider *The Helen Morgan Story* to be one of Curtiz's weaker works,[10] but several sequences are as visually effective as any in his earlier films. The warehouse robbery, for instance, with its claustrophobic atmosphere, its deep shadows pierced by sudden bursts of machine gun fire, its images of Larry trapped behind crates, fired on by unseen assailants from above, reminds of us of a similar scene in *Angels with Dirty Faces*, made almost twenty years earlier.

Like *Jim Thorpe: All-American*, *The Helen Morgan Story* ends with a testimonial dinner honoring its main character, and the scene seems even more hollow and contrived than the earlier one. There is no flashback structure to prepare us for it; we do not even have a narrator's words promising us a bright, new future for Helen.[11] A surprise for her, the dinner is held in what was once her own nightclub; she is led to it from an alcoholic sanatorium. The scene's only purpose is to enable the film to end with an image of Helen reminiscent of her days of glory, perched on a piano singing a torch song. Exactly what happens after this scene is deliberately unclear, but everything else in the film implies that for Helen there can be no happy ending.

I began this study of Curtiz's films by asking what kinds of connections could be found in his films of different genres. The heroes of an earlier chapter move from cynicism to idealism, from being imprisoned within themselves to an openness in human relationships. The heroes of this chapter move in the opposite direction, from youthful ambition to bitter disillusion, from a trust in others to a suspicion of all relationships; they are among Curtiz's most pessimistic films. But another look shows how closely connected they are to Curtiz's films in one of the lightest, most positive genres, the musical biography of show business success. *Yankee Doodle Dandy* (1942), *Night and Day* (1946), and *The Best Things in Life are Free* (1956) also center on intensely ambitious heroes, but their stories are the mirror images of Helen Morgan's and Jim Thorpe's. In each one, ambition threatens to overwhelm the hero's personal relationships. However, since these are comedies of success, the hero recognizes the threats, conquers them and wins both popular acclaim and private happiness.

Yankee Doodle Dandy, probably Curtiz's best known film after *Casablanca,* celebrates the talent that made George M. Cohan a theatrical institution. Cohan, as a boy, is shown to be an arrogant, self-centered brat, who earns a beating from both his father and a bunch of boys from an audience. When he is a young adult, Cohan's cockiness in telling theater managers how to run their business keeps losing jobs for his family, his fianceé, and himself. The crucial scene of the film's first section has Cohan (Jame Cagney) overhearing his family planning to refuse yet another booking because the producers do not want him. Awakened to a sense of family responsibility, George lies to his parents and sister, telling them to accept the offer because he has one of his own. George's ambition and perseverance finally pay off, however, for George eventually produces his own Broadway shows and has his family head the cast.

Thus, the film's two worlds, theater and family, cannot truly be said to be in conflict, for the Cohans are the perfect fusion of the two, a theatrical family. Whatever conflict does arise stems from George's own self-absorption and by the middle of the film George is a changed man and all the conflicts are happily resolved.

Further, Curtiz treats Cohan's immense energy and drive as positive qualities, celebrating them with his own cinematic energy, his lively camera movement, rapid pacing of dialogue and action and his high-spirited treatment of the musical numbers. Moreover, he tempers our sense of George being singularly devoted to theater by emphasizing his equal devotion to his family. Using his talent for turning possibly sentimental material into emotionally effective scenes, Curtiz creates a number of memorable dramatic moments, such as when George makes his father a partner in all his theatrical ventures.

The conflict between theater and family appears in more serious form in *Night and Day,* [12] based on Cole Porter's life. Here, as in *Four Daughters* and *Daughters Courageous,* Curtiz stresses the role of home and family as a haven from the outside world. The scenes on the Porter estate, particularly the Christmas scene near the beginning, are reminiscent of those in the earlier films and the family scenes in *Yankee Doodle Dandy.* After exchanging presents, the Porters cluster around the piano, singing together as Cole (Cary Grant) plays, while the warm glow of the fireplace keeps the winter's cold away. [13]

Nevertheless, there is dissension within the family. Cole's ambition to write music conflicts with his grandfather's (C. Aubrey Smith) desire for him to practice law. In this context we easily sympathize with Cole; his grandfather, however amiable, seems stuffy and archaic in his objections. Indeed, the grandfather eventually reconciles himself with Cole, admitting that while many people know his grandson's music, few sing legal briefs.

Ironically though, this reconciliation occurs just after Cole's marriage breaks up, and in this case we cannot sympathize with Cole. He dedicates himself to work so totally that he ignores his wife, Linda (Alexis Smith); he constantly promises to go away with her, then breaks that promise by starting a new show. Cole's failure to separate the worlds of family and theater becomes most obvious when he invites one show's entire cast and crew to rehearse at his estate. Curtiz vividly contrasts this scene with the earlier Christmas one. Here the singing and joking are done by strangers who run carelessly through the house, oblivious to Linda, leaving her alone and useless in what should be her own backyard. Cole violates the sanctity and privacy of the home; he allows the theater to invade and overwhelm the family. However, we are still in the realm of the success musicals, so *Night and Day* ends with a second reconciliation, between a repentant Cole and a forgiving Linda.

In *The Best Things in Life Are Free,* the family is a metaphoric unit, the song-writing trio of Buddy daSilva (Gordon Macrae), Ray Henderson (Dan Dailey), and Lew Brown (Ernest Borgnine). Like the Cohans, they are equally involved in theater, but Buddy's ambition threatens to break them apart. There is one real family in the film, Ray and his wife (Phyllis Avery) and their low-key but strong relationship is contrasted with Buddy's more intense, on-again, off-again romance with Kitty Kane (Sheree North).

Further, while Ray stays quietly at home, Buddy hobnobs with the rich and famous at fancy parties. His social connections almost cause disaster when a gangster threatens one of the group's shows. Eventually, their success brings them to Hollywood where Buddy's dreams reach full bloom. Invited to produce films, he abandons his partners, who return to New York. But, again, the film ends with a reconciliation, and an appropriately festive comic conclusion, a song.[14]

Even some of Curtiz's nonbiographical musicals deal with the conflicts between theater and family. In *My Dream Is Yours* (1949), for example, Doris Day plays a widowed mother (Martha Gibson) torn between her responsibilities to her son and her ambition for a singing career; eventually she manages to satisfy both.

I said that *Mildred Pierce* turns 180 degrees away from the realm of comic triumph inhabited by the swashbucklers. With the musicals, we seem to have come full circle back to that realm. The musical heroes defeat "villains" both internal, overweening ambition, and external, initial theatrical setbacks, to form a "new society," their family and friends, which reconciles the oppositions that tear apart the tragic figures. In the end they manage to live in both worlds, to balance the demands of personal relationships and individual ambitions, private life and public life, family and career, aprons and minks.

Conclusion

In the preceding pages I have tried to begin the difficult but necessary task of examining the films of Michael Curtiz. What makes this work so difficult is the vast number and striking diversity of these films. Earlier, I compared two of them to one by a recognized auteur, Howard Hawks. Although Hawks worked in a wider variety of genres than many other equally recognized auteurs (such as Alfred Hitchcock, Frank Capra, and John Ford), he did not work in as many as Curtiz and was certainly less prolific. The point is not that Curtiz is therefore a better or worse director than Hawks, but simply that critics find it easier to identify and discuss a consistent personal vision in the films of less prolific, less broad-ranging directors. Yet I believe that Andrew Sarris's words about Hawks apply equally to Curtiz:

> That one can discern the same directorial signature over a wide variety of genres is proof of artistry. That one can still enjoy the genres for their own sake is proof of the artist's professional urge to entertain.[1]

The most obvious aspect of Curtiz's directorial signature is his expression-istic visual style, and its most obvious feature is its unusual camera angles and carefully detailed, crowded, complex compositions, full of mirrors and reflec-tions, smoke and fog, and physical objects, furniture, foliage, bars, and windows, that stand between the camera and the human characters and seem to surround and often entrap them. Curtiz also favors dramatic, nonrealistic lighting (in which the light appears from sources impossible or illogical in real situations), marked by strong contrasts between masses of bright light and deep shadow. Often these shadows are used like physical objects to impede our view of the characters, falling across them in bar-like stripes. Curtiz moves his camera whenever possible, using every device from the short, forward movement towards a character, to underline a significant speech or reaction, to long, elaborate, technically difficult crane and tracking shots. He also frequently employs subjective shots, in which the camera sees only what one character sees, forcing the audience to become that character, and the high crane shot, which locates a character within a larger environment.

These techniques are not merely visual embellishments. Like most other studio directors, Curtiz did not write his own scripts, but he did use his style to emphasize selectively certain themes and motifs within them; the dramatic implications of Curtiz's style become another aspect of his directorial signature. Thus, Curtiz seems to define his characters by their environment, often suggesting they are trapped by that environment. In fact, environment becomes a form of fate, and Curtiz's characters often struggle against fate, trying to mold their own lives, shape their own destinies. The typical Curtiz hero is a morally divided figure, forced by circumstance, his own personality, or a combination of these, to make a serious moral decision. I have called the alternatives he must choose from the two worlds of Curtiz's films, and have suggested that the opposition between these worlds structures nearly all of his films.

In the swashbucklers the worlds represent, in a rather straightforward manner, good and evil, innocence and corruption. It is not so much the hero who is divided as it is his society. The conflict remains external, fought between hero and villain; when the hero defeats the villain, he purges the society of its evil. As we move away from the swashbuckler, towards the romantic or tragic melodrama, the conflict moves inward and the hero faces more ambiguous alternatives: private happiness or public duty; neutrality or commitment; family or career; cynicism or idealism. Heroism, he discovers, demands painful sacrifices, usually of his love or his life. Finally, in the *film noir*, the hero contains the villain within himself. The swashbucklers' tyrants are obsessed with ambition, which finally leads to their ruin. In the *film noir* it is the hero who feels that ambition, and he too ends up ruined.

In looking at the films of these different genres, I have, for convenience's sake, moved chronologically, from *Captain Blood* of 1935 to *Mildred Pierce* of 1945 and *The Helen Morgan Story* of 1957. However, I must emphasize that this movement does not imply a thematic development within Curtiz's career, a progressive darkening of his vision. Nor does it necessarily imply changes within public taste to which Curtiz responded. Curtiz made films in all genres throughout his life. For example, in 1947, two years after *Mildred Pierce*'s dark, scathing attack on American values and family life, in the same year as his equally dark thriller, *The Unsuspected*, Curtiz celebrated the American family in one of his most commercially successful films, the sentimental, nostalgic, technicolored *Life with Father*. In the late forties and early fifties, simultaneously with such pessimistic films as *Bright Leaf* and *Young Man with a Horn*, Curtiz made a number of light musicals, comedies, and biopics, such as *My Dream Is Yours* (1949), *The Lady Takes a Sailor* (1949), and *The Will Rogers Story* (1952). Finally, some of Curtiz's darkest films, the chilling and perverse horror pictures, *Dr. X* (1932) and *Mystery of the Wax Museum* (1933), were made before his swashbucklers. Moreover, the swashbucklers themselves contain elements of cruelty and sadism that would not be out of place in the horror films.

Thus, the chronological movement we have outlined actually indicates the relations between the genres, the way one shades gradually into another. Curtiz's style emphasizes these connections, for it seeks out the central dramatic tensions common to all of them.

Although I have tried to show that the metaphoric worlds within Curtiz's films can represent complex groups of oppositions, it might be objected that, in reducing the films to these basic conflicts, I have oversimplified them. After all, almost every drama involves conflict, usually between some form of good and evil. Or, it may seem that Curtiz himself is simplistic, that on an intellectual level his examination of moral issues is not especially profound. But this is precisely the point. As John Baxter says, Curtiz is not an "artist of ideas."[2] We never find in his films a character who speaks for him, enunciating his philosophy or morality, as we often find in Hawks's or Ford's films.

The ultimate purpose of all his visual and dramatic devices is to make us share his characters' emotions, to involve us in their struggles, external and internal. To this end he does "reduce" his stories to their elemental conflicts. He searches for the essential emotional bedrock on which every script, every scene, is built, and then he uses all his skill to make us participate in that conflict.

I noted that some critics have called Curtiz cynical, and some of his work deserves that adjective. But we have also seen Curtiz's romantic side, and that should not surprise us; cynicism and romanticism are often the two halves of one personality. In this light, it seems appropriate that *Casablanca*'s Rick Blaine is Curtiz's most popular character, for he is a shining example of the man who uses cynicism to hide his true romanticism. If Curtiz's films do express any personal vision, it would seem to be his belief in the primacy of human emotions. Nothing, not war, nor politics, nor great fortunes, is more important than that "hill of beans" which is the story of human feeling. D.W. Griffith, talking about the goal of his filmmaking, reportedly said, "The task I'm trying to achieve is above all to make you see."[3] Of Curtiz we could say his task is above all to make us feel.

I called this study of Curtiz's films a beginning, and I must repeat that here. I have tried to give some shape to Curtiz's enormous output, to suggest an approach to his films. I have tried at least to touch on almost all of his major films, but there are many others that I was unable even to mention. At least some of Curtiz's European and American silent films still exist. It would be worthwhile to examine them closely, to determine exactly what he brought with him from Europe and how it influenced his first American work.[4] One genre I have not looked at here is Curtiz's horror films, and these too could be studied profitably.[5] I also neglected *The Sea Wolf* (1941), an unusual mixture of *film noir* and sea adventure, called the best of the many versions of the Jack London novel and one of Curtiz's strongest, richest movies.[6] Curtiz's late, non-Warners films need reassessing. Those critics who have considered Curtiz have dismissed them as inferior, without trying to relate them to his earlier work.[7] Several of them, such as *The Boy from Oklahoma* (1954), *The Hangman* (1959), and *The Adventures of Huckleberry Finn* (1960), with their long, static takes and simple, uncluttered compositions, seem more relaxed, mellow, and perhaps more boring than we might expect. But others, such as *King Creole* (1958), retain the distinctive Curtiz look and atmosphere.[8] For too long an undiscovered director, Curtiz deserves the sustained critical attention others have received. Curtiz's talking shadows remain with us, waiting to speak to those who are willing to listen.

Plate 1. *Captain Blood*. Blood behind bars.

Plate 2. *Captain Blood*. Blood behind bars.

Plate 3. *Captain Blood*. Blood behind bars.

Plate 4. *Captain Blood*.

Plate 5. *Captain Blood*

Plate 6. *Captain Blood*

Plate 7. *Captain Blood*. The water wheel

Plate 8. *Captain Blood*. The gallows

Plate 9. *Captain Blood*

Plate 10. *Captain Blood*

Plate 11. *Captain Blood*

Plate 12. *Adventures of Robin Hood.*
The duel as myth

Plate 13. *Private Lives of Elizabeth
and Essex.* Essex in Prison

Plate 14. *Casablanca.* Laszlo "shadowed"

Plate 15. *Casablanca.*

Plate 16. *Casablanca.*

Plate 17. *Casablanca*. Rick at his safe.

Plate 18. *Casablanca*. The airport scene

Plate 19. *Casablanca*. The airport scene

Plate 20. *Casablanca*. The airport scene

Plate 21. *Casablanca.* The final shot

Plate 22. *Angels with Dirty Faces.*
Rocky's execution

Plate 23. *Angels with Dirty Faces.*
Rocky's execution

Plate 24. *Angels with Dirty Faces.*
Rocky's execution

Plate 25. *Mildred Pierce.* The waterfront

Plate 26. *Mildred Pierce.* Wally trapped

Plate 27. *Mildred Pierce.* Wally trapped

Plate 28. *Mildred Pierce.* Wally trapped

Plate 29.   *Mildred Pierce*. Mildred sees the light

Plate 30.   *Mildred Pierce*. Mildred sees the light

Plate 31.   *Mildred Pierce*. Mildred sees the light

Plate 32.   *Mildred Pierce*. Mildred sees the light

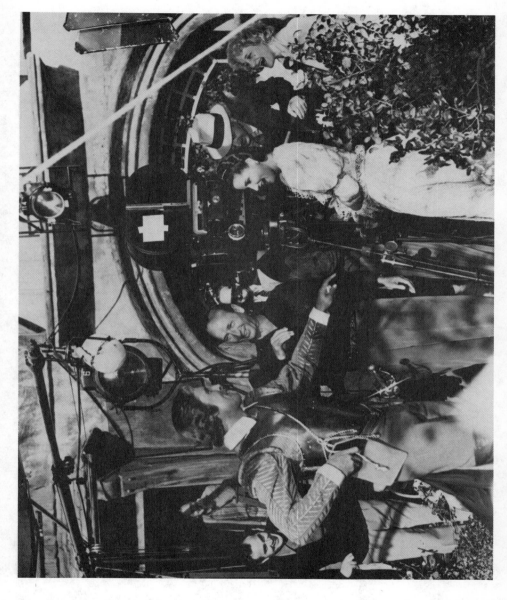

Plate 33. Errol Flynn *(l)*, Curtiz *(center)*, and Brenda Marshall *(r)* on the set of *The Sea Hawk*.

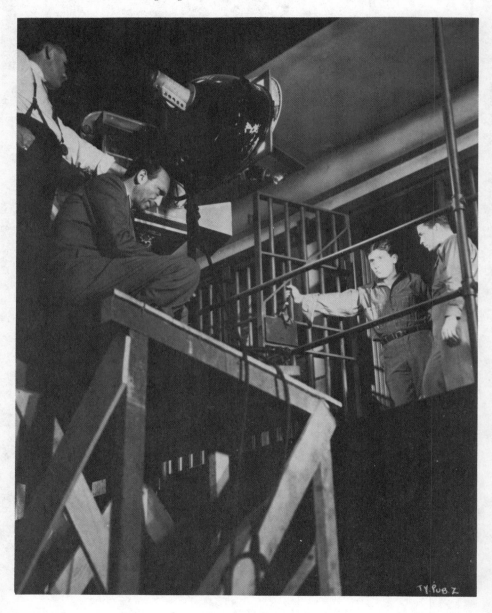

Plate 35. Publicity still from *The Sea Hawk* imitating Curtiz's complex compositions.

Plate 36. Bars and shadows. Publicity still of Bogart in *Passage to Marseille.*

Notes

Introduction

1. Curtiz himself once said something similar in an article written, or at least signed, by him, for a popular magazine: "... motion pictures are not a pure art. They are the composite of all five arts: literature, painting, architecture, music and sculpturing...." See Michael Curtiz, "Hollywood Is a Fertile Field for Creativeness and Ingenuity," *PIC*, April 1947, p. 108.

2. Davis's articles will be referred to within the text where appropriate. A complete list of them will be found in the bibiliography.

3. Again, these will be cited where appropriate and are listed in the bibiliography.

4. Kingsley Canham, *The Hollywood Professionals: Michael Curtiz, Raoul Walsh, Henry Hathaway* (New York: A.S. Barnes & Co., 1973).

5. John Baxter, *Hollywood in the Thirties* (New York: A.S. Barnes & Co., 1968), p. 52.

6. Charles Higham and Joel Greenberg, *Hollywood in the Forties* (New York: Paperback Library, 1970), p. 19.

7. Don Whittemore and Philip Alan Cecchettini, *Passport to Hollywood: Film Immigrants: Anthology* (New York: McGraw Hill, 1976), pp. 188-228.

8. William R. Meyer, *The Warner Brothers Directors: The Hard Boiled, the Comic and the Weepers* (New Rochelle, N.Y.: Arlington House Publishers, 1978), pp. 75-107.

9. The American Film Institute, *The American Film Heritage: Impressions from the American Film Institute Archives* (Washington, D.C.: Acropolis Books, Ltd., 1972). This anthology includes three articles of interest: John Davis and Tom Flinn, "Michael Curtiz," pp. 32-39; Tom Shales, *"The Mystery of the Wax Museum,"* pp. 28-31; David Thaxton, *"Mission to Moscow,"* pp. 40-42.

10. Andrew Sarris, in *The American Cinema* (New York: E.P. Dutton, 1968), pp. 174-76, summarizes this position.

11. Ina Rae Hark, "The Visual Politics of *The Adventures of Robin Hood,*" *Journal of Popular Film,* 5 (Winter 1976), 16.

12. For discussions of the Supreme Court decision, and its impact on the major studios, see Ernest Borneman, "The United States versus Hollywood: The Case Study of an Antitrust Suit," in *The American Film Industry,* ed. Tino Balio (Madison: University of Wisconsin Press, 1976), pp. 332-45; and Michael Conant, "The Impact of the *Paramount* Decrees," ibid, pp. 346-70.

13. Baxter, p. 8.

14. John Baxter, in *Hollywood in the Thirties,* pp. 50-69, echoes many of my observations in the following paragraphs, which are drawn from my own viewing of Warner Brothers thirties films. See also Russell Campbell, "Warner Brothers in the Thirties: Some Tentative Notes," *Velvet Light Trap,* No. 1 (June 1971), 2-4.

15. See, for example, any of the older standard film histories, such as Paul Rotha and Richard Griffith, *The Film Till Now* (New York: Funk and Wagnalls, 1949); Lewis Jacobs, *The Rise of the American Film* (New York: Harcourt, Brace, 1939); Arthur Knight, *The Liveliest Art* (New York: New American Library, 1957).

16. See François Truffaut, "Un Certain tendance du cinéma français," *Cahiers du cinéma,* No. 31 (January 1954), 15-29; and André Bazin, "De la politique des Auteurs," *Cahiers du cinéma,* No. 70 (April 1957), 2-11.

17. Andrew Tudor, *Theories of Film* (New York: Viking Press, 1974), p. 123.

18. Ibid., p. 130.

19. Andrew Sarris, "Notes on the Auteur Theory in 1962," *Film Culture,* No. 27 (Winter 1962-63), 1-8. Sarris updated his ideas in "Notes on the Auteur Theory in 1970," *Film Comment,* 6 (Fall 1970), 7-9, and in "The Auteur Theory Revisited," *American Film,* 2 (July-August 1977), 49-53.

20. Kael's attack on Sarris, "Circles and Squares: Joys and Sarris," is reprinted in her collection of articles, *I Lost It at the Movies* (New York: Bantam Books, 1966), pp. 264-88. It first appeared in *Film Quarterly,* 16 (Spring 1963), 12-16. Sarris' reply, "Auteur Theory and the Perils of Pauline," appeared in *Film Quarterly,* 16 (Summer 1963), 26-33. See also Ian Cameron et al., "*Movie* vs. Kael," *Film Quarterly* 17 (Fall 1963), 57-64.

21. See, for example: Phil Hardy, *Samuel Fuller* (New York: Praeger Publishers, 1970); Jim Kitses, *Horizons West: Anthony Mann, Budd Betticher and Sam Peckinpah: Studies of Authorship within the Western* (Bloomington: Indiana University Press, 1970); David Will and Paul Willeman, eds., *Roger Corman,* Edinburgh Film Festival '70 in association with *Cinema* Magazine (Edinburgh, 1970). Each of these works argues that although the director may not write his scripts, his interpretation of them in visual and dramatic form enables one to identify them as his distinctive work.

22. F. Anthony Macklin, "Interview with Andrew Sarris," *Film Heritage,* 8 (Summer 1973), 26-36.

23. Michael Curtiz, "Hollywood Is a Fertile Field for Creativeness and Ingenuity," *PIC,* April 1947, pp. 76-77, 108.

24. Tudor, p. 131.

25. For studies of writers see: Richard Corliss, *Talking Pictures* (New York: Penguin Books, 1975).
    For studies of cameramen see: Charles Higham, *Hollywood Cameramen* (Bloomington: Indiana University Press, 1970); Richard Koszarski, "The Men with the Movie Cameras: 60 Filmographies," *Film Comment,* 8 (Summer 1972), 27-57.
    For a study of editors see: Win Sharples, Jr. et al., "Prime Cut: 75 Editors' Filmographies and Supporting Material," *Film Comment,* 13 (March-April 1977), 6-29.
    For studies of genres see: John Cawelti, *The Six-Gun Mystique* (Bowling Green, Ohio: Bowling Green University Popular Press, 1971); Stuart Kaminsky, *American Film Genres: Approaches to a Critical Theory of Popular Film* (Dayton, Ohio: Pflaum Publishing, 1974);

Kitses, *Horizons West;* Colin McArthur, *Underworld U.S.A.* (New York: Viking Press, 1972); Leland Poague, "The Problem of Film Genre: A Mentalistic Approach," MS; Douglas Pye, "Genre and Movies," *Movie,* No. 20, (Spring 1975), pp. 29-43; Stanley Solomon, *Beyond Formula: American Film Genres* (New York: Harcourt, Brace, Jovanovich, 1976); Tudor, *Theories of Film;* Peter Wollen, *Signs and Meaning in the Cinema* (Bloomington: Indiana University Press, 1969); Robin Wood, "Ideology, Genre, Auteur," *Film Comment,* 13 (January-February 1977), 46-51.

For a study of the actor's ability to shape his films to suit his personality, see: Patrick McGilligan, "James Cagney: The Actor as Auteur," *Velvet Light Trap,* No. 7 (Winter 1972-73), 3-15.

26. Tudor, p. 131.

27. All biographical information in the following pages is drawn primarily from: Jack Edmund Nolan, "Michael Curtiz," *Films in Review,* 21 (November 1970), 525-48; Whittemore and Cecchettini, pp. 189-99; Pete Martin, "Hollywood's Champion Language Assassin," *Saturday Evening Post,* 220 (August 2, 1947), 22-23, 58, 63, 64, 66; supplemented by newspaper and magazine clippings in the Curtiz file at the Lincoln Center Branch of the New York Public Library (hereafter referred to as "Curtiz file"). See also István Nemeskurty, *Word and Image: History of the Hungarian Cinema,* trans. Zsuzsanna Horn (Budapest: Corvina Press, 1968). Curtiz himself wrote, or at least signed, two articles in English, one in *PIC,* previously cited, and "Talent Shortage Is Causing Two Year Production Delay," *Films and Filming,* 2 (June 1956), 9.

28. See Jack Warner, with Dean Jennings, *My First Hundred Years in Hollywood* (New York: Random House, 1964), pp. 275-76, for a brief account of Curtiz's successful efforts to get his parents out of Europe in 1938, before the Nazis could catch them.

29. This confusion continued throughout his life and when he died the *New York Times* obituary (April 12, 1962, 35:1) printed the latter story; the *New York Herald-Tribune* obituary (April 12, 1962, 12:2) repeated the former.

30. Ironically, Lily Damita later married Curtiz's first American "discovery," Errol Flynn.

31. As I have said, we do not know precisely how many films Curtiz made in Europe, nor how many of them still exist. Furthermore, as far as I have been able to discover, none of the European films is available for study in the U.S., although the George Eastman House in Rochester does have a print of *Atlantis.* The British Film Institute in London has prints of: *Wege des Schrekens* (Austria—1922), *Die Slavenkoenigin* (Austria—1924, known in U.S. as *Moon of Israel*), *Fiaker Nr. 13* (Austria—1926), *Die goldene Schmetterling* (Austria—1926). However, when I visited the institute, only the first two were available for screening and study.

32. Nolan quotes Curtiz as saying, after becoming production head of Phoenix Films, "An actor's success is no more than the success of the director, whose concept of the whole brings into harmony the portrayal of each character." See Nolan, p. 527.

33. For a revealing and well written account of the making of one of these films, *Sodom and Gomorrah* (Austria—1922), see Richard Berczeller, "Sodom and Gomorrah," *New Yorker,* 50 (October 14, 1974), 48-54.

34. Warner, p. 160.

35. Ibid., p. 10. The Curtiz file has articles with further details about this matter.

36. Pete Martin, pp. 22-23.

37. Again, see the Curtiz file and Martin's article for various accounts of the origin of these phrases.

38. David Niven, *Bring on the Empty Horses* (New York: Dell Publishing, 1976). In the 1945 Western, *San Antonio,* the studio played a private joke on Curtiz by having actor S.Z. Sakall point to a herd of wild horses and say, "Look, empty horses."

39. Nolan, p. 533.

40. Warner, p. 206. For other reminiscences about Curtiz, see James Cagney, *Cagney by Cagney* (New York: Pocket Books, 1977); Errol Flynn, *My Wicked Wicked Ways* (New York: Berkeley Publishing Corp., 1974); Karyn Kay and Gerald Peary, "Talking to Pat O'Brien," *Velvet Light Trap,* No. 15 (Fall 1975), 29-32.

41. Among the articles in the Curtiz file, see especially Mary Morris, "Mary Morris Meets Movie Maker Michael Curtiz," *PM,* Sept. 17, 1944, pp. M12-M13.

42. Canham, p. 15. See also the comments by Curtiz in Warner, passim, and Charles Higham, *Warner Brothers: A History of the Studio: Its Pictures, Stars, and Personalities* (New York: Charles Scribner's Sons, 1975) (hereafter referred to as *Warners*).

43. Tom Flinn, "Interview with William Dieterle: the Plutarch of Hollywood," *Velvet Light Trap,* No. 15 (Fall 1975), 27.

44. Whittemore and Cecchetini, p. 195. They suggest that he took over the direction of *The Adventures of Robin Hood* because "Curtiz, acknowledged to be the foremost director at Warner and accustomed to receiving all the best scripts, thought he should have been given *Robin Hood* from the start. His prestige gave him the power to persuade Jack Warner to make the change" (p. 195).

45. John Davis, *"Captain Blood," Velvet Light Trap,* No. 1 (June 1971), 28-29.

46. Howard Koch, *Casablanca: Script and Legend* (Woodstock, New York: Overlook Press, 1973), pp. 24-25. For a complete discussion of this incident, see the chapter on *Casablanca.*

47. The film itself won an Oscar for "best picture."

48. See note 25 for a list of recent books and articles on film genres.

49. Tudor, pp. 131-35.

50. Ibid., p. 138.

51. Ibid., p. 139.

52. Ibid., p. 145.

53. Stanley Solomon, *Beyond Formula: American Film Genres* (New York: Harcourt Brace Jovanovich, Inc, 1976), p. 3.

54. Ibid., p. 3.

55. Ibid., pp. 3-4.

56. Ibid., p. 5.

57. Wood, p. 47.

58. Ibid.

59. The books by Solomon and Kaminsky cited above, which are surveys of a broad range of genres, do not even mention the swashbuckler.

60. Quoted in Pete Martin, p. 66.

Chapter 1

1. Stuart Kaminsky, *American Film Genres* (Dayton, Ohio: Pflaum Publishing, 1974).

2. Stanley Solomon, *Beyond Formula* (New York: Harcourt Brace Jovanovich, 1976).

3. John Cawelti, *Adventure, Mystery and Romance: Formula Stories as Art and Popular Culture* (Chicago: University of Chicago Press, 1976).

4. James Robert Parish and Don E. Stanke, *The Swashbucklers* (New Rochelle, N.Y.: Arlington House Publishers, 1976).

5. Tony Thomas, *Cads and Cavaliers: The Film Adventurers* (South Brunswick, N.J.: A.S. Barnes, 1973).

6. Tony Thomas, *The Great Adventure Films* (Secaucus, N.J.: Citadel Press, 1976).

7. Ian Cameron, *Adventure in the Movies* (New York: Crescent Books, 1974); published in England as *Adventure and the Cinema* (London: Studio Vista, 1973).

8. Gordon Gow's article "The Swashbucklers" (*Films and Filming*, 18 [January 1972], 34-40) tries a similar survey in far fewer pages and is therefore even sketchier. Other works touching on the genre include: Rudolf Arnheim, "Epic and Dramatic Film" *Film Culture*, 3, No. 1 (1957), 9-10; Raymond Durgnat, "Epic," *Films and Filming*, 10 December 1963), 9-12; John Peter Dyer, "Some Mighty Spectacles," *Films and Filming*, 4 (February 1958), 13-15, 34; William K. Everson, "Film Spectacles—Are Both a Genre of Their Own and a Help to Other Kinds of Pictures," *Films in Review*, 5 (November 1954), 459-71; William K. Everson, *The Bad Guys* (New York: Citadel Press, 1964); Kevin Gough-Yates, "The Hero," *Films and Filming*, 12 (December 1965), 11-16, continued in vol. 12 (January 1966), 11-16, 12 (February 1966), 25-30, 12 (March 1966), 25-30; Gough-Yates, "The Heroine," *Films and Filming*, 12 (May 1966), 23-27, continued in 12 (June 1966), 27-32, 12 (July 1966), 38-43, 12 (August 1966), 45-50; David Robinson, "Spectacle," *Sight and Sound*, 25 (Summer 1966), 22-26, 55-56; Richard Whitehall, "Days of Strife and Nights of Orgy: The Roman Spectaculars," *Films and Filming*, 9 (March 1963), 8-14.

9. Jeffrey Richards, "The Swashbuckling Revival," *Focus on Film*, No. 27 (Summer 1977), 7-29. (Hereafter referred to as "Swashbuckling.")

10. Jeffrey Richards, *Swordsmen of the Screen* (London: Routledge and Kegan Paul, 1977). (Hereafter referred to as *Swordsmen*.)

11. For discussions of these critical tendencies, see Northrop Frye, *The Secular Scripture* (Cambridge, Mass.: Harvard University Press, 1976), especially Chapter 1; and Paul Zweig, *The Adventurer* (New York: Basic Books, 1974), especially pp. 3-18.

12. Richards, in "Swashbuckling," p. 10, makes this point, but William Meyer believes there "is no doubt that the Hungarian [Curtiz] is to the swashbuckler what John Ford is to the Western." (See Meyer, p. 83.)

13. See any of the studies of the western cited in the introduction. But also see Cawelti's *Adventure, Mystery and Romance*, Chapter 1, which discusses both the appeal and difficulty of asserting relationships between popular culture and social history.

14. See especially Andrew Bergman, *We're in the Money: Depression America and its Films* (New York: New York University Press, 1971).

15. Richards, "Swashbuckling," pp. 9, 19.

16. Richards, *Swordsmen*, p. 3.

17. Edward Connor, "Swashbucklers on the Screen," preface to Parish and Stanke, *The Swashbucklers*, p. 16.

18. Richards, "Swashbuckling," p. 13.

19. Ibid.

20. Ibid.

21. See Lion Feuchtwanger, *The House of Desdemona: The Laurels and Limitations of Historical Fiction*, trans. Harold Basilius (Detroit: Wayne State University Press, 1963), pp. 44-64.

22. Ibid., pp. 30-44.

23. Richards, "Swashbuckling," pp. 12-13.

24. Ibid.

25. See Frank Rahill, "The Cape and Sword Hero," in *The World of Melodrama* (University Park: Pennsylvania State University Press, 1967), pp. 75-84, for a concise history of the genre and its relation to later films. Another useful history of early melodrama is: David Grimstead, *Melodrama Unveiled: American Theater and Culture. 1800-1850* (Chicago: University of Chicago Press, 1968).

26. See John Belton, "Souls made Great by Adversity," *Focus,* No. 9 (Spring 1973), 16. Raymond Durgnat has also theorized about film and literary melodrama in "Ways of Melodrama," *Sight and Sound,* 2 (August-September 1951), 34-40.

27. Peter Brooks, "The Aesthetics of Astonishment," *Georgia Review,* No. 30 (Fall 1976), 628-29. Two other important articles by Brooks on melodrama are: "The Text of Muteness," *New Literary History,* 5 (Spring 1974), 549-64, and "Romantic Antipastoral and Urban Allegories," *Yale Review,* 64 (Autumn 1974), 11-26. All three appear, in somewhat altered form, in *The Melodramatic Imagination* (New Haven: Yale University Press, 1976). Another useful approach to melodrama is found in Earl F. Bargainnier, "Melodrama as Formula," *Journal of Popular Culture,* 9 (Winter 1975), 726-33.

28. Robert B. Heilman, "Fashions in Melodrama," *Western Humanities Review* 13 (Winter 1959), 3.

29. John Fell discusses this in "Darling, This Is Bigger than Both of Us," *Cinema Journal,* 12 (Spring 1973), 58.

30. Richards, "Swashbuckling," p. 9.

31. Richards, *Swordsmen*, p. 3.

32. Much of Northrop Frye's *A Natural Perspective: The Development of Shakespearean Comedy and Romance* (New York: Harcourt, Brace and World, 1965) deals with this issue of dramatic convention and the audience's expected familiarity with the conventions.

33. Richrd Whitehall has also suggested this comparison. See Whitehall, p. 9.

34. Richards, "Swashbuckling," pp. 18-19.

35. Thomas Agabiti, "Samuel Fuller's 'Run of the Arrow' and the Mythos of Romance: An Archetypal Analysis," *Film Reader,* 2 (January 1977), p. 98.

36.   Agabiti also specifically cites *Captain Blood* as an example of a pirate movie "in the romance category" (p. 98).

37.   See Northrop Frye, *Anatomy of Criticism* (Princeton: Princeton University Press, 1957), pp. 186-206, and *The Secular Scripture* (Cambridge: Harvard University Press, 1976), esp. pp. 49-54.

38.   Frye, *Anatomy*, p. 187.

39.   Ibid., p. 163. See also *A Natural Perspective* (hereafter referred to as *Perspective*), pp. 72-73, and "The Argument of Comedy," *English Institute Essays* (New York: Columbia University Press, 1949), pp. 58-73.

40.   Frye, *The Secular Scripture* (hereafter cited as *Scripture*), p. 171. See also Fredric Jameson's similar comparison of comedy and romance in "Magical Narratives: Romance as Genre," *New Literary History*, 7 (Fall 1975), pp. 135-67, esp. p. 153.

41.   Frye, *Anatomy*, p. 163.

42.   Other than contemporary reviews of his books, almost nothing has been written about Sabatini, but see: A. St. John Adcock, *The Glory that Was Grub Street* (New York: Fred A. Stokes, 1928), pp. 283-286; Robert Birkmyre, "R.S.," *Bookman*, 46 (June 1914), 111-112; Brad Darrach, "Rapier Envy, Anyone?" *Time*, 108 (August 9, 1976), 70-73.

43.   For details about the 1924 version of *Captain Blood*, see John Davis, "*Captain Blood,*" *Velvet Light Trap*, No. 1 (June 1971), 27; and Richards, *Swordsmen*, pp. 251-52.

44.   See Davis, "*Captain Blood,*" p. 27, for further information about this cycle, as well as speculations about why it appeared in the mid thirties.

45.   Some sources, such as Canham, p. 17, cite Donat's poor health as his reason for rejecting the role, but Jack Warner himself, in his autobiography, claims it was a salary dispute. See Warner, p. 234.

46.   See John Davis, "*Captain Blood,*" pp. 28-31, for further details on the film's production history.

47.   Frye, *Scripture*, p. 54.

48.   Ibid., p. 104.

49.   Ibid., p. 148.

50.   John Davis, "*Captain Blood,*" p. 26.

51.   Paul Zweig, *The Adventurer* (New York: Basic Books, 1974), pp. 32, 34, 35-36, 40.

52.   Ibid., p. 48.

53.   Throughout this work, unless otherwise noted, all dialogue is quoted directly from the films' soundtrack, and not from printed scripts.

54.   See Maurice Willson Disher, *Blood and Thunder: Midvictorian Melodrama and Its Origins* (London: Frederick Muller, Ltd., 1949), pp. 120-25, and Rahill, pp. 146-51, for concise histories of the bandit-hero in popular literature and drama.

55.   See John Davis, "*Captain Blood,*" pp. 27, 30, and John Davis, "Notes on Warner Brothers Foreign Policy: 1918-1948," *Velvet Light Trap*, No. 4 (Spring 1972), 26-28.

56.   Richards, "Swordsmen," p. 256.

57. In "The Swashbuckling Revival," Richards points out that swashbuckling villains are usually "the dark side of the mirror . . . [they] embody some of the same qualities as the hero: courage, resourcefulness, swordsmanship. But they are fatally flowed by ambition, greed, or simply *hubris*" (pp. 10-11).

58. Zweig, pp. 61-80 (Chapter 5, "The Flight from Women").

59. See Davis, "*Captain Blood*," p. 31, for a brief discussion of the film's music and sound effects.

60. Davis, "*Captain Blood*," p. 28.

61. Ibid.

62. See ibid., p. 30, for a concise discussion of Blood's "fatalism."

63. Katherine Hume discusses this idea in "Romance: A Perdurable Pattern," *College English*, 36 (October 1974), 129-46, esp. p. 145.

Chapter 2

1. For brief histories of Robin Hood's literary career, see Maurice Keen, *The Outlaws of Medieval Legend* (London: Routledge and Kegan Paul, 1961); Rudy Behlmer, "Robin Hood on the Screen," *Films in Review*, 16 (February 1965), 91-92; and Jeffrey Richards, *Swordsmen*, pp. 187-91.

2. See Behlmer, pp. 92-93, and Richards, *Swordsmen*, pp. 191-94, for brief discussions of early Robin Hood films.

3. This opinion is shared by many, including Richards. See *Swordsmen*, p. 196.

4. Behlmer, p. 98.

5. For additional, if less relevant, production details, including a list of the tableware and furnishings used in the Nottingham feast scene, see Charles Higham, *Warner Brothers: A History of the Studio* (New York: Charles Scribner's Sons, 1975), pp. 123-26. See also Richards, *Swordsmen*, pp. 196-97.

6. This opinion is shared by Whittemore and Cecchetini, p. 195, and by Ina Rae Hark, "The Visual Politics of *The Adventures of Robin Hood*," Journal of Popular Film, 5 (Winter 1976), 16-17.

7. Ironically, although Hark mentions the film's "cinematic consistency," much of her article discusses the visual contrasts between the forest and court scenes; see especially pp. 11-13, which mention camera movement. Hark is obviously unfamiliar with Curtiz's other films, or at least has not noticed their own stylistic consistency.

8. Frye, *Anatomy*, p. 182.

9. Ibid.

10. Frye, "The Argument of Comedy," *English Institute Essays* (New York: Columbia University Press, 1949), p. 71.

11. Jeffrey Richards, for example, says the film has the "strongly plotted narrative line" the Fairbanks version lacks. See *Swordsmen*, p. 196.

12. Ibid.

13. Hark, p. 13.

14. Ibid.

15. Richards, *Swordsmen*, p. 194.

16. Hark, p. 16.

17. Peter Brooks, "The Aesthetics of Astonishment," *Georgia Review*, No. 30 (Fall, 1976), pp. 629-30.

18. It turns out to be merely hanging.

19. Hark, p. 10.

20. Ernest Callenbach, "Comparative Anatomy of Folk Myth Films: *Robin Hood* and *Antonio Das Mortes*," *Film Quarterly*, 23 (Winter 1969-70), 43.

21. Hark, p. 7.

22. Ibid.

23. Callenbach, p. 44.

24. Hark, p. 6.

25. Jack Edmund Nolan calls the film "*Romeo and Juliet* in Sherwood Forest, including a balcony scene." See "Michael Curtiz," *Films in Review*, 21 (November 1970), 544.

26. Callenbach, p. 42.

27. Hark, p. 9.

28. Hark, pp. 8-9.

29. Hark, p. 9.

30. Not above borrowing from himself, Curtiz used this image to end the battle between Blood and the French at the end of *Captain Blood*. He used it again, nearly twenty years later, to indicate the end of a battle in *The Vagabond King* (1956).

Chapter 3

1. Originally a screen writer, Daves later became a director; his first feature, *Destination Tokyo*, was produced by Warners in 1943.

2. Koch later co-wrote *Casablanca* for Curtiz with Philip and Julius Epstein.

3. Miller had co-authored *The Adventures of Robin Hood* with Norman Reilley Raine.

4. Tony Thomas, *The Great Adventure Films* (Secaucus, N.J.: Citadel Press, 1976), p. 106. See also Richards, *Swordsmen*, pp. 237-38.

5. See the next chapter for a discussion of this film.

6. Charles Higham, *Warner Brothers: A History of the Studio: Its Pictures, Stars and Personalities* (New York: Charles Scribner's Sons, 1975), pp. 127-28. For further information on *The Sea Hawk*'s production history, see Richards, *Swordsmen*, pp. 240-41, and Thomas, *The Great Adventure Films*, pp. 106-8.

7. Thomas, p. 108.

8. Ibid. This cut version is the one now generally available and, unfortunately, the only one I have been able to see.

9.   Jean-Loup Bourget, "Social Implications in the Hollywood Genres," *Journal of Modern Literature*, 3 (April 1973), 198-99.

10. John Davis, *"Captain Blood," Velvet Light Trap*, No. 1 (June 1971), p. 27.

11. Richards, "Swashbucklers," p. 11.

12. Ibid., p. 18.

13. Ibid.

14. Even Northrop Frye, who generally favors apolitical criticism, talks of the inherently "revolutionary quality of romance." See *The Secular Scripture*, especially pages 23-25, 139-40, 163-65.

15. John Davis refers several times to Blood's anarchism. See *"Captain Blood,"* p. 30. Although Richards claims that Blood's anger is directed at only one man, King James II, he does note that Blood preys on all ships, while the 1924 version's Blood attacked only Spanish ships. See *Swordsmen*, pp. 252-53.

16. Callenbach, p. 42.

17. Richards, "Swashbucklers," p. 12.

18. Hark, p. 13.

19. See John Davis, "Notes on Warner Brothers Foreign Policy," passim; Andrew Bergman, passim; Hark, pp. 3-6, and Jack Warner, passim. Warner Brothers films are rather open in their propagandistic intent. Perhaps the most famous instance is Busby Berkely's "Shanghai Lil" number in *Footlight Parade* (1933), in which dancers form themselves into huge portraits of FDR and the NRA eagle. In 1942 Warners produced *Mission to Moscow* (directed by Curtiz) at FDR's request, according to Warner, as a plea for better relations with Russia, our ally against the Axis.

20. Davis, *"Captain Blood,"* p. 30.

21. Hark, p. 4.

22. Ibid., p. 6.

23. Tony Thomas, p. 108.

24. Richards, *Swordsmen*, p. 5.

25. Ina Hark talks about Robin's fitness for leadership in terms that are equally applicable to Blood and Thorpe. See pp. 9-10 and 14-15 of her article.

26. Curtiz emphasizes the price they pay for their faith in him with a close shot of a sailor wincing under the lash.

27. The patriotic Thorpe is perhaps the most "American" of our heroes, the capitalist privateer who enriches his country while enriching himself.

28. Callenbach discusses this idea as it applies to *The Adventures of Robin Hood*. See his article, pp. 43-44.

29. For a related but somewhat different psychological interpretation of romance literature, see Hume, "Romance: A Perdurable Pattern," pp. 129-46.

30. Callenbach, p. 43.

31. He is thus related to the traditional blocking characters of comedy. Frederic Jameson points out the Oedipal implications of these figures in "Magical Narratives: Romance as Genre," *New Literary History*, 7 (Fall, 1975), 153.

32. For an engaging history of movie villains, including the characters played by Rathbone and Daniell in Curtiz's films, see William K. Everson, *The Bad Guys* (New York: Citadel Press, 1964).

33. Perhaps, then, Elizabeth is the benevolent father-figure. At any rate, she later comments on her rough ways with men, telling Maria, "I daresay each of us must choose between loving a man or ruling him. I choose to rule. I don't quarrel with your choice, Maria. You have your song and I have my scepter." The phallic implication here is typical of the script's subtle wit.

34. The woman-shy hero is, of course, a well-established variation of the typical hero, appearing in films at least as early as the 1924 *Robin Hood* and probably earlier. In *Robin Hood* the hero is so terrified of a group of eager ladies that he falls into a moat; later King Richard ties him to a stake and promises a gift to the one who wins him.

35. See John Baxter, *Hollywood in the Thirties* (New York: A.S. Barnes, 1968), p. 52.

36. Richards, *Swordsmen*, p. 240.

37. He reminds us, of course, of the similar figure in *Captain Blood* who kept time for the slaves walking the water wheel.

38. Richards, *Swordsmen*, p. 438.

39. Ibid., p. 238.

40. Hark, p. 7.

41. Martha is played by Una O'Connor, who also played Emma.

42. Richards rightly notes that these orders are pure nonsense. See *Swordsmen*, p. 240.

43. Music is one of any film's most effective means of manipulating audience emotion, but the music in *The Sea Hawk* is especially important. Erich Wolfgang Korngold, who wrote the scores for all three films, thought of his movie music as operas without words, and composed individual melodies for every major character and situation. For information about his working methods and assessments of his contributions to the Curtiz swashbucklers, see: Rudy Behlmer, "Erich Wolfgang Korngold: Established Some of the Filmmusic Basics Film Composers Now Ignore," *Films in Review*, 18 (February 1967), 86-100; Alan Cleave, "Record Review: *The Sea Hawk*," *Moviemaker*, No. 7 (May 1973), p. 328; Peter G. Davis, "Lights, Action, Korngold," *New York Times*, March 24, 1974, II, 26:3; Charles Higham, *Warner Brothers*, pp. 119-20, 125-26; James R. Silke, *Here's Looking at You, Kid* (Boston: Little, Brown & Company, 1976), pp. 146-51; Tony Thomas, *Music for the Movies* (South Brunswick and New York: A.S. Barnes, 1973), pp. 124-40. Warner Brothers' other major composer during the thirties and forties was Max Steiner, who wrote the music for many Curtiz films, including *Casablanca, Passage to Marseille*, and *Mildred Pierce*, discussed in later chapters. For discussions of Steiner's work see Thomas, pp. 107-23, and Steiner's own article in *We Make the Movies*, ed. Nancy Naumburg (New York: W.W. Norton and Company, 1937), pp. 216-38.

44. If occasionally the good guys lose a battle, as in *The Sea Hawk's* Panama sequence, we know it is only a temporary setback.

45. Curtiz's heroes all have lines minimizing or justifying their acts of violence. Peter Blood claims to have killed "as few as possible," Robin only "those that deserved it, the cruel and unjust," Thorpe only those who would enslave England.

46. See Ian Cameron, *Adventure in the Movies*, p. 89, and Richards, "Swashbuckler," pp. 9 and 19. Cameron compares battle scenes to dance numbers in musicals.

47. John Davis discusses Curtiz's working methods for *Captain Blood*'s battle scenes in his article "*Captain Blood*," pp. 30-31.

48. Compare this with the battle scenes in *Hercules* (1959, directed by Pietro Francisci) and the other Italian pseudo-swashbucklers of the early sixties. Their violence seems absurd or repulsive or both because, without the serious intent and deliberately demythologizing context of later films like *Mash* and *The Wild Bunch*, they revel in screams, bloody faces, and battered corpses. For a useful appraisal of these films, see Richard Whitehall, "Days of Strife and Nights of Orgy," *Films and Filming*, 9 (March 1963), 8-14.

49. Many shots used in the battle montages of both *The Sea Hawk* and *Captain Blood* are stock sea fight footage. Others, first shot for *Captain Blood*, appear again in *The Sea Hawk*. One of them, a mast crashing diagonally across the screen, actually appears twice in *Captain Blood*'s climactic battle; the second time it is "flipped" to reverse the angle of the mast's direction.

50. Richards, "Swashbucklers," p. 9. Throughout his book, *Swordsmen of the Screen*, Richards comments extensively on the duels appearing in each of the films he discusses. See pp. 237-41 for *The Sea Hawk*, pp. 252-56 for *Captain Blood*, and pp. 196-200 for *The Adventures of Robin Hood*. For a more compact and equally valuable discussion of film dueling, see Rudy Behlmer, "Swordplay on the Screen," *Films in Review*, 16 (June-July 1965), 362-75. (Behlmer concentrates on the Curtiz-Flynn films on pp. 366-67.) Behlmer details the job of the fencing master, who works with the director in conceiving and choreographing each swordfight routine, and coaches (and sometimes doubles for) the actors involved in them. The fencing master for the three Curtiz swashbucklers was Fred Cavens who, along with Ralph Faulkner, was Hollywood's leading fencing director in the thirties and forties. Behlmer also explains that some shooting scripts are quite spare in their description of a duel scene, while others go into lengthy detail which is often changed when the film is actually shot. He cites Curtiz's *The Sea Hawk* as an example of the latter.

51. John Davis, among others, retells the well-known story of Curtiz in his passion for realism removing the protective tips from the actors' swords during the shooting of this duel. See "*Captain Blood*," p. 29.

52. Behlmer remarks the Curtiz "loved to use scenery and props to increase the theatricality and violence of his duels." In *The Adventures of Robin Hood* "hero and villain fought their way down a winding staircase, upset a giant candelabra, locked blades over a heavy table, slashed candles, etc." See "Swordplay on the Screen," p. 366.

Chapter 4

1. Flynn had risen to stardom in *Captain Blood*, and between 1935 and 1941 Curtiz directed ten of his sixteen films. However, their mutual dislike grew throughout this period until 1941 when the direction of *They Died with Their Boots On* was reassigned to Raoul Walsh.

2. For notes on the production of *The Charge of the Light Brigade* see Higham, *Warner Brothers*, pp. 121-23, and Parish and Stanke, *The Swashbucklers*, pp. 276-78.

3. John Davis, "Notes on Warner Brothers Foreign Policy," *Velvet Light Trap*, No. 4 (Spring 1972), p. 27.

4. Jeffrey Richards writes about *The Charge of the Light Brigade* in *Visions of Yesterday* (London: Routledge and Kegan Paul, 1973), passim.

5. Jeffrey Richards, "Swashbuckling," p. 18.

6. Ibid.

7. Ibid., p. 19.

8. Solomon, p. 16. Other studies of the western usually discuss this central theme.

9. David Morse, "Under Western Eyes: Variations on a Genre," in Whittemore and Cecchettini, p. 203.

10. Ibid.

11. Morse, pp. 203-204.

12. Ibid., p. 204.

13. Ibid.

14. Both Morse (pp. 206-8) and Solomon (pp. 26-29) correctly point out the often unnoticed connection between the outlaw villains of the rural western and the gangster villains of the urban crime film. Morse says that Surret can be seen as a "gangster boss" whose saloon, with "its alcohol, gambling and girls reflects the stranglehold which organised crime achieved over speakeasies and illegal liquor sales, prostitution and the numbers racket" (p. 207). Surret has a hired hit man, Yancy; uses violence to build his empire; and flees town when the "heat is on."

15. See Solomon, pp. 12-29, and Robert Warshow, "Movie Chronicle: The Westerner," *The Immediate Experience* (New York: Atheneum, 1971), pp. 135-54.

16. *Virginia City*, as we will see, also deals with reconciling North and South. We saw how *The Sea Hawk*'s political content indicated the studio's awareness of the external dangers facing America in 1940. Although I have no evidence other than the films' content, I would speculate that the emphasis on national unity in *Virginia City* and *Santa Fe Trail*, both also released in 1940, reflect the studio's attempt to rally the country in the face of these dangers. Davis' article on Warner Brothers' foreign policy, cited earlier, shows how the studio inserted political propaganda in its films, but it does not discuss these two westerns.

17. Linda Pepper and John Davis, "John Brown's Body Lies A'Rolling in his Grave," *Velvet Light Trap*, No. 8 (1973), pp. 14-19. Pepper and Davis point out that the three Curtiz-Flynn westerns I am talking of here were all written by Virginian Robert Buckner, whose scripts reveal his unmistakable sectional bias.

18. Pepper and Davis, p. 17.

19. Ibid.

20. Canham, p. 22.

21. Pepper and Davis, p. 17.

22. Ibid., p. 19.

23. Canham, p. 25.

24. Parish and Stanke report that Bogart's dislike for both Flynn and Scott caused difficulties during *Virginia City*'s production. See *The Swashbucklers*, p. 291.

25. For comments on the film's lack of historicity, see John Peter Dyer, "From Boadicea to Bette Davis," *Films and Filming*, 5 (January 1959), pp. 13-15, 32, and James Morgan, "Coronation U.S.A.," *Sight and Sound*, 23 (July-September 1953), 43-46.

26. I noted, in the last chapter, that many of the same sets and costumes were used the following year for *The Sea Hawk*. See Parish and Stanke, pp. 290-92, and Richards, *Swordsmen*, pp. 237-38.

27. Daniell also played the villain, Wolfingham, in *The Sea Hawk*. On the other hand, the somewhat unusual roles taken by Alan Hale and Olivia de Havilland suggest this film is different from the swashbucklers. Hale is Flynn's enemy, rather than his sidekick; de Havilland plays the minor role of Penelope, a lady-in-waiting who loves but is rejected by Essex.

28. Parish and Stanke (p. 290) explain that the film's title was designed to satisfy Flynn's desire for equal billing. I do not know when or if the film was officially renamed, but I have seen prints with Anderson's original title.

29. Ina Rae Hark, p. 9.

30. While both *Casablanca* and *The Private Lives of Elizabeth and Essex* involve this conflict, the specific kind of politics in one is the reverse of the other. *The Private Lives of Elizabeth and Essex*, made in 1939, reflects America's prewar isolationism. Elizabeth thinks Essex would be a bad king because he would drag England into a costly, bloody, unnecessary war. *Casablanca*, made in 1942, is clearly an anti-isolationist fable. In fact, the nation's mood had changed enough by 1940 so that *The Sea Hawk*, made then, presents another Elizabeth who comes to learn the dangers of isolationism. John Davis discusses this further in "Notes on Warner Brothers Foreign Policy," cited earlier.

Chapter 5

1. *Casablanca*'s release date is sometimes given as 1943. Actually, it premiered in November, 1942, but went into general release in early 1943. The confusion comes from its being eligible for and winning the Academy Award as Best Picture of 1943. The award itself was presented in 1944.

2. The other awards were for Best Picture and Best Screenplay. Curtiz's short, *Sons of Liberty* (1939) won the Best Short Subject award for that year, but Curtiz himself did not get any award.

3. *Casablanca*'s production history is described by Howard Koch (co-author of the screenplay) in "The Making of Casablanca," *Casablanca: Script and Legend*, ed. Koch (Woodstock, N.Y.: Overlook Press, 1973), pp. 17-27, from which most of the above paragraph is taken. Additional information can be found in Richard Schickel, "Some Nights in *Casablanca*," in *Favorite Movies: Critics Choice*, ed. Philip Nobile (New York: Macmillan, 1973), pp. 114-25, and in Ronald Haver, "Finally, the Truth about *Casablanca*," *American Film*, 1 (June 1976), 10-16.

4. Richard Anobile, "Interview with Ingrid Bergman," in *Casablanca*, ed. Richard Anobile (New York: Avon Books, 1974), p. 6.

5. Ronald Haver, pp. 15-16.

6. Koch, p. 17.

7. The worst I have seen is John J. Croft, "*Casablanca* Revisited," *Classic Film Collector*, No. 42 (Spring, 1974), p. 43. On the other hand, although none of the following are particularly scholarly, they each offer useful insights: Arkadin, "Film Clips," *Sight and Sound*, 37 (Autumn 1968), 210-11; Lenny Rubenstein, "*Casablanca*," *Cineaste*, 8 (Summer 1977), 34-35; John Stickney, "Last Word on *Last Tango* and *Casablanca*," *Mademoiselle*, 77 (July 1973), 128-29, 150-51.

8. William Donnely, "Love and Death in *Casablanca*," *Persistence of Vision: A Collection of Film Criticism*, ed. Joseph McBride (Madison: Wisconsin Film Society Press, 1968), pp. 103-7.

9. Donnely, p. 103.

10. Fiedler's pattern of male/male relationships appears often in Howard Hawks' films, whose *To Have and Have Not* will be discussed later. Curtiz's own films, however, usually emphasize erotic male/female relationships. The hero may have a best buddy, but his primary loyalty is usually to the heroine.

11. Both Donnely and Richard Corliss discuss this allegorical theory. See Donnely, pp. 103-4, and Richard Corliss, "Analysis of the Film," in Koch, p. 187.

12. Harvey Greenberg, *The Movies on Your Mind* (New York: Saturday Review Press, 1975), p. 88.

13. Ibid., p. 99.

14. Ibid., p. 94.

15. Ibid., p. 97.

16. Corliss, p. 195.

17. Barry Day, "Casablanca," *Films and Filming*, 20 (August 1974), 21.

18. Schickel, p. 199.

19. Corliss, p. 195.

20. Schickel, p. 123.

21. Michael Wood, *America in the Movies* (New York: Basic Books, 1975), p. 24.

22. Ibid., p. 25.

23. Ibid., p. 28.

24. See Wood, pp. 24-50. Wood himself mentions Rhett as another self-consciously cynical figure, but he doesn't draw the parallel between him and Rick as closely as I have.

25. Barbara Deming, *Running Away from Myself* (New York: Grossman Publishers, 1969), p. 17.

26. Jean-Loup Bourget, "Romantic Dramas of the Forties: An Analysis," *Film Comment*, 10 (January 1974), 48-49.

27. Michael Wood, p. 25.

28. Schickel, p. 125.

29. Corliss, p. 193.

30. Ibid., p. 195.

31. Koch, pp. 24-25. Corliss refers to the flashback as occurring in 1937, apparently assuming that Rick went from running guns in 1935 and fighting in Spain in 1936 directly to Paris and Ilsa. Obviously, this is wrong, since the affair ended the day the Germans entered Paris, in June of 1940. This is a trivial point, but it does show that Rick has not been nursing his emotional wounds for too long a time when Ilsa reappears.

32. Carl remarks that "the leading banker in Amsterdam is now the pastry chef in our kitchen." The original script, published in *Best Film Plays of 1943-1944*, ed. John Gassner and Dudley

Nichols (New York: Crown Publishers, 1945), pp. 631-94, included speeches describing Carl as a mathematics professor from Leipzig and Sascha as the czar's favorite sword-swallower, but these were cut from the final script and do not appear in the two published versions of it (in the previously cited books edited by Koch and Anobile) nor in the film itself. What remains is Abdul, a doorman (Dan Seymour), referring once to Carl as "Professor" and Rick calling Sascha a "crazy Russian." The other changes between original script and actual film provide an object lesson in polishing a script to smooth its trip to the screen. Briefly, in the final version, jokes are changed, lines cut, scenes rearranged or omitted, all with the aim of speeding the pace by eliminating unnecessary detail. Perhaps the most significant change, probably Curtiz's work, moves the final scene from Rick's cafe to the airport, obviously a more expressive locale.

Chapter 6

1. See, for example: Joseph McBride, ed., *Focus on Howard Hawks* (Englewood Cliffs, N.J.: Prentice Hall, Inc., 1972); Andrew Sarris, *The American Cinema* (New York: E.P. Dutton, 1968), pp. 52-56; Donald Willis, *The Films of Howard Hawks* (Metuchen, N.J.: Scarecrow Press, 1975); Peter Wollen, *Signs and Meaning in the Cinema* (Bloomington: Indiana University Press, 1969), pp. 80-94; Robin Wood, *Howard Hawks* (New York: Doubleday, 1968).

2. Ironically, Curtiz directed a "remake" in 1951, *The Breaking Point*, which also claimed to be based on Hemingway's novel. Actually, Curtiz's film differs from Hawks' as much as they both differ from the novel. Don Siegel (who did the montages in *Casablanca*) directed a third version, *The Gun Runners*, in 1956, which did emulate Curtiz's film's plot. Finally, John Huston used the climax of the Curtiz and Siegel films, a shipboard shoot-out, for *Key Largo* (1948). F.M. Laurence discusses this last point in "Death in the Matinee: the Film Endings of Hemingway's Fiction," *Literature/Film Quarterly*, 2 (Winter 1974), 44-51.

3. Robin Wood, "To Have (Written) and Have Not (Directed)," *Film Comment*, 9 (May-June 1973), 33-34; hereafter referred to as "To Have." Even contemporary reviewers, familiar with the studios' habit of imitating successful films, spotted the connection. Bosley Crowther, for example, said: *"To Have and Have Not is Casablanca moved west to the somewhat less hectic Caribbean, but along the same basic parallel. And, although there are surface alterations in some of the characters, you will meet here substantially the same people as in that other geo-political romance."* (See Bosely Crowther, rev. of *To Have and Have Not, New York Times*, October 12, 1944, 24:1).

4. Wood, "To Have," p. 33.

5. Schickel, p. 118.

6. Sarris, *The American Cinema*, p. 55.

7. Wollen, *Signs and Meaning in the Cinema*, p. 82.

8. Wollen, p. 86.

9. Robin Wood, "To Have," p. 35.

10. Ibid., p. 34.

11. Michael Wood, pp. 37-38.

12. Ibid., p. 35.

13. Ibid.

14.   Ibid.

15.   Ibid., p. 33.

16.   Ibid., p. 35.

17.   Ibid., p. 34.

18.   Peter Wollen, among other Hawks critics, notes that Hawks reduces the genres to two, the adventure-melodrama and the "crazy comedies." I would suggest that these two genres are closer than Wollen thinks; that the adventure-melodramas, with their emphasis on the "new society" of the heroic group, its equal, often sparring hero and heroine, are forms of comedy similar to the swashbuckler.

     Molly Haskell, in *From Reverence to Rape* (Baltimore: Penguin Books, 1974), also thinks *To Have and Have Not* superior to *Casablanca*, but for somewhat different reasons. Writing from a feminist perspective, searching for nonsexist films, she applauds Hawks not for his glorification of male camaraderie but for his interest in the "tensions and possibilities of a heterosexual relationship between equals" (p. 25). *To Have and Have Not* concerns a "more important meaning to the idea of involvement...[than commitment to a cause] the involvement of a man with a woman, a scarier and deeper risk of oneself, perhaps than death" (p. 212). For Haskell, *Casablanca* "reaps the conventional glory for an act—rejection—that is easiest" while Morgan's true heroism is accepting "the consequences of heterosexual love" (p. 213). Haskell's insights are a useful and important critique of the traditional view of Hawks. But, like Wood, she ignores the question of dramatic form when comparing *Casablanca* and *To Have and Have Not*. Further, I question whether Slim is the "dazzlingly adult woman" (p. 26) she claims her to be, or simply a very young woman hiding her vulnerability behind a façade of toughness. Her exaggerated sultriness seems almost a parody of the adolescent image of the aggressive female.

19.   Bosley Crowther, for example, considered it ponderous and slow, complaining that it never "escapes from its own mechanical toils." See his review of *Passage to Marseille* in the *New York Times*, February 17, 1944, 12:5.

20.   Michael Wood, p. 26.

Chapter 7

1.   Jack Shadoian, "Michael Curtiz' *20,000 Years in Sing-Sing*," *Journal of Popular Film* 2 (Spring 1973), 172-73.

2.   Ibid., p. 172.

3.   Ibid., p. 176.

4.   Shadoian, passim. See also John Baxter, *Hollywood in the Thirties*, p. 53, and Charles Higham, *Warner Brothers*, p. 96.

5.   Andrew Bergman's *We're in the Money* (New York: New York University Press, 1971) talks about this. See especially pp. 152-53, 160-61 on *Angels with Dirty Faces*.

6.   Child actors Billy Halop, Leo Gorcey, Gabriel Dell, Huntz Hall, Bernard Punsley, and Bobby Jordan were called the Dead End Kids because their first film appearance was in *Dead End* (1937), William Wyler's screen version of Sidney Kingsley's stage success. The group made several other dramatic films together (including *Angels Wash Their Faces*, 1939, directed by Ray Enright) and, after personnel and name changes, became a comedy group and appeared in a long series of comedies as the Bowery Boys.

7. Stephen Louis Karpf, *The Gangster Film: Emergence, Variation and Decay of a Genre, 1930-1940* (New York: Arno Press, 1973), p. 126.

8. Coincidentally, Bancroft starred as Bull Weed in one of the very first gangster films, Von Sternberg's *Underworld* (1926).

9. Colin MacArthur argues this same point. See *Underworld U.S.A.* (New York: Viking Press, 1972), p. 39.

10. David Thomson views the ending in a similar fashion. See *America in the Dark* (New York: William Morrow and Company, 1977), pp. 169-70.

11. See James Cagney, *Cagney on Cagney* (New York: Pocket Books, 1976), p. 90. Pat O'Brien also claims no one knew if Rocky was really yellow at the end. See Karyn Kay and Gerald Peary, "Talking to Pat O'Brien," *Velvet Light Trap*, No. 15 (Fall 1975), p. 31.

12. Neil Hurley calls this a rare film treatment of the operation of grace. See *Toward a Film Humanism* (New York: Delta Books, 1970), pp. 130-31.

13. Both John Baxter and Stephen Karpf suggest, correctly I believe, that Nick's feelings for his sister border on the incestuous, and compare him to Camonte in Hawks' *Scarface* (1932). See Baxter, *Hollywood in the Thirties*, p. 57, and Karpf, p. 111.

14. Howard Gelman has written of how Curtiz helped Garfield develop this role, his first in films, into what became his screen persona. See Howard Gelman, "John Garfield: Hollywood was the Dead End," *Velvet Light Trap*, No. 7 (Winter 1972-73), pp. 16-20.

15. The official sequel is *Four Wives*, which Curtiz directed in 1939 and which continues the Lemp family saga; a third chapter, *Four Mothers*, appeared in 1940, directed by William Keighley. But since Mickey died in the first film, he made only a ghostly appearance in the second and none in the third.

16. In *Hollywood in the Thirties*, John Baxter refers to Gabriel's "socialist oriented" dialogue which assails "every institution in sight." See Baxter, p. 57.

17. Gelman talks of the "strong ethnic" quality Garfield projected in his roles, with his "heavily New York accented prose and clipped manners...straight from the city ghettoes." See Howard Gelman, p. 17.

18. Paul Zweig, looking at literary history, suggest that as we move from older, mythic tales to the modern novel, the "substance of adventure has been displaced inward." The novel celebrates "not heroics, but psychology, not the voyage out, but the voyage in." See Zweig, pp. 226-27, 132-33.

19. Kingsley Canham notes that in *Daughters Courageous*, the "treatment by which the strongest performances come from the...irresponsible characters, is strongly representative of Curtiz."

Chapter 8

1. See Joyce Nelson, " 'Mildred Pierce' Reconsidered," *Film Reader 2*, January 1977, pp. 65-70, and June Sochen, "*Mildred Pierce* and Women in Film," *American Quarterly*, 30 (Spring 1978) pp. 3-20, and Pam Cook, "Duplicity in *Mildred Pierce*," in *Women in Film Noir*, ed. E. Ann Kaplan (London: British Film Institute, 1978) pp. 68-82.

2. For notes on the production of *Mildred Pierce*, see Higham, *Warner Brothers*, pp. 184-85, and Sochen, pp. 1-2.

3. Higham, p. 184.

4. Sochen, p. 1.

5. According to Higham, Turney's screenplay adopted this ending, but Wald wanted it changed, "despite Cain's violent objections in a series of letters" (Higham, pp. 184-85). Cain repeated his objections in an interview held before his recent death. See Peter Brunette and Gerald Peary, "Tough Guy: James M. Cain Interviewed," *Film Comment*, 12 (May-June, 1976), 50-57.

6. John Davis tells us that several scenes "dealing with Veda's intensely disappointing discovery that the musical talent so carefully nurtured by her mother was essentially an illusion" were "deleted from the final scripts because of time limitations." See "The Tragedy of *Mildred Pierce*," *Velvet Light Trap*, No. 6 (Fall 1972), p. 29.

7. Amir Massoud Karimi, *Toward a Definition of the American Film Noir (1941-1949)* (New York: Arno Press, 1976), p. 28. Karimi's book was originally a dissertation, written in 1970 for the University of Southern California. The Borde-Chaumeton book was published in Paris in 1955 by Les Editions de Minuit.

8. A complete bibliography on *film noir* would take far more space than I have here, and Karimi includes a fairly extensive one up to 1970. However, I should mention three of the more important books that include discussions of *film noir:* Lawrence Alloway, *Violent America* (New York: Museum of Modern Art, 1971); Charles Higham and Joel Greenberg, *Hollywood in the Forties* (New York: Paperback Library, 1970); Michael Wood, *America in the Movies* (New York: Basic Books, 1975). To these I would add: Barbara Deming, *Running Away from Myself* (New York: Grossman Publishers, 1969). Deming never once uses the term *film noir*, since she first wrote her book in 1950, before it was popularized. But she perceives the implicit pessimism of many forties films, and this perception constitutes the "discovery" of *film noir*. See also: Alain Silver and Elizabeth Ward, eds., *Film Noir: An Encyclopedic Reference to the American Style* (Woodstock: Overlook Press, 1979).

   Among the major recent articles on *film noir* are: Alfred Appel, Jr., "The End of the Road: Dark Cinema and Lolita," *Film Comment*, 10 (Summer 1974), 25-31; Charles Gregory, "Living Life Sideways," *Journal of Popular Film*, 5 (Fall-Winter 1976), 289-311; Paul Jensen, "The Return of Dr. Caligari: Paranoia in Hollywood," *Film Comment*, 7 (Winter 1971-72), 36-45; J.A. Place and L.S. Peterson, "Some Visual Motifs of Film Noir, *Film Comment*, 10 (January-February 1974), 30-35; Robert G. Porfirio, "No Way Out: Existential Motifs in the Film Noir," *Sight and Sound*, 45 (Autumn 1976), 212-17; Paul Schrader, "Notes on Film Noir," *Film Comment*, 8 (Spring 1972), 8-13; John S. Whitney, "A Filmography of Film Noir," *Journal of Popular Film*, 5 (Fall-Winter, 1976), 321-71.

   Film Comment, 10 (November-December 1974) contains a special section devoted to *film noir*, which includes the following articles: Alfred Appel, Jr., "Film Noir: The Director: Fritz Lang's American Nightmare," pp. 12-17; Mitchell S. Cohen, "Film Noir: The Actor: Villains and Victims," pp. 27-29; Raymond Durgnat, "The Family Tree of Film Noir," pp. 6-7; Stephen Farber, "Film Noir: The Society: Violence and the Bitch Goddess," pp. 8-11; Richard T. Jameson, "Film Noir: Today: Son of Noir," pp. 30-33; Paul Jensen, "Film Noir: The Writer: Raymond Chandler and the World You Live in," pp. 18-26.

   Velvet Light Trap, No. 5, Summer 1972, devoted to "The Forties in Hollywood," has a number of articles on *film noir*, including: John Belton, "Prisoners of Paranoia: The World of Edgar G. Ulmer," pp. 17-20; Mark Bergman, "Hollywood in the Forties Revisited," pp. 2-5; Tom Flinn, "Three Faces of Film Noir: *Stranger on the Third Floor, Phantom Lady*, and *Criss Cross*," pp. 11-16. It also contains an important article on another of Curtiz's *films noirs The Unsuspected* (1947): John Davis, "Curtiz's *The Unsuspected*," pp. 21-24.

   Among the more interesting older articles on *film noir* are: Penelope Houston, "The Heroic Fashion," *Sight and Sound*, 21 (October-December, 1951), 61-63; John Russel Taylor, "The

High Forties," *Sight and Sound*, 30 (Autumn 1961), pp. 188-91; Andrew Sarris, "The High Forties Revisited," *Film Culture*, No. 24, pp. 62-70.

Finally, I might mention my own article, "The Dark Night of the Screen: Messages and Melodrama in the American Movie," *American Quarterly*, 27 (March 1975), 88-98.

9. Some critics do not consider it a genre at all; see the articles by Durgnat and Schrader cited above.

10. Karimi, p. 155.

11. Ibid., p. 29.

12. Ibid., p. 31.

13. Ibid., p. 33.

14. Ibid., pp. 155 and 43-45.

15. Ibid., pp. 56-68.

16. Ibid., p. 83. See also Higham and Greenberg, pp. 19-21.

17. Karimi, pp. 167-68.

18. We recall that Stanley Solomon identified film genres by their visual and aural "iconography" which give them a central "core of narrative meaning" (Solomon, pp. 3-5). I will shortly use the word "iconography" with Solomon's discussion in mind.

19. Wood, p. 98. However, Wood specifically cites *Mildred Pierce* as an exception, a film in which the visual mood is an appropriate "metaphor for the stormy, tortured confusion of her [Mildred's] feelings" (p. 99).

20. Wood, p. 98.

21. Higham and Greenberg, p. 21.

22. See Donald Deschner, "Anton Grot, Warners Art Director 1927-1948," *Velvet Light Trap*, No. 15 (Fall 1975), pp. 19-22, for information on Grot, who invented the "ripple machine" that created these effects. Grot also used the machine for his work on *The Sea Hawk*. The other Curtiz films on which he worked are: *The Mad Genius* (1931), *Dr. X* (1932), *The Mystery of the Wax Museum* (1933), *Bright Lights* (1930), *Captain Blood* (1935), *The Sea Wolf* (1941), *The Private Lives of Elizabeth and Essex* (1939).

23. Joyce Nelson notes that:

> All of the scenes within the present (which includes the third flashback) seem much more suggestive of film noir style than are the two lengthy segments from Mildred's past, her discourse. Thus, the film's present is characterized by greater contrasts in areas of light and dark, certain unsettling variations in camera distance and angle, claustrophobic sets and framing devices, lines and angles which splinter the composition of the frame, events taking place at night, a mood of suspicion and distrust. In comparison, the two segments from Mildred's past are more evenly illustrated, use little variation in camera angle, are more harmoniously composed with traditionally balanced three-shots and two-shots, mainly concern events taking place in the light of day, and attempt to clarify rather than cloud relationships.

Nelson's basic observation is correct, but she ignores the significant *film noir* elements within the flashbacks that help keep the film's tone consistent, help maintain that "mood of suspicion and distrust." For example, when Veda tells her mother, "I've been so miserable. I made a mistake" by marrying Ted Forrester, Curtiz focuses on her emotionless, frozen face, while the background music becomes a high-pitched warning. Veda's handling of the whole Forrester affair, manipulating those involved, lying shamelessly, faking emotions she doesn't feel, qualifies her as a junior league Brigid O'Shaugnessy.

Furthermore, the flashbacks are filled with hints of the potential violence arising from the characters' selfish ambition. When Mildred realizes, after Bert leaves her, that she is "dead broke," and "with Bert gone...I'd stay broke," we see, under these words of narration, her hand in close-up rummaging through a drawer and finding the gun used later to kill Monty. This potential violence breaks out in a fairly regular pattern, as I will discuss later.

24.   Hitchcock's *Stage Fright* (1950) depends on this principle for its plot. The hero, accused of murder, explains his innocence in what becomes a flashback. At the film's end we learn he really is guilty; the flashback was a lie. Audiences and critics were so taken aback by this unprecedented violation of film convention that the film was not one of Hitchcock's bigger hits. See Kristin Thompson, "The Duplicitous Text: an Analysis of *Stage Fright*," *Film Reader 2*, January 1977, pp. 52-64.

25.   Davis, "Mildred Pierce," p. 28.

26.   Molly Haskell, *From Reverence to Rape* (Baltimore; Penguin Books, 1974), pp. 180-81.

27.   This line subtly prefigures Monty's fate; he does "drop dead" from the idea of marrying Veda.

28.   This line relates Veda even more closely to Monty, who earlier told Mildred: "Yes, I take money from you ... but not enough to make me like kitchens or cooks. They smell of grease.

29.   Michael Wood, pp. 103-4.

30.   Ibid., p. 107.

31.   See, for example, Sochen, p. 9.

32.   The prologue even contains a miniature of this: Mildred first invites Wally to the beach house, apparently to sleep with him at last, then rejects his sexual advances.

33.   Davis, p. 28.

34.   Nelson, p. 69.

35.   Michael Wood talks about the theme of deceptive appearances being crucial to *film noir;* see pp. 97-125, especially pp. 105 and 111-25. Other critics have noted the use of mirrors and reflections in *film noir;* see especially Schrader, and Place and Peterson, cited above.

36.   Parker Tyler, *Magic and Myth of the Movies* (New York: Simon and Schuster, 1974), p. 225.

37.   Ibid., p. 227.

38.   Ibid., p. xxviii.

39.   Ibid., pp. 226-27.

40.   Haskell, p. 180.

41.   Ibid., p. 154.

42.   For further, detailed information on the "woman's film," see Haskell, pp. 153-88 and 189-230, as well as Marjorie Rosen's *Popcorn Venus* (New York: Coward, McCann, and Geoghegan, 1973), pp. 189-244.

43.   Haskell, p. 179.

44. Ibid., p. 169.

45. Ibid., p. 170.

46. John Davis notes that our first impression of Mildred changes when we see her at the police station and realize she "is simply too scared to be a real *femme fatale*" (see p. 27).

47. Sochen, p. 9.

48. Ibid., p. 18.

49. Nelson, p. 68.

50. Ibid., p. 69.

51. Ibid., p. 67.

52. Ibid.

53. Ibid., p. 70.

54. Ibid.

55. Ibid., p. 69.

56. Ibid., p. 70.

57. Ibid., p. 69.

58. Ibid., p. 70.

59. Davis, "Mildred Pierce," p. 28.

60. Nelson, p. 70.

61. In the next chapter I discuss the similar question of the obligatory happy endings imposed on *Young Man with a Horn, Jim Thorpe: All-American,* and *The Helen Morgan Story.*

62. Thomson, p. 217.

Chapter 9

1. The other two are *The Breaking Point* (1950) and *Force of Arms* (1951). Tom Flinn and John Davis have written an interesting study of the first: "*The Breaking Point,*" *Velvet Light Trap,* No. 14 (Fall 1975), pp. 17-20.

2. Whittemore and Cecchettini, talking of the "thematic similarities" within Curtiz's films, suggest that he "probes the nature of ambition with such insistence . . . that this particular facet of human desire seems to be the axis on which his stories turn." See p. 199.

3. In an earlier chapter I noted and challenged Baxter's description of Curtiz as cynical, but for this scene, if for no other, he does deserve Baxter's adjective, "pitiless." See *Hollywood in the Thirties,* p. 52.

4. Not coincidentally, Ranald MacDougall, who received screenplay credit for *Mildred Pierce,* also received it for *Bright Leaf.*

5. *Young Man with a Horn* uses the traditional melodramatic contrast between the light and dark woman. Jo, the "good woman," is blonde; Amy, the bad, is brunette. *Bright Leaf* reverses the usual associations; the villainous Margaret is blonde, while Sonia is brunette. In a later, non-Warners Curtiz film, *The Egyptian* (1954, produced by Twentieth Century Fox), two women

again represent moral alternatives: Nefer (Bella Darvi) is an evil whore who helps destroy the hero; Merit (Jean Simmons) is a warm-hearted peasant who loves him. Both of them are dark haired.

6. There is even a subtle suggestion of a lesbian relationship between Amy and a friend.

7. We saw this same device, put to somewhat different use, in *Mildred Pierce*.

8. This was a common studio practice at the time and happens occasionally even now. The Dorothy Baker novel on which the film is based, itself said to be partly based on Bix Beiderbecke's tragically brief life, ends with Rick's death.

9. It should be obvious that I am not at all concerned with the accuracy of this or any other of Curtiz's biographical films (or biopics, as they are called). While the issue of accuracy raises some interesting questions, they are irrelevant to my interests, the style and structure of the individual film, and its relationship to other Curtiz films. For these purposes, we can consider the biopics fiction.

10. See, for example, Nolan, p. 537; Canham, pp. 45-53, esp. p. 50; Whittemore and Cecchettini, pp. 198-99; and Meyer, pp. 99-101.

11. Walter Winchell does narrate the film, and acts as master of ceremonies at the dinner, but rather than offering any hope for Helen, he talks about her as if she were already a memory, saying that Broadway's lights "have dimmed" for the once great star.

12. Doug McClelland has written about this film in "*Night and Day:* Jane Wyman Was the One," *Filmograph*, 4, No. 1 (1973), 33-36.

13. Higham and Greenberg call this the film's best scene. See *Hollywood in the Forties*, p. 204.

14. What makes the similarities between *The Best Things in Life Are Free* and the other films discussed in this chapter especially noteworthy is that it was made at Twentieth Century Fox, after Curtiz left Warner Brothers. Despite the change of studio, Curtiz's structure and style, with its idiosyncratic emphases, remain evident; the film even begins with a crane shot that locates its main characters within their environment.

Conclusion

1. Sarris, *The American Cinema*, p. 55.

2. Baxter, *Hollywood in the Thirties*, p. 58.

3. Quoted in George Bluestone, *Novels into Film* (Berkeley: University of California Press, 1968), p. 1.

4. John Davis and Tom Flinn have written on one of Curtiz's silent films, his first in the U.S., *The Third Degree* (1927). See "*The Third Degree*," *Silent Picture*, No. 18 (1973), pp. 37-42.

5. Two fine articles have been written about Curtiz's horror films. See John Davis, "When Will They Ever Learn? A Tale of Mad Geniuses, Scientists, Artists and A Director (Also Mad)," *Velvet Light Trap*, No. 15 (Fall 1974), pp. 11-17 (about *The Mad Genius* [1931], *Dr. X, Mystery of the Wax Museum*, and *The Walking Dead* [1936]); and Jeffrey Richards, "Discoveries: *The Walking Dead* and *Strangler of the Swamp*," *Focus on Film*, No. 15 (Summer 1973), pp. 59-62.

6. See Whittemore and Cecchettini, pp. 199-202, and Tom Flinn and John Davis, "Warners' War of the Wolf," in *The Classic American Novel and the Movies*, ed. Gerald Peary and Roger

Shatzkin (New York: Frederick Unger Publishing Co., 1977), pp. 192-205, for intelligent and admiring articles on *The Sea Wolf*.

7.   See Nolan, p. 537, Canham, pp. 45-53, Whittemore and Cecchetini, pp. 198-99, and Meyer, pp. 99-101.

8.   *King Creole* even has its two worlds represented by two women, a dramatic device we saw in many of Curtiz's films of the early fifties discussed in the last chapter.

Filmography

To prepare this filmography I collated those that appear in the works previously cited by Canham (abbreviated as C), Nolan (abbreviated as N), Meyer (abbreviated as M), and Nemeskurty, the Curtiz filmography found in James Robert Parish and Michael Pitts, *Film Directors: A Guide to Their American Films* (Metuchen, N.J.: Scarecrow Press, 1974), pp. 88-91 (abbreviated as P), and the Curtiz filmography found in the Swedish magazine *Sunset Boulevard*, No. 3, (Winter 1971), pp. 17-22 (abbreviated as S). In addition, I have cross-checked Curtiz's American films in the American Film Institute Catalog (volumes F2 and F6) and the U.S. Copyright Office's Catalog of Copyright Entries for Motion Pictures (volumes covering 1912-1969).

An accurate, complete list of Curtiz's European films has not yet been, and may never be, established. I have tried to indicate the discrepancies between the existing filmographies of the European works. A complete list of Curtiz's American films has been established. However, some films were publicly shown before being officially registered with the copyright office. I have indicated these films; for all others, the year given is the year of copyright.

I have included selected production credits for the American films, although they were not available for all films. I have used the following abbreviations to indicate these credits: Producer—Prod; Screenwriter—Sc; Director of Photography—Ph; Film Editor—Ed. I have also indicated the studios that released Curtiz's American films, using the following abbreviations: WB—Warner Brothers; Fox—Twentieth Century Fox; Par—Paramount: UA—United Artists; BV—Buena Vista; MGM—Metro-Goldwyn-Mayer. For the silent films, running time is given in reels; e.g., 8r means eight reels.

Má es Holnap (Today and Tomorrow) (Hungary, 1912). Curtiz also credited as co-scriptwriter and actor.

Az Utolsó Bohèm (The Last Bohemian) (Hungary, 1912).

Rablélek (Captive Soul) (Hungary, 1913).

Atlantis (Denmark, 1913). Directed by August Blom, with Curtiz as an actor.

? (Denmark, 1913). Film of unknown title, directed by Curtiz, released in 1914 after his return to Hungary.

Házasokik Az Uram (My Husband's Getting Married) (Hungary, 1913).

Az Èjszaka Rabja (Prisoner of the Night) (Hungary, 1914). Curtiz also credited as actor.

Aranyásó (Golddigger) (Hungary, 1914).

Bánk Bán (Hungary, 1914).

A Tolonc (The Vagrant) (Hungary, 1914).

A Kölesonkert Csecsemök (The Borrowed Babies) (Hungary, 1914).

A Hercegnö Pongyolában (The Princess in a Nightrobe) (Hungary, 1914).

Akit Ketten Szeretnek (Loved by Two) (Hungary, 1915). Curtiz also credited as actor.

A Farkas (The Wolf) (Hungary, 1916).

A Karthauzi (The Carthusian) (Hungary, 1916).

Makkhetes (Seven of Clubs) (Hungary, 1916).

A Fekete Szivárvány (The Black Rainbow) (Hungary, 1916).

Az Ezust Kecske (The Silver Goat) (Hungary, 1916).

Doktor Úr (The Doctor) (Hungary, 1916).

A Magyar Föld Ereje (The Strength of the Hungarian Soil) (Hungary, 1916).

A Medikus (The Medic) (Hungary, 1916).

Zoárd Mester (Master Zoard) (Hungary, 1917).

A Vörös Samson (The Red Samson) (Hungary, 1917).

Az Utolsó Hajnal (The Last Dawn) (Hungary, 1917).

A Senki Fia (Nobody's Son) (Hungary, 1917).

A Szentjóbi Erdo Titka (The Secret of St. Job Forest) (Hungary, 1917).

A Kuruzsló (The Charlatan) (Hungary, 1917).

A Föld Embere (The Man of the Soil) (Hungary, 1917).

A Halálsengö (The Death Bell) (Hungary, 1917).

Az Ezredes (The Colonel) (Hungary, 1917).

Egy Krajcár Története (The Story of a Penny) (Hungary, 1917).

A Béke Útja (The Road to Peace) (Hungary, 1917).

Az Arendás Zsidó (Jean the Tenant) (Hungary, 1917).

Tatárjárás (Tartar Invasion) (Hungary, 1917).

Az Orvos (The Doctor) (Hungary, 1917). Listed only in M and P.

Tavasz a Télben (Spring in Winter) (Hungary, 1917).

A Napraforgos Holgy (The Lady with Sunflowers) (Hungary, 1918).

Szamarbor (Hungary 1917-18). Listed only in S.

Lulu (Lulu) (Hungary, 1918).

Kilencvenkilenc (Ninety-nine) (Hungary, 1918).

Az Ördög (The Devil) (Hungary, 1918).

A Csúnya Fiu (The Ugly Boy) (Hungary, 1918).

Alraune (The Disguise) (Hungary, 1918).

Judas (Hungary, 1918)

A Vig Özvegy (The Merry Widow) (Hungary, 1918).

Varázskeringö (Magic Waltz) (Hungary, 1918).

Lu, a Kokott (Lu, a Coquette) (Hungary, 1918).

Jön az Öcsem (My Brother is Coming) (Hungary, 1919)

A Skorpio (Hungary, 1918). Listed only in S, this may be a Hungarian version of part one of Fritz Lang's serial, *Die Spinnen.*

A Wellington Rejtely (The Wellington Enigma) (Hungary or Sweden, 1919).

Liliom (Liliom) Hungary, (1919—unfinished).

Odette et l'Histoire des Femmes Illustrés (Sweden, 1919). Although all sources except S list this, they all describe it as a doubtful attribution.

Die Dame mit dem Schwarzen Handschuh (Austria, 1919).

Der Stern von Damaskus (Austria, 1919).

Die Gottesgeissel (Austria, 1920).

Die Dame mit den Sonnenblumen (Austria, 1920).

Labyrinth des Grauens (Austria, 1920). Not listed in S or N; C says it is the same film as *Wege des Schrecken.*

Wege des Schrecken (Austria, 1921).

Boccaccio (Austria, 1920). Listed only in C.

Frau Dorothys Bekenntnis (Austria, 1921).

Miss Tutti Frutti (Austria, 1921).

Herzogin Satanella (Austria, 1921).

Cherchez La Femme (Austria, 1921). Listed only in C and S, this may be the same film as *Herzogin Satanella.*

Sodom und Gomorrha: Part one (Austria, 1922).

Sodom und Gomorrha: Part two (Austria, 1923). Curtiz is credited as co-scriptwriter on both parts of *Sodom und Gomorrha.*

Der Junge Medarus (Austria, 1923). Co-directed by Sascha Kolowrat.

Namenlos (Austria, 1923).

Die Lawine (Austria, 1923).

Avalanche (Austria, 1924). C says this is the same film as *Die Lawine.*

Ein Speil Ums Leben (Austria, 1924).

General Babka (Austria, 1924).

The Uncle from Sumatra (Austria, 1924).

Harun Al Raschid (Austria, 1924).

Die Slavenkönigin (Moon of Israel) (Austria, 1924).

Das Spielzeug von Paris (Red Heels) (Germany-Austria, 1925).

Der golden Schmetterling (The Road to Happiness) (Germany-Austria, 1926).

Flaker Nr. 13 (Germany-Austria, 1926).

The Third Degree (WB, 1926). Sc: Graham Baker. Ph: Hal Mohr. Ed: Clarence Kolster. With: Jason Robards, Sr., Dolores Costello. 8r.

A Million Bid (WB, 1927). Sc: Robert Dillon. Ph: Hal Mohr. With: Dolores Costello, Warner Oland. 7r.

The Desired Woman (WB, 1927). Sc. Anthony Coldeway. Ph: Conrad Wells. Prod: Darryl F. Zanuck. With: Irene Rich, William Russell. 7r.

Good Time Charley (WB, 1927). Sc: Ilona Fulop. Ph: Barney McGill. Prod: Darryl F. Zanuck. With: Warner Oland, 7r.

Tenderloin (WB, 1928). Sc: E.T. Lowe, Jr. Ph: Hal Mohr. Prod: Darryl F. Zanuck. With: Conrad Nagel, Dolores Costello. 8r. Curtiz's first talking film. The films listed hereafter are all part-talking or all-talking.

Noah's Ark (WB, first shown 1928, copyright 1929). Sc: Anthony Coldeway. Ph: Hal Mohr, Barney McGill. Ed: Harold McCord. With: Dolores Costello, George O'Brien. 11r.

The Glad Rag Doll (WB, 1929). Sc: Graham Baker. Ph: Byron Haskin. With: Dolores Costello, Ralph Graves. 8r.

Madonna of Avenue A (WB, 1929). Sc: Ray Doyle. Ph: Byron Haskin. Ed: Ray Doyle. With Dolores Costello, Grant Withers. 8r.

The Gamblers (WB, 1929). Sc: J. Grubb Alexander. Ph: William Reese. Ed: Thomas Pratt. With: H.B. Warner, Lois Wilson. 8r.

Hearts in Exile (WB, 1929). Sc: Harvey Gates. Ph: William Reese. Ed: Thomas Pratt. With: Dolores Costello, Grant Withers. 9r.

Mammy (WB, 1930). Sc: Gordon Ribgy, Joseph Jackson. Ph: Barney McGill. With: Al Jolson, Lowell Sherman. With scenes in Technicolor. 84m.

Under a Texas Moon (WB, 1930). Sc: Gordon Rigby. Ph: William Reese. Ed: Ralph Dawson. With: Frank Fay, Myrna Loy. Technicolor. 82m.

The Matrimonial Bed (WB, 1930). Sc: Seymour Hicks, Harvey Thew. Ph: Dev Jennings. With: Lilyan Tashman, Frank Fay. 98m.

Bright Lights (WB, 1930). Sc: Humphrey Pearson, Henry McCarthy. Ph: Lee Garmes. With: Dorothy Mackaill, Frank Fay. Technicolor. 73m.

A Soldier's Plaything (WB, 1930). Sc: Percey Vekroff. Ph: J.O. Taylor. Ed: Jack Killifer. With: Ben Lyon, Harry Langdon. 71m.

River's End (WB, 1930). Sc: Charles Kenyon. Ph. Robert Kurrle. Ed: Ralph Holt. With: Charles Bickford, Evelyn Knapp. 74m.

Daemon des Meeres (WB, 1931). Sc: Oliver H.P. Garrett, Ulrich Steindorff. Ph: Robert Kurrle. With: William Dieterle, Anton Pointer. 75m. A German-language version of *Moby Dick,* filmed at the same time as Lloyd Bacon's English language film with John Barrymore.

God's Gift to Women (WB, 1931). Sc: Joseph Jackson, Raymond Griffith. Ph: Robert Kurrle. Ed: James Gribbon. With: Joan Blondell, Frank Fay. 71m.

The Mad Genius (WB, 1931). Sc: J. Grubb Alexander, Harvey Thew. Ph: Barney McGill. Ed: Ralph Dawson. With: John Barrymore, Marian Marsh. 75m.

The Woman from Monte Carlo (WB, 1932). Sc: Harvey Thew. Ph: Ernest Haller. Ed: Harold McLernon. With: Lil Dagover, Walter Huston. 68m.

Alias the Doctor (WB, 1932). Sc: Houston Branch, Charles Kenyon. Ph: Barney McGill. Ed: William Holmes. With: Richard Barthelmess, Marian Marsh. 69m.

The Strange Love of Molly Louvain (WB, 1932). Sc: Erwin Gelsey, Brown Holmes. Ph: Robert Kurrle. Ed: James Borby. With: Ann Dvorak, Lee Tracy. 70m.

Doctor X (WB, 1932). Sc: Earl Baldwin, Robert Tasker. Ph: Ray Rennahan, Richard Tower. Ed: George Amy. With: Lionel Atwill, Fay Wray. Technicolor. 80m.

Cabin in the Cotton (WB, 1932). Sc: Paul Green. Ph: Barney McGill. Ed: George Amy. With: Bette Davis, Richard Barthelmess. 79m.

20,000 Years in Sing Sing (WB, 1933). Sc: Wilson Mizner, Brown Holmes. Ph: Barney McGill. Ed: George Amy. With: Spencer Tracy, Bette Davis. 78m.

The Mystery of the Wax Museum (WB, 1933). Sc: Don Mullaly, Carl Erickson. Ph: Ray Rennahan. Ed: George Amy. With: Lionel Atwill, Fay Wray. Technicolor. 78m.

The Keyhole (WB, 1933). Sc: Robert Presnell. Ph: Barney McGill. Ed: Ray Curtis. With: Kay Francis, George Brent. 69m.

Private Detective 62 (WB, 1933). Sc: Rian James. Ph: Tony Gaudio. With: William Powell, Margaret
Lindsay. 67m.

Goodbye Again (WB, 1933). Sc: Ben Markson. Ph: George Barnes. Ed: Thomas Pratt. With: Warren William, Joan Blondell. 65m.

The Kennel Murder Case (WB, 1933). Sc: Robert N. Lee, Peter Milne. Ph: William Reese. Ed: Harold McLarnin. With: William Powell, Mary Astor. 73m.

Female (WB, 1933). Sc: Gene Markey, Kathryn Scola. Ph: Sid Hickox. Ed: Jack Killifer. With: Ruth Chatterton, George Brent. 60m.

Mandalay (WB, 1934). Sc: Austin Parker, Charles Kenyon. Ph: Tony Gaudio. Ed: Thomas Pratt. With: Kay Francis, Ricardo Cortez. 65m.

Jimmy the Gent (WB, 1934). Sc: Bertram Milhauser. Ph: Ira Morgan. Ed: Tom Richards. With: James Cagney, Bette Davis. 66m.

The Key (WB, 1934). Sc: Laird Doyle. Ph: Ernest Haller. Ed: William Clemens, Thomas Richards. With: Edna Best, William Powell. 72m.

British Agent (WB, 1934). Sc: Laird Doyle. Ph: Ernest Haller. Ed: Tom Richards. With: Leslie Howard, Kay Francis. 81m.

The Case of the Curious Bride (WB, 1935). Prod: Harry Joe Brown. Sc: Brown Holmes, Tom Reed. Ph: David Abel. Ed: Terry Morse. With: Warren William, Margaret Lindsay. 68m.

Black Fury (WB, 1935). Prod: Robert Lord. Sc: Abem Finkel, Carl Erickson. Ph: Byron Haskin. Ed: Tom Richards. With: Paul Muni, Karen Morley. 92m.

Front Page Woman (WB, 1935). Prod: Samuel Bischoff. Sc: Laird Doyle, Roy Chanslor, Lillie Hayward. Ph: Tony Gaudio. Ed: Terry Morse. With: Bette Davis, George Brent. 82m.

Little Big Shot (WB, 1935). Prod: Sam Bischoff. Sc: Jerry Wald, Julius J. Epstein, Robert Andrews. Ph: Tony Gaudio. Ed: Jack Killifer. With: Sybil Jason, Glenda Farrell. 78m.

Captain Blood (WB, 1935). Prod: Harry Joe Brown. Sc: Casey Robinson. Ph: Hal Mohr. Ed: George Amy. With: Errol Flynn, Olivia de Havilland. 119m.

The Walking Dead (WB, 1936). Sc: Ewart Adamson, Peter Milne, Robert Adams, Lillie Hayward. Ph: Hal Mohr. Ed: Thomas Pratt. With: Boris Karloff, Ricardo Cortez. 66m.

The Charge of the Light Brigade (WB, 1936). Prod: Hal Wallis. Sc: Michael Jakoby, Rowland Leigh. Ph: Sol Polito, Fred Jackman. Ed: George Amy. With: Errol Flynn, Olivia de Havilland. 115m.

Mountain Justice (WB, 1936). Sc: Norman Reilly Raine, Luci Ward. Ph: Ernest Haller. Ed: George Amy. With: George Brent, Josephine Hutchinson. 83m.

Stolen Holiday (WB, 1936). Prod: Hal Wallis. Sc: Casey Robinson. Ph: Sid Hickox. Ed: Terry Morse. With Claude Rains. 84m.

Kid Galahad (WB, 1937). Prod: Hal Wallis. Sc: Seton I. Miller. Ph: Tony Gaudio. Ed: George Amy. With: Edward G. Robinson, Bette Davis. 101m.

The Perfect Specimen (WB, 1937). Prod: Hal Wallis. Sc: Norman Reilly Raine, Lawrence Riley, Brewster Morse, Fritz Falkenstein. Ph: Charles Rosher. Ed: Terry Morse. With: Errol Flynn, Joan Blondell. 98m.

Gold Is Where You Find It (WB, 1938). Prod: Hall Wallis. Sc: Warren Duff, Robert Buckner. Ph: Sol Polito. Ed: Clarence Kolster. With: Errol Flynn, Olivia de Havilland. Technicolor. 94m.

The Adventures of Robin Hood (WB, 1938). Co-director: William Keighley. Prod: Hal Wallis. Sc: Norman Reilly Raine, Seton I. Miller. Ph: Tony Gaudio, Sol Polito, W. Howard Green. Ed: Ralph Dawson. With: Errol Flynn, Basil Rathbone. Technicolor. 105m.

Four Daughters (WB, 1938). Prod: Hal Wallis. Sc: Julius J. Epstein, Lenore Coffee. Ph: Ernest Haller. Ed: Ralph Dawson. With: Claude Rains, John Garfield. 90m.

Four's a Crowd (WB, 1938). Prod: David Lewis. Sc: Casey Robinson, Sig Herzig. Ph: Ernest Haller. Ed: Clarence Kolster. With: Errol Flynn, Olivia de Havilland. 91m.

Angels with Dirty Faces (WB, 1938). Prod: Sam Bischoff. Sc: John Wexley, Warren Duff. Ph: Sol Polito. Ed: Owen Marks. With: James Cagney, Pat O'Brien. 99m.

Dodge City (WB, 1939). Prod: Robert Lord. Sc: Robert Buckner. Ph: Sol Polito. Ed: George Amy. With: Errol Flynn, Olivia de Havilland. Technicolor. 105m.

Sons of Liberty (WB, 1939). Sc: Crane Wilbur. With: Claude Rains. Technicolor. 20m. Curtiz's only American short.

Daughters Courageous (WB, 1939). Prod: Henry Blanke. Sc: Julius J. Epstein, Philip G. Epstein. Ph: James Wong Howe. Ed: Ralph Dawson. With: Priscilla Lane, John Garfield. 107m.

The Private Lives of Elizabeth and Essex (WB, 1939). Prod: Hal Wallis. Sc: Norman Reilly Raine, Aeneas Mackenzie. Ph: Sol Polito, W. Howard Greene. Ed: Owen Marks. With: Bette Davis, Errol Flynn. Technicolor. 105m.

Four Wives (WB, first shown 1939, copyright, 1940). Prod: Hal Wallis. Sc: Julius and Philip Epstein. Ph: Sol Polito. Ed: Ralph Dawson. With: Claude Rains, Priscilla Lane. 110m.

Virginia City (WB, 1940). Prod: Hal Wallis. Sc: Robert Buckner. Ph: Sol Polito. Ed: George Amy. With: Errol Flynn, Miriam Hopkins. 121m.

The Sea Hawk (WB, 1940). Prod: Hal Wallis. Sc: Howard Koch, Seton I. Miller. Ph: Sol Polito. Ed: George Amy. With: Errol Flynn, Brenda Marshall. 126m cut to 109m.

Santa Fe Trail (WB, 1940). Prod: Jack Warner. Sc: Robert Buckner. Ph: Sol Polito. Ed: George Amy. With: Errol Flynn, Olivia de Havilland. 110m.

The Sea Wolf (WB, 1941). Prod: Henry Blanke. Sc: Robert Rossen. Ph: Sol Polito. Ed: George Amy. With: Edward G. Robinson, John Garfield. 110m.

Dive Bomber (WB, 1941). Prod: Hal Wallis. Sc: Frank Wead, Robert Buckner. Ph: Bert Glennon, Winton Hoch. Ed: George Amy. With: Errol Flynn, Ralph Bellamy. Technicolor. 137m.

Captains of the Clouds (WB, 1942). Prod: Hal Wallis. Sc: Arthur Horman, Richard Macauley, Norman Reilly Raine. Ph: Winton Hoch, Sol Polito. Ed: George Amy. With: James Cagney, Alan Hale. Technicolor. 113m.

Yankee Doodle Dandy (WB, first shown 1942, copyright 1943). Prod: Hal Wallis. Sc: Robert Buckner, Edmund Joseph. Ph: James Wong Howe. Ed: George Amy. With: James Cagney, Walter Huston. 126m.

Casablanca (WB, first shown 1942, copyright 1943). Prod: Hal Wallis. Sc: Julius Epstein, Philip Epstein, Howard Koch. Ph: Arthur Edeson. Ed: Owen Marks. With: Humphrey Bogart, Ingrid Bergman. 102m.

Mission to Moscow (WB, 1943). Prod: Robert Buckner. Sc: Howard Koch. Ph: Bert Glennon. Ed: Owen Marks. With: Walter Huston, Ann Harding. 123m.

This Is the Army (WB, 1943). Prod: Hal Wallis. Sc: Casey Robinson, Capt. Claude Binyon. Ph: Bert Glennon, Sol Polito. Ed: George Amy. With: George Murphy, Joan Leslie. Technicolor. 121m.

Passage to Marseille (WB, 1944). Prod: Hal Wallis. Sc: Casey Robinson, Jack Moffitt. Ph: James Wong Howe. Ed: Owen Marks. With: Humphrey Bogart, Peter Lorre. 110m.

Janie (WB, 1944). Prod: Alex Gottlieb. Sc: Charles Hoffman, Agnes Johnston. Ph: Carl Guthrie. Ed: Owen Marks. With: Joyce Reynolds, Robert Hutton. 106m.

Roughly Speaking (WB, 1945). Prod: Henry Blanke. Sc: Louise Randall Pierson. Ph: Joseph Walker. Ed: David Weisbart. With: Rosalind Russell, Jack Carson. 117m.

Mildred Pierce (WB, 1945). Prod: Jerry Wald. Sc: Ranald MacDougall. Ph: Ernest Haller. Ed: David Weisbart. With: Joan Crawford, Zachary Scott. 111m.

Night and Day (WB, 1946). Prod: Arthur Schwartz. Sc: Charles Hoffman, Leo Townsend, William Bowers. Ph: J. Peverell Marley, William V. Skall. Ed: David Weisbart. With: Cary Grant, Alexis Smith. Technicolor. 128m.

Life with Father (WB, 1947). Prod: Robert Buckner. Sc: Donald Ogden Stewart. Ph: J. Peverell Marley, William V. Skall. Ed: George Amy. With: William Powell, Irene Dunne. Technicolor. 118m.

The Unsuspected (WB, 1947). A Michael Curtiz Production. Prod: Charles Hoffman. Sc: Ranald MacDougall. Ph: Woody Bredell. Ed: Frederick Richards. With: Claude Rains, Joan Caulfield. 103m.

Romance on the High Seas (WB, 1948). A Michael Curtiz Production. Prod: Alex Gottlieb. Sc: Julius and Philip Epstein. Ph: Woody Bredell. Ed: Rudi Fehr. With: Doris Day, Jack Carson. Technicolor. 99m.

My Dream Is Yours (WB, 1949). A Michael Curtiz Production. Prod: Michael Curtiz. Sc: Harry Kurnitz, Dane Lussier. Ph: Ernest Haller. Ed: Folmar Blangsted. With: Doris Day, Jack Carson. Technicolor. 101m.

Flamingo Road (WB, 1949). A Michael Curtiz Production. Prod: Jerry Wald. Sc: Robert Wilder. Ph: Ted McCord. Ed: Folmar Blangsted. With: Joan Crawford, Sydney Greenstreet. 94m.

The Lady Takes a Sailor (WB, 1949). Prod: Harry Kurnitz. Sc: Everett Freeman. Ph: Ted McCord. Ed: David Weisbart. With: Jane Wyman, Dennis Morgan. 99m.

Young Man with a Horn (WB, 1950). Prod: Jerry Wald. Sc: Carl Foreman, Edmund North. Ph: Ted McCord. Ed: Alan Crosland, Jr. With: Kirk Douglas, Juano Hernandez. 113m.

Bright Leaf (WB, 1950). Prod: Henry Blanke. Sc: Ranald MacDougall. Ph: Karl Freund. Ed: Owen Marks. With: Gary Cooper, Lauren Bacall. 110m.

The Breaking Point (WB, 1950). Prod: Jerry Wald. Sc: Ranald MacDougall. Ph: Ted McCord. Ed: Alan Crosland, Jr. With: John Garfield, Phyllis Thaxter. 97m.

Jim Thorpe—All-American (WB, 1951). Prod: Everett Freeman. Sc: Douglas Morrow, Everett Freeman. Ph: Ernest Haller. Ed; Folmar Blangsted. With: Burt Lancaster, Charles Bickford. 107m.

Force of Arms (WB, 1951). Prod: Anthony Veiller. Sc: Orin Jannings. Ph: Ted McCord. Ed: Owen Marks. With: William Holden, Nancy Olson. 110m.

I'll See You in My Dreams (WB, 1951). Prod: Louis Edelman. Sc: Jack Rose and Melville Shavelson. Ph: Ted McCord. Ed: Owen Marks. With: Danny Thomas, Doris Day. Warnercolor. 110m.

The Story of Will Rogers (WB, 1952). Prod: Robert Arthur. Sc: Stanley Roberts, Frank Davis. Ph: Wilfred Cline. Ed: Folmar Blangsted. With: Will Rogers, Jr., Jane Wyman. Warnercolor. 109m.

The Jazz Singer (WB, 1953). Prod: Louis Edelman. Sc: Frank Davis, Leonard Stern, Louis Meltzer. Ph: Carl Guthrie. Ed: Alan Crosland, Jr. With: Danny Thomas, Peggy Lee. Technicolor. 110m.

Trouble Along the Way (WB, 1953). Prod: Melville Shavelson. Sc: Melville Shavelson, Jack Rose. Ph: Archie Stout. Ed: Owen Marks. With: John Wayne, Donna Reed. 110m.

The Boy from Oklahoma (WB, 1953). Prod: David Weisbart. Sc: Winston Miller, Frank Davis. Ph: Robert Burks. Ed: James Moore. With: Will Rogers, Jr., Nancy Olson. Warnercolor. 88m.

The Egyptian (Fox, 1954). Prod: Darryl Zanuck. Sc: Philip Dunne, Casey Robinson. Ph: Leon Shamroy. Ed: Barbara McClean. With: Edmund Purdom, Jean Simmons. Cinemascope. DeLuxe Color. 140m.

White Christmas (Par, 1954). Prod: Robert Emmet Dolan. Sc: Norman Krasna, Norman Panama, Melvin Frank. Ph: Loyal Griggs. Ed: Frank Bracht. With: Bing Crosby, Danny Kaye. VistaVision. Technicolor. 120m.

We're No Angels (Par, 1955). Prod: Pat Duggan. Sc: Ranald MacDougall. Ph: Loyal Griggs. Ed: Arthur Schmidt. With: Humphrey Bogart, Peter Ustinov. VistaVision. Technicolor. 103m.

The Scarlet Hour (Par, 1956). Prod: Michael Curtiz. Sc: Rip Van Ronkel, Frank Tashlin, John Meredyth Lucas. Ph: Lionel Lindon. Ed: Everett Douglas. With: Tom Tryon, Carol Omhart. VistaVision. 95m.

The Vagabond King (Par, 1956). Prod: Pat Duggan. Sc; Ken Englund, Noel Langley. Ph: Robert Burks. Ed: Arthur Schmidt. With: Oreste, Kathryn Grayson. VistaVision. Technicolor. 88m.

The Best Things in Life Are Free (Fox, 1956). Prod: Henry Ephron. Sc: William Bowers, Phoebe Ephron. Ph: Leon Shamroy. Ed: Dorothy Spencer. With: Dan Dailey, Gordon MacRae. Cinemascope. DeLuxe Color. 104m.

The Helen Morgan Story (WB, 1957). Prod: Martin Rackin. Sc: Stephen Longstreet, Oscar Saul, Dean Reisner, Nelson Gidding. Ph: Ted McCord. Ed: Frank Bracht. With: Ann Blythe, Paul Newman. Cinemascope. 118m.

The Proud Rebel (BV, 1958). Prod: Samuel Golwyn, Jr. Sc: Joe Petracca, Lillie Hayward. Ph: Ted McCord. Ed: Aaron Stell. With: Alan Ladd, Oliva de Havilland. Technicolor. 103m.

King Creole (Par, 1958). Prod: Hal Wallis. Sc: Herbert Baker, Michael Gazzo. Ph: Russell Harlan. Ed: Warren Low. With: Elvis Presley, Carolyn Jones. VistaVision. 115m.

The Hangman (Par, 1959). Prod: Frank Freeman, Jr. Sc: Dudley Nichols. Ph: Loyal Griggs. Ed: Terry Morse. With: Robert Taylor, Tina Louise. 86m.

The Man in the Net (UA, 1959). Prod: Walter Mirisch. Sc: Reginal Rose. Ph: John Seitz. Ed: Richard Heermance. With: Alan Ladd, Carolyn Jones. 97m.

The Adventures of Huckleberry Finn (MGM, 1960). Prod: Sam Goldwyn, Jr. Sc: James Lee. Ph: Ted McCord. Ed: Frederic Steinkamp. With: Eddie Hodges, Archie Moore. Cinemascope. Metrocolor. 107m.

A Breath of Scandal (Par, 1960). Prod: Carlo Ponti, Marcello Girosi. Sc: Walter Bernstein. Ph: Mario Montuori. Ed: Howard Smith. With: Sophia Loren, John Gavin. Technicolor. 98m.

Francis of Assisi (Fox, 1961). Prod: Plato A. Skouras. Sc: Eugene Vale, James Forsythe, Jack Thomas. Ph: Piero Portalupi. Ed: Louis Loeffler. With: Bradford Dillman, Dolores Hart. Cinemascope. DeLuxe Color. 111m.

The Comancheros (Fox, 1961). Prod: George Sherman. Sc: James Edward Grant, Flair Huffaker. Ph: William Clothier. Ed: Louis Loeffler. With: John Wayne, Ina Balin. Cinemascope. DeLuxe Color. 107m.

Bibliography

Adcock, A. St. John. *The Glory That Was Grub Street*. New York: Fred A. Stokes, 1928.

Agabiti, Thomas. "Samuel Fuller's 'Run of the Arrow' and the Mythos of Romance: An Archetypal Analysis." *Film Reader 2*, January 1977, pp. 96-110.

Alloway, Lawrence. *Violent America*. New York: Museum of Modern Art, 1971.

Anobile, Richard, ed. *Casablanca*. New York: Avon Books, 1974.

Appel, Alfred, Jr. "The End of the Road: Dark Cinema and *Lolita*." *Film Comment*, 10 (Summer 1974), 25-31.

_____. "Film Noir: The Director: Fritz Lang's American Nightmare." *Film Comment*, 10 (November-December 1974), 12-17.

Arkadin. "Film Clips." *Sight and Sound*, 37 (Autumn 1968), 210-11.

Arnheim, Rudolf. "Epic and Dramatic Film." *Film Culture* 3, No. 1 (1957), 9-10.

Bargainnier, Earl F. "Melodrama as Formula." *Journal of Popular Culture*, 9 (Winter 1975), 726-33.

Baxter, John. *Hollywood in the Thirties*. New York: A.S. Barnes, 1968.

Bazin, André. "De la politique des auteurs." *Cahiers du cinéma*, No. 70 (April 1954), pp. 2-11.

Behlmer, Rudy. "Erich Wolfgang Korngold—Established Some of the Filmmusic Basics Composers Now Ignore." *Films in Review*, 18 (February 1967), 86-100.

_____. "Robin Hood on the Screen." *Films in Review*, 16 (February 1965), 91-102.

_____. "Swordplay on the Screen." *Films in Review*, 16 (June-July 1965), 362-75.

Belton, John. "Souls Made Great by Adversity." *Focus*, No. 9 (Spring 1973), pp. 16-22.

_____. Prisoners of Paranoia: The World of Edgar G. Ulmer." *Velvet Light Trap*, No. 5 (Summer 1972), pp. 17-20.

Berczeller, Richard. "Sodom and Gomorrah." *New Yorker*, 50 (October 14, 1974), 48-54.

Bergman, Andrew. *We're in the Money: Depression America and Its Films*. New York: New York University Press, 1971.

Bergman, Mark. "Hollywood in the Forties Revisited." *Velvet Light Trap*, No. 5 (Summer 1972), pp. 2-5.

Birkmyre, Robert. "R.S." *Bookman*, 46 (June 1914), 111-12.

Bluestone, George. *Novels into Film*. Berkeley: University of California Press, 1968.

Borde, Raymond, and Chaumeton, Etienne. *Panorama du film noir américain (1941-1953)*. Paris: Les Editions de Minuit, 1955; rpt. Paris: Les Editions d'Aujourd'hui, 1976.

Borneman, Ernest. "The United States versus Hollywood: The Case Study of an Antitrust Suit." In *The American Film Industry*. Ed. Tino Balio. Madison: University of Wisconsin Press, 1976.

Bourget, Jean-Loup. "Romantic Dramas of the Forties: An Analysis." *Film Comment*, 10 (January 1974), 46-51.

_____. "Social Implications in the Hollywood Genres." *Journal of Modern Literature*, 3 (April 1973), 191-200.

Brooks, Peter. "The Aesthetics of Astonishment." *Georgia Review*, No. 30 (Fall 1976), pp. 615-39.
_____. *The Melodramatic Imagination*. New Haven: Yale University Press, 1976.
_____. "Romantic Antipastoral and Urban Allegories." *Yale Review*, 69 (Autumn 1974), 11-26.
_____. "The Text of Muteness." *New Literary History*, 5 (Spring 1974), 549-64.
Brunette, Peter, and Peary, Gerald. "Tough Guy: James M. Cain Interviewed." *Film Comment*, 12 (May-June 1976), 50-57.
Cagney, James. *Cagney by Cagney*. New York: Pocket Books, 1977.
Callenbach, Ernest. "Comparative Anatomy of Folk Myth Films: *Robin Hood* and *Antonio Das Mortes*." *Film Quarterly* 23 (Winter 1969-70), 42-47.
Cameron, Ian. *Adventure in the Movies*. New York: Crescent Books, 1974; published in England as *Adventure and the Cinema*. London: Studio Vista, 1973.
Cameron, Ian, et al. "*Movie* vs. Kael." *Film Quarterly*, 17 (Fall 1963), 57-64.
Campbell, Russell. "Warner Brothers in the Thirties." *Velvet Light Trap*, No. 1 (June 1971), pp. 2-4.
Canham, Kingsley. *The Hollywood Professionals: Volume I. Michael Curtiz, Raoul Walsh, Henry Hathaway*. New York: A.S. Barnes & Co., 1973.
Cawelti, John. *Adventure, Mystery and Romance: Formula Stories as Art and Popular Culture*. Chicago: University of Chicago Press, 1976.
_____. *The Six-Gun Mystique*. Bowling Green, Ohio: Bowling Green University Popular Press, 1971.
Cleave, Alan. "Record Review: *The Sea Hawk*." *Movie Maker*, No. 7 (May 1973), p. 328.
Cohen, Mitchell S. "Film Noir: The Actor: Villains and Victims." *Film Comment*, 10 (November-December 1974), 27-29.
Conant, Michael. "The Impact of the Paramount Decrees." In *The American Film Industry*. Ed. Tino Balio. Madison: University of Wisconsin Press, 1976.
Cook, Pam. "Duplicity in *Mildred Pierce*." In *Women in Film Noir*. Ed. E. Ann Kaplan, London: British Film Institute, 1978, pp. 68-82.
Corliss, Richard. "Analysis of the Film." In *Casablanca*. Ed. Howard Koch. Woodstock, New York: The Overlook Press, 1973, pp. 185-98.
_____. *Talking Pictures*. New York: Penguin Books, 1975.
Croft, John J. "*Casablanca* Revisited." *Classic Film Collector*, No. 42 (Spring 1974), p. 43.
Crowther, Bosley. " 'Passage to Marseille,' a Heavy Action Drama in Which Free Frenchmen Figure, with Bogart, at the Hollywood." *New York Times*, February 17, 1944, 12:5.
_____. " 'To Have and Have Not,' With Humphrey Bogart, at the Hollywood—Arrival of other New Films at Theatres Here." *New York Times*, October 12, 1944, 24:1.
Curtiz File. Newspaper and magazine clippings at the Lincoln Center Branch of the New York Public Library.
Curtiz, Michael. "Hollywood Is a Fertile Field for Creativeness and Ingenuity." *PIC*, April 1947, pp. 76-77, 108.
_____. "Talent Shortage is Causing Two Year Production Delay." *Films and Filming*, 2 (June 1956), 9.
Darrach, Brad. "Rapier Envy, Anyone?" *Time*, 108 (August 9, 1976), pp. 70-73.
Davis, John. "*Captain Blood*." *Velvet Light Trap*, No. 1 (June 1971), pp. 26-31.
_____. "Curtiz's *The Unsuspected*." *Velvet Light Trap*, No. 5 (Summer 1972), pp. 21-24.
_____. "Notes on Warner Brothers Foreign Policy: 1918-1948." *Velvet Light Trap*, No. 4 (Spring 1972), pp. 23-34.
_____. "The Tragedy of *Mildred Pierce*." *Velvet Light Trap*, No. 6 (Fall 1972), pp. 27-30.
_____. "When Will They Ever Learn: A Tale of Mad Geniuses, Scientists, Artists and a Director (Also Mad)." *Velvet Light Trap*, No. 15 (Fall 1975), pp. 11-17.
Davis, John, and Flinn, Tom. "Michael Curtiz." In *The American Film Heritage: Impressions from the American Film Institute Archives*. Ed. American Film Institute. Washington, D.C.: Acropolis Books, Ltd., 1972, pp. 32-39.

_____. "The Third Degree." *Silent Picture*, No. 18 (1973), pp. 37-42.

Davis, Peter G. "Lights, Action, Korngold." *New York Times*, March 24, 1974, II, 26:3.

Day, Barry, "*Casablanca*." *Films and Filming*, 20 (August 1974), 20-24.

Deming, Barbara, *Running Away from Myself: A Dream Portrait of America Drawn from the Films of the Forties*. New York: Grossman Publishers, 1969.

Deschner, Donald. "Anton Grot, Warners Art Director—1927-48." *Velvet Light Trap*, No. 15 (Fall 1975), pp. 19-22.

Disher, Maurice Willson. *Blood and Thunder: Mid-Victorian Melodrama and its Origins*. London: Frederick Muller, Ltd., 1949.

Donnely, William. "Love and Death in *Casablanca*." In *Persistence of Vision: A Collection of Film Criticism*. Ed. Joseph McBride. Madison: Wisconsin Film Society Press, 1968, pp. 103-107.

Durgnat, Raymond. "Epic." *Films and Filming*, 10 (December 1963) 9-12.

_____. "The Family Tree of Film Noir." *Film Comment*, 10 (November-December 1974), 6-7.

_____. "Ways of Melodrama." *Sight and Sound*, 21 (August-September 1951), 34-40.

Dyer, John Peter. "From Boadicea to Bette Davis." *Films and Filming*, 5 (January 1959), 13-15, 32.

_____. "Some Mighty Spectacles." *Films and Filming*, 4 (Febuary 1958), 13-15, 34.

Everson, William K. *The Bad Guys*. New York: Citadel Press, 1964.

_____. "Film Spectacles—Are Both a Genre of Their Own and a Help to Other Kinds of Pictures." *Films in Review*, 5 (November 1954), 459-71.

Farber, Stephen. "Film Noir: The Society: Violence and the Bitch Goddess." *Film Comment*, 10 (November-December 1974), pp. 8-11.

Fell, John. "Darling, This is Bigger than Both of Us." *Cinema Journal*, 12 (Spring 1974), 56-64.

Feuchtwanger, Lion. *The House of Desdemona: The Laurels and Limitations of Historical Fiction*. Trans. Harold Basilius. Detroit: Wayne State University Press, 1963.

Flinn, Tom. "Interview with William Dieterle, the Plutarch of Hollywood." *Velvet Light Trap*, No. 15 (Fall 1975), pp. 23-28.

_____. "Three Faces of Film Noir: *Stranger on the Third Floor, Phantom Lady*, and *Criss Cross*." *Velvet Light Trap*, No. 5 (Summer 1972), pp. 11-16.

Flinn, Tom, and Davis, John. "The Breaking Point." *Velvet Light Trap*, No. 14 (Winter 1974), pp. 17-20.

_____. "Warners' War of the Wolf." In *The Classic American Novel and the Movies*. Ed. Gerald Peary and Roger Shatzkin. New York: Frederick Ungar Publishing Co., 1977, pp. 192-205.

Flynn, Errol. *My Wicked Wicked Ways*. New York: Berkley Publishing Corp., 1974.

Frye, Northrop. *Anatomy of Criticism: Four Essays*. Princeton, N.J.: Princeton University Press, 1957.

_____. "The Argument of Comedy." *English Institute Essays—1948*. New York: Columbia University Press, 1949, pp. 58-73.

_____. *A Natural Perspective: The Development of Shakesperean Comedy and Romance*. New York: Harcourt, Brace & World, 1965.

_____. *The Secular Scripture*. Cambridge, Mass.: Harvard University Press, 1976.

Gassner, John, and Nichols, Dudley, eds. *Best Film Plays of 1943-1944*. New York: Crown Publishers, 1945, pp. 631-94.

Gelman, Howard. "John Garfield: Hollywood Was the Dead End." *Velvet Light Trap*, No. 7 (Winter 1972-73), pp. 16-20.

Gough-Yates, Kevin. "The Hero." *Films and Filming*, 12 (December 1965), 11-16; 12 (January 1966), 11-16; 12 (Febuary 1966), 25-30; 12 (March 1966), 25-30.

_____. "The Heroine." *Films and Filming*, 12 (May 1966), 23-27; 12 (June 1966), 27-32; 12 (July 1966), 38-43; 12 (August 1966), 45-50.

Gow, Gordon. "The Swashbucklers." *Films and Filming*, 18 (January 1972), 34-40.

Greenberg, Harvey. *The Movies on Your Mind*. New York: Saturday Review Press, 1975), pp. 79-105.

Gregory, Charles. "Living Life Sideways." *Journal of Popular Film*, 5 (Fall-Winter 1976), 289-311.
Grimstead, David. *Melodrama Unveiled: American Theater and Culture 1800-1850*. Chicago: University of Chicago Press, 1968.
Hardy, Phil. *Samuel Fuller*. New York: Praeger Publishers, 1970.
Hark, Ina Rae. "The Visual Politics of *The Adventures of Robin Hood.*" *Journal of Popular Film*, 5 (Winter 1976), 3-17.
Haskell, Molly. *From Reverence to Rape: The Treatment of Women in the Movies*. Baltimore: Penguin Books, 1974.
Haver, Ronald. "Finally, the Truth about *Casablanca.*" *American Film*, 1 (June 1976), 10-16.
Heilman, Robert B. "Fashions in Melodrama." *Western Humanities Review*, 13 (Winter 1959), 3-15.
Higham, Charles. *Hollywood Cameramen*. Bloomington: Indiana University Press, 1970.
_____. *Warner Brothers: A History of the Studio: Its Pictures, Stars and Personalities*. New York: Charles Scribner's Sons, 1975.
Higham, Charles and Greenberg, Joel. *Hollywood in the Forties*. New York: Paperback Library, 1970.
Houston, Penelope. "The Heroic Fashion." *Sight and Sound* 21 (October-December 1951), 61-63.
Hume, Katherine. "Romance: A Perdurable Pattern." *College English*, 36 (October 1974), 129-46.
Hurley, Neil P. *Toward a Film Humanism*. New York: Delta Books, 1970.
Jacobs, Lewis. *The Rise of the American Film*. New York: Harcourt, Brace, 1939.
Jameson, Fredric. "Magical Narrative: Romance as Genre." *New Literary History*, 7 (Fall 1975), 135-67.
Jameson, Richard T. "Film Noir: Today: Son of Noir." *Film Comment*, 10 (November-December 1974), 30-33.
Jensen, Paul. "Film Noir: The Writer: Raymond Chandler and the World You Live In." *Film Comment*, 10 (November-December 1974), 18-26.
_____. "The Return of Dr. Caligari: Paranoia in Hollywood." *Film Comment*, 7 (Winter 1971-72), 36-45.
Kael, Pauline. "Circles and Squares." *Film Quarterly*, 16 (Spring 1963), 12-26.
_____. *I Lost It at the Movies*. New York: Bantam Books, 1966, pp. 264-88.
Kaminsky, Stuart. *American Film Genres: Approaches to a Critical Theory of Popular Film*. Dayton, Ohio: Pflaum Publishing, 1974.
Karimi, Amir Massoud. *Toward a Definition of the American Film Noir*. New York: Arno Press, 1976.
Karpf, Stephen Louis. *The Gangster Film: Emergence, Variation and Decay of a Genre, 1930-1940*. New York: Arno Press, 1973.
Kay, Karyn, and Peary, Gerald. "Talking to Pat O'Brien." *Velvet Light Trap*, No. 15 (Fall 1975), pp. 29-32.
Keen, Maurice. *The Outlaws of Medieval Legend*. London: Routledge and Kegan Paul, 1961.
Kitses, Jim. *Horizons West: Anthony Mann, Budd Boetticher, Sam Peckinpah: Studies of Authorship within the Western*. Bloomington: Indiana University Press, 1970.
Knight, Arthur. *The Liveliest Art*. New York: New American Library, 1957.
Koch, Howard, ed. *Casablanca: Script and Legend*. Woodstock, N.Y.: The Overlook Press, 1973.
Koszarski, Richard. "The Men with the Movie Camera—60 Filmographies." *Film Comment*, 8 (Summer 1972), 27-57.
Laurence, F.M. "Death in the Matinee: the Film Endings of Hemingway's Fiction." *Literature/Film Quarterly*, 2 (Winter 1974), 44-51.
MacArthur, Colin. *Underworld, U.S.A*. New York: Viking Press, 1972.
Macklin, F. Anthony. "Interview with Andrew Sarris." *Film Heritage*, 8 (Summer 1973), 26-36.
Martin, Pete. "Hollywood's Champion Language Assassin." *Saturday Evening Post*, 220 (August 2, 1947), 22-23, 58, 63-64, 66.

McBride, Joseph, ed. *Focus on Howard Hawks.* Englewood Cliffs, New Jersey: Prentice-Hall, Inc., 1972.

McClelland, Doug. *"Night and Day:* Jane Wyman was the One." *Filmograph,* 4 (1973), 33-36.

McGilligan, Patrick. "James Cagney: The Actor as Auteur." *Velvet Light Trap,* No. 7 (Winter 1972-73), pp. 3-15.

Meyer, William R. *The Warner Brothers Directors: The Hard Boiled, The Comic, and the Weepers.* New Rochelle, N.Y.: Arlington House Publishers, 1978), pp. 75-107.

"Michael Curtiz Filmografi." *Sunset Boulevard,* No. 3 (Winter 1971), pp. 17-22. [In Swedish]

Morgan, James. "Coronation U.S.A." *Sight and Sound,* 23 (July-September 1953), 43-46.

Morris, Mary. "Mary Morris Meets Movie Maker Michael Curtiz." *PM,* September 17, 1944, pp. M12-M13.

Morse, David. "Under Western Eyes: Variations on a Genre." In *Passport to Hollywood: Film Immigrants: Anthology.* Ed. Don Whittemore and Philip Alan Cecchetini. New York: McGraw-Hill, 1976, pp. 202-15.

Nelson, Joyce. " 'Mildred Pierce' Reconsidered." *Film Reader 2,* January 1977, pp. 65-70.

Nemeskurty, István. *Word and Image: History of the Hungarian Cinema.* Trans. Zsuzsanna Horn. Budapest: Corvina Press, 1968.

Niven, David. *Bring on the Empty Horses.* New York: Dell Publishing Co., Inc., 1976.

Nolan, Jack Edmund. "Michael Curtiz." *Films in Review,* 21 (November 1970), pp. 525-48.

Obituary. "Michael Curtiz." *New York Herald Tribune,* April 12, 1962, 12:2.

Obituary. "Michael Curtiz." *New York Times,* April 12, 1962, 35:1.

Parish, James Robert, and Pitts, Michael. *Film Directors: A Guide to Their American Films.* Metuchen, N.J.: Scarecrow Press, 1974, pp. 88-91.

Parish, James Robert, and Stanke, Don E. *The Swashbucklers.* New Rochelle, N.Y.: Arlington House Publishers, 1976. With a preface by Edward Connor, "Swashbucklers on the Screen," pp. 15-23.

Pepper, Linda, and Davis, John. "John Brown's Body Lies A'Rolling in His Grave." *Velvet Light Trap,* No. 8 (1973), pp. 14-19.

Place, J.A., and Peterson, L.S. "Some Visual Motifs of Film Noir." *Film Comment,* 10 (January-February 1974), 30-35.

Poague, Leland. "The Problem of Film Genre: A Mentalistic Approach." Unpublished manuscript.

Porfirio, Robert G. "No Way Out: Existential Motifs in the Film Noir." *Sight and Sound,* 45 (Autumn 1976), 212-17.

Pye, Douglas. "Genre and Movies." *Movie,* No. 20 (Spring 1975), pp. 29-43.

Rahill, Frank. *The World of Melodrama.* University Park, Pennsylvania: Pennsylvania State University Press, 1967.

Richards, Jeffrey. "Discoveries: *The Walking Dead* and *Strangler of the Swamp." Focus on Film,* No. 15 (Summer 1973), pp. 59-62.

————. "The Swashbuckling Revival." *Focus on Film,* No. 27 (Summer 1977), pp. 7-29.

————. *Swordsmen of the Screen.* London: Routledge and Kegan Paul, 1977.

————. *Visions of Yesterday.* London: Routledge and Kegan Paul, 1973.

Robinson, David. "Spectacle." *Sight and Sound,* 25 (Summer 1955), 22-26, 55-56.

Rosen, Marjorie. *Popcorn Venus.* New York: Coward, McCann & Geoghegan, 1973.

Rosenzweig, Sidney. "The Dark Night of the Screen: Messages and Melodrama in the American Movie." *American Quarterly,* 27 (March 1975), 88-98.

Rotha, Paul, and Griffith, Richard. *The Film Till Now.* New York: Funk and Wagnalls, 1949.

Rubenstein, Lenny. "Casablanca." *Cinéaste,* 8 (Summer 1977), 34-35.

Sarris, Andrew. *The American Cinema: Directors and Directions 1929-1968.* New York: E.P. Dutton, 1968.

————. "Auteur Theory and the Perils of Pauline." *Film Quarterly,* 16 (Summer 1963), 26-33.

_____. "The Auteur Theory Revisited." *American Film* 2 (July-August 1977), 49-53.

_____. "The High Forties Revisited." *Film Culture*, No. 24 (Spring 1962), pp. 62-70.

_____. "Notes on the Auteur Theory in 1970." *Film Comment*, 6 (Fall 1970), 7-9.

_____. "Notes on the Auteur Theory in 1962." *Film Culture*, No. 27 (Winter 1962-63), pp. 1-8.

Schickel, Richard. "Some Nights in Casablanca." In *Favorite Movies: Critics Choice*. Ed. Philip Nobile. New York: Macmillan, 1973, pp. 114-25.

Schrader, Paul. "Notes on Film Noir." *Film Comment*, 8 (Spring 1972), 8-13.

Shadoian, Jack. "Michael Curtiz' *20,000 Years in Sing-Sing*." *Journal of Popular Film*, 2 (Spring 1973), 165-79.

Shales, Tom. "*The Mystery of the Wax Museum*." In *The American Film Heritage: Impressions from the American Film Institute Archives*. Ed. The American Film Institute. Washington, D.C.: Acropolis Books, Ltd., 1972, pp. 28-31.

Sharples, Win, Jr., et al. "Prime Cut: 75 Editors' Filmographies with Supporting Materials," *Film Comment*, 13 (March-April 1977), 6-29.

Silke, James R. *Here's Looking at You Kid: Fifty Years of Fighting Working and Dreaming at Warner Brothers*. Boston: Little, Brown, 1976.

Silver, Alain, and Ward, Elizabeth, eds. *Film Noir: An Encyclopedic Reference to the American Style*. Woodstock, New York: The Overlook Press, 1979.

Sochen, June. "*Mildred Pierce* and Women in Film." *American Quarterly*, 30 (Spring 1978), pp. 3-20.

Solomon, Stanley. *Beyond Formula: American Film Genres*. New York: Harcourt, Brace, Jovanovich, 1976.

Steiner, Max. "Scoring the Film." In *We Make the Movies*. Ed. Nancy Naumburg. New York: W.W. Norton, 1973, pp. 216-38.

Stickney, John. "Last Word on *Last Tango* and *Casablanca*." *Mademoiselle*, 77 (July 1974), 138-39, 150-51.

Taylor, John Russell. "The High Forties." *Sight and Sound*, 30 (Autumn 1961), 188-91.

Thaxton, David. "Mission to Moscow." In *The American Film Heritage: Impressions from the American Film Institute Archives*. Ed. The American Film Institute. Washington, D.C.: Acropolis Books, Ltd., 1972, pp. 40-42.

Thomas, Tony. *Cads and Cavaliers: The Film Adventurers*. South Brunswick, N.J.: A.S. Barnes, 1973.

_____. *The Great Adventure Films*. Secaucus, N.J.: Citadel Press, 1976.

_____. *Music for the Movies*. South Brunswick and New York: A.S. Barnes, 1973.

Thompson, Kristin. "The Duplicitous Text: An Analysis of *Stage Fright*." *Film Reader 2*, January 1977, pp. 52-64.

Thomson, David. *America in the Dark: Hollywood and the Gift of Unreality*. New York: William Morrow and Co., 1977.

Truffaut, François. "Un certaine tendance du cinéma français." *Cahiers du cinéma*, No. 31 (January 1954), pp. 15-29.

Tudor, Andrew. *Theories of Film*. New York: Viking Press, 1974.

Tyler, Parker. *Magic and Myth of the Movies*. New York: Simon and Schuster, 1947.

Warner, Jack L., with Jennings, Dean. *My First Hundred Years in Hollywood*. New York: Random House, 1964.

Warshow, Robert. *The Immediate Experience*. New York: Atheneum, 1971.

Whitehall, Richard. "Days of Strife and Nights of Orgy: The Roman Spectaculars." *Films and Filming*, 9 (March 1963), 8-14.

Whitney, John S. "A Filmography of Film Noir." *Journal of Popular Film*, 5 (Fall-Winter 1976), 321-71.

Whittemore, Don, and Cecchettini, Philip Alan. *Passport to Hollywood: Film Immigrants: Anthology*. New York: McGraw-Hill, 1976, pp. 188-228.

Will, David, and Willeman, Paul, eds. *Roger Corman*. Edinburgh Film Festival '70 in Association with *Cinema* Magazine, Edinburgh, 1970.

Willis, Donald. *The Films of Howard Hawks*. Metuchen, N.J.: The Scarecrow Press, 1975.

Wollen, Peter. *Signs and Meaning in the Cinema*. Bloomington: Indiana University Press, 1969.

Wood, Michael. *America in the Movies*. New York: Basic Books, 1975.

Wood, Robin. *Howard Hawks*. New York: Doubleday, 1968.

,_____. "Ideology, Genre, Auteur." *Film Comment*, 13 (January-February 1977), 46-51.

_____. "To Have (Written) and Have Not (Directed)." *Film Comment*, 9 (May-June 1973), 30-35.

Zweig, Paul, *The Adventurer*. New York: Basic Books, 1974.

Index

Academy award winners, 7, 8, 30, 77, 122
Adventurer, 20, 24
Adventures of Huckleberry Finn, The, 160
Adventures of Robin Hood, The, 29-41, 47, 49-51, 52, 66, 67; comic in, 33; compared to Dwan-Fairbanks version, 35; literary history, 29-30; role of minor characters, 55; synopsis, 29
Angels with Dirty Faces, 109, 111-13
Arden, Eve: in Mildred Pierce, 121
Atlantis, 5
Atwill, Lionel: in Captain Blood, 14, 22
Auteur theory, 4, 5, 9
Avery, Phyllis, 155

Bacall, Lauren, 97; in Bright Leaf; in Young Man with a Horn, 148
Bainter, Fay, 116
Battle sequences: role of, 56-57
Beery, Wallace, 35
Beggars of the Sea, 44
Bennet, Enid, 35
Bennett, Bruce: in Mildred Pierce, 121
Bergman, Ingrid: in Casablanca, 77
Best Things in Life are Free, The, 154, 155
Bickford, Charles: in Jim Thorpe . . . , 150
Big Sleep, The, 123
Blom, August, 5
Blythe, Ann: in Helen Morgan Story, 152; in Mildred Pierce, 121
Bogart, Humphrey, 71-72; in Casablanca, 77; in Kid Galahad, 113; in Passage to Marseille, 97, 101; in To Have and Have Not, 97
Bois, Curt, 89
Borgnine, Ernest, 155
Boy from Oklahoma, The, 160
Bright Leaf, 145-47; moral worlds, 146
Brooke, Clifford, 55
Butler, Rhett, 83
Byron, Arthur, 109

Cabot, Bruce, 66
Cagney, James, 111, 154
Calhern, Louis, 110
Captain Blood, 14-28, 47, 49-51, 52, 66; and Robin Hood, 34, 36; synopsis, 14-15
Carlson, Richard, 152
Carmichael, Hoagy: in Young Man with a Horn, 148
Carson, Jack: in Mildred Pierce, 121; in Bright Leaf, 146
Casablanca, 8, 68, 77-95, 105, 186n. 30; criticism of, 78; Freudian reading, 79; minor figures in, 79, 85; production history, 78
Charge of the Light Brigade, The, 61-65, 70; synopsis, 61-62
Cianelli, Edward, 103
Cohan, George, M., 154
Color: use of, 39
Comancheros, The, 8
Composition in depth, 40
Confessions of a Nazi Spy, 48
Cooper, Gary, 145
Cooper, Melville: in Robin Hood, 29, 32-39
Cording, Harry: in Robin Hood, 36
Corey, Jeff: in Bright Leaf, 146
Crawford, Joan: in Mildred Pierce, 121, 122
Crisp, Donald: in Bright Leaf, 145; in Daughters Courageous, 116; in Sea Hawk, 45
Curtiz, Michael: accent, 7; biography, 5-9; other accounts, 1-2; see also sound; two worlds metaphor; visual style

Dailey, Dan, 155
Dalio, Marcel, 97
Damita, Lily, 6, 175
Daniell, Henry, 73, 186 n. 27; in Sea Hawk, 43
Dantine, Helmut, 85, 101
Daughters Courageous, 109, 116-18
Daves, Delmer, 44

Davis, Bette, 7; in *Charge of the Light Brigade*, 73; in *Kid Galahad*, 114; in *20,000 Years in Sing-Sing*, 110
Dawson, Ralph, 30
Day, Doris, 148, 155
de Grasse, Sam, 35
de Havilland, Olivia, 62, 186 n. 27; in *Captain Blood*, 14; in *Robin Hood*, 29, 32-41
DeMille, Cecil B., 6
Dickey, Paul, 35
Dieterle, William, 8
Dr. X, 158
Dodge City, 61, 65-68; synopsis, 66-67
Donat, Robert, 18, 179n. 45
Doraine, Lucy, 5, 6
Dorn, Philip, 101
Double Indemnity, 122, 123
Douglas, Kirk: in *Young Man . . . ,* 147
Duels, 58-59, 184 n. 50

Electra complex, 140
Epstein, Julius, 78
Epstein, Philip, 78

Fairbanks, Douglas, Jr., 15
Faulkner, William, 97, 122
Film noir, 10, 122-25, 128, 132, 138, 158; literary origins, 124
Flashback: *Casablanca*, 90; *Jim Thorpe . . . ,* 151; *Mildred Pierce*, 122-23, 151; *Passage to Marseille*, 102
Flynn, Errol, 62, 66, 68, 71, 73, 175 n. 30; in *Captain Blood*, 14, 19; in *Robin Hood*, 29, 32; in *Sea Hawk*, 43
Four Daughters, 109, 115-16
Furthman, Jules, 97

Garbo, Greta, 6
Garfield, John, 115, 116
Genre, 8-10; definitions, 9
Gesamtkunstwerk, 1
Glass Key, The, 123
Gone with the Wind, 83
Grant, Cary, 154
Greek chorus, 55-56
Green world, 30, 31-41
Greenstreet, Sydney: in *Passage to Marseille*, 101
Grot, Anton, 44

Hale, Alan, 71, 73, 186 n. 27; in *Dodge City*, 66; in *Robin Hood*, 29
Hangman, The, 160
Hassel, George: in *Captain Blood*, 14, 23
Hawks, Howard, 97; style, 98-99
Heflin, Van, 70
Helen Morgan Story, The, 145, 152-53

Henried, Paul: in *Casablanca*, 77
Hero, 49, 51, 183 n. 45; rebel, 22, 67, 73; relationship with heroine, 24, 61-62; in *Sea Hawk*, 50; in swashbucklers, 18, 20, 67
Hopkins, Miriam, 72
Hunter, Ian: in *Robin Hood*, 29, 35, 38

Imprisonment, 62; in *Captain Blood*, 20, 24-26; in *Casablanca*, 88-89; in *Passage to Marseille*, 104; in *20,000 Years in Sing-Sing*, 109-10
Iron Mask, The, 15

Jim Thorpe: All-American, 145, 150-52
Jory-Victor, 66

Keighley, William, 30
Kertesz, Mihaly, 5
Kid Galahad, 109, 113-15
Killers, The, 141
King Creole, 160
Knowles, Patric, 63; *Robin Hood*, 29, 32-39
Koch, Howard, 8, 44, 78
Korngold, Erich Wolfgang, 18, 30, 44, 183 n. 43

Lady from Shanghai, 141
Lady Takes a Sailor, The, 158
Lancaster, Burt: in *Jim Thorpe . . . ,* 150
Lane, Lola, 115, 116
Lane, Priscilla, 115, 116
Lane, Rosemary, 115, 116
La Torre, Charles, 103
Laura, 123
Le Beau, Madeleine: in *Casablanca*, 82
Liliom, 6
Litvak, Anatole, 48
Loder, John, 101
Lorre, Peter, 77, 101
Love, Montague: in *Robin Hood*, 33; in *Sea Hawk*, 43
Love Story, 84
Lynn, Jeffrey, 115

MacDonald, Francis, 55
MacDougall, Randy, 122
Macrae, Gordon, 155
Ma Es Holnap, 5
Maltese Falcon, The, 123
Mark of Zorro, The, 15
Marshall, Brenda: in *Sea Hawk*, 43
Massey, Raymond, 68
McHugh, Frank, 67
Meredyth, Bess, 7
Mildred Pierce, 121-43, 155; synopsis, 121; woman's film, 140-43
Miller, Seton I., 30, 44
Molnar, Walter, 97

Moon of Israel, 6-7
Morally divided character, 65; Marian, 38; Rick, 82-83; Rocky, 113
Moran, Dolores, 97
Morocco, 100
Murder, My Sweet, 123
Mundin, Herbert: in *Robin Hood,* 29, 32-39
My Dream is Yours, 155
Mystery of the Wax Museum, 158

Neal, Patricia: in *Bright Leaf,* 146
Newman, Paul: in *The Helen Morgan Story,* 152
Night and Day, 154-55
Nightmare world, 19
Noah's Ark, 6

O'Brien, Pat, 111
Odette et l'histoire des femmes illustrée, 6
O'Neill, Henry, 68
Oppositions, 31-34, 64, 67, 71, 73, 98, 99; in *Angels...,* 112; in *Casablanca,* 85-87, 93-94; in *Kid Galahad,* 113; in *Mildred Pierce,* 136; in *Santa Fe Trail,* 69, 71

Page, Gail, 115, 116
Page, Joy, 85
Pallette, Eugene: in *Robin Hood,* 29
Passage to Marseille, 101-108; darkness, 105; structure, 102
Phoenix Films, 6
Polito, Sol, 44
Private Lives of Elizabeth and Essex, The, 44, 61, 73-75, 84, 186 n. 30

Raine, Norman Reilly, 30
Rains, Claude: in *Casablanca,* 77; in *Daughters Courageous,* 116; in *Four Daughters,* 115; in *Passage to Marseille,* 101; in *Robin Hood,* 29, 32-39; in *Sea Hawk,* 43
Rathbone, Basil: in *Captain Blood,* 14; in *Robin Hood,* 29, 32
Reagan, Ronald, 70
Robinson, Edward G., 113
Robson, Flora: in *Sea Hawk,* 43
Roman Holiday, 84

Sabatini, Rafael, 18, 44
Sakall, S.Z., 89, 176
Santa Fe Trail, The, 61, 68-71
Sarris, Andrew, 4
Sascha Film Co., 6
Sazerac, 72
Scott, Randolph, 71
Scott, Zachary: in *Mildred Pierce,* 121
Sea Hawk, The, 43-59; role of minor

characters, 55; social and political comment in, 44-50; synopsis, 43
Sea Wolf, The, 159
Seastrom, Victor, 5
Selznick, David O., 78
Shadow shot, 58-59
Slave Queen, The, (Die Slavenkönigin), see Moon of Israel
Smith, C. Aubrey: in *Night and Day,* 154
Sokoloff, Vladimir, 101
Sound: for effect, 26, 44, 127
Steiner, Max, 18
Stephenson, Henry, 63
Stiller, Mauritz, 5
Strange Love of Martha Ivers, The, 123-24
Student Prince, The, 84
Studio system, 2
Swashbuckler, 10, 14-18, 158; as comedy, 17-18; as melodrama, 16; as morality play, 17; as romance, 17; hero in, 20-21; literary ancestors, 16; neglect of, 14; politics, 46-47, 49; tripartite structure, 35, 62

Talking shadows, 1, 28
Tobias, George, 101
To Have and Have Not, 97-101; compared to *Casablanca,* 98-101
Tracy, Spencer, 109
Turney, Catherine, 122
20,000 Years in Sing-Sing, 109-11
Two worlds metaphor, 19-20, 31-41, 52-54; 67, 74-75, 85-87, 93, 103

Unsuspected, The, 8

Veidt, Conrad: in *Casablanca,* 77
Villains, 45, 71, 73-74, 131, 180 n. 57; in *Captain Blood,* 23-24; in *Robin Hood,* 36-37; in *Sea Hawk,* 49-51; in swashbucklers, 18, 94
Virginia City, 61, 68, 71-73
Visual style, 6, 25-28, 39, 71, 74, 109, 157; deep focus photography, 149, 151; moving camera, 27, 54; subjective shot, 27 windows and mirrors, 149

Wald, Jerry, 122
War films, 107
Warner Brothers, 47; "proletarian," 3, 4
Warner, Jack, 6
Warner ocean, 44
Weyl, Carl Jules, 30
Wilder, Billy, 122
Will Rogers Story, The, 158
Williams, Guinn, 66, 71

Yankee Doodle Dandy, 154
Young Man with a Horn, 145, 147-50